CAPTAIN RANSOM, TEXAS RANGER

An American Hero
1874 - 1918

PAT HILL GOODRICH

ILLUSTRATOR...STONEWALL

Pat Hill Goodrich, author of the award-winning *The Savvy Samoyed*

Registration No. 122-54-00

Writers Guild of America East

U. S. Copyright Office
     PAU-2-502-389
     TXU-1-011-045

Captain Ransom, Texas Ranger
Copyright © 2007 by Pat Hill Goodrich

Requests for information should be addressed to:
Pat Hill Goodrich
PO Box 418
Pinehurst, Texas 77362

or

Evangel Publishing House
2000 Evangel Way
P.O. Box 189
Nappanee, Indiana 46550
Phone: (800) 253-9315
Internet: www.evangelpublishing.com

Cover Design by Mark Sharon

ISBN-10: 1-933858-30-3
ISBN-13: 978-1-933858-30-2
Library of Congress Control Number: 2007936569

Printed in the United States of America by Evangel Press, Nappanee, IN

DEDICATION

To my Bill, the late William Ashley Goodrich, Jr., MD

…the love of my life…

The Texas Ranger

"There was a freedom and ease about this character that gave him individuality and charm. He followed no fixed military rules, wore no uniform, and took part in no parades. He was enlisted for active service and was ready to go at any moment to be called to duty. Well-armed and mounted...always ready for the worst...the Ranger has stood in a class alone. His protection extended to all kinds of people. He restored and encouraged order and confidence, built up that which had been destroyed, and put an end to viciousness and vice.

"The Ranger has given to us a lofty type of manhood. He who protects the helpless, rescues the perishing, and cares for the dying...fulfills the holy law of God. The Texas Ranger's spurs were won by service of danger, and his badge of knighthood was the bright lone star. Like King Richard of old, he was lion-hearted, and every happy home in Texas owes him gratitude and honor."

—Miss Katie Daffan

From *The Texas Literature Reader*
Compiled by Davis Foute Eagleton
Professor of English, Austin College
The Southern Publishing Co.
Dallas, Texas 1919

Former Texas Rangers Association

3805 BROADWAY, ~~████████~~, SAN ANTONIO, TEXAS 78209
(210) 822-9011

I've had the privilege to read the entire manuscript of <u>Captain Henry Ransom - The Life and Times of a Texas Ranger</u>. It's an excellent piece of work on the part of its researcher and writer.

In keeping with family values, the author has the knack of making the reader visualize his/her own childhood and relate to having been reared under the way of life by pioneer parents and grandparents. As you read each chapter, it's not hard to imagine that each character, as portrayed, takes on a true-life personality.

With "Been there--done that" on my mind, I see that nothing much has changed over the years in the life of a 20th Century (1905-1998) Texas Ranger, down to and including the need for voluminous report writing to their superiors in Austin--always considered by me to be one of the "necessary evils" of the job!

Respectfully,

Jerome H. Preiss

JEROME H. PREISS *("Geronimo")*
Texas Ranger Co. "D" (Retired)

This book is endorsed by Joe Davis. Joe was a Texas Ranger for 24 years and in law enforcement for 30 years. He's president of the Former Texas Rangers Foundation and a past president of the Former Texas Rangers Association. Joe says "Our wives are our greatest supporters. Without them we could not have done our jobs."

ABOUT THE AUTHOR

Pat Hill Goodrich is an award-winning author, script writer, and artist. A sixth generation Texan, she is an accomplished pianist and harpist, as well as a Texas history enthusiast. Recently she papered the State with petitions requesting the Legislature to declare March the official Texas history month. This was done unanimously by both the House and Senate.

She founded two heritage societies, Descendants of Austin's Old Three Hundred, and the Siege of Bexar Descendants. After teaching six years in public schools, she founded and directed a private school from grades 1 to 12, using a classic curriculum. During this time she hosted a radio talk show.

Forthcoming books include details about a little known but strategic battle in 1835 and another titled *Chasing The Elusive Caduceus.*

Her movie script based on this book won first place in the biographical section of an international competition with entries from 34 different countries. Plans are made for its future production.

Indexed are many names of Rangers active at this time, along with excerpts from some of their actual letters and wires to the Adjutant Generals. Readers may discover new Texas Rangers in their family.

Illustrator: Stonewall, well-known Quarter Horse breeder and Western artist.

PRIMARY SOURCES

This book would not have been possible without the generous assistance and encouragement from the following: the former Beatrice Ransom, author's mother and the daughter of Captain Ransom's first marriage; Henry Brown Ransom, Jr., son of Will Ransom, the Captain's brother; his son, Henry Ransom, Jr.; Stonewall Hill, brother of the author and grandson of Captain Ransom; Justus W. Hill, author's father; Abby Cole Cagle and Artie Cole Echols, cousins of Martha Ella Cole, the Captain's first wife; Terrell Radford Rogers, grandson of Victoria Adelaide Ransom Davis, oldest sister of Captain Ransom, and his wife, the former Geraldine Harmon, genealogist; Robert Lee Ransom, grandson of Captain Ransom's second marriage; Mrs. Olene Baker Chapman, daughter of Jules Baker (she donated family photo on cover); Ernest Ensley Rogers, grandson of Victoria Ransom Davis; Miss Hulen, sister of General John A. Hulen; Ruby Lee Ransom and Jonathan Lane Ransom, daughter and son of Captain Ransom's second marriage; Stephen Ransom, a cousin; Mrs. Tom (Izora) Cooke, wife of Anna Hope Ransom's brother; Mrs. David Arnold (Hazel), granddaughter of Sheriff Jack Yarbrough of Sweetwater, Texas; William K. Ransom, cousin, descendant of Confederate General Matt Ransom; Texas Ranger Captain A. Y. Allee of Carrizo Springs; Fay Ransom and Sadie Mae Ransom Riemer, wife and sister of Henry B. Ransom, Jr.; Orville Benton and wife, the former Myrle Grubbs; Texas Ranger Jerome ("Geronimo") Preiss, President of Former Texas Rangers and Their Descendants Association; Billie Lee Danz of Daughters of the Republic in Texas; Jim Locke; Virginia Diaz; Patrick Kegans, grandson of "Bud" Kegans, close friend of Captain Ransom; Orville Stoessel, Bastrop; Jack Stearn, Wallis; J. Luke Hill, San Felipe; George Teague, Houston; County Sheriff "Buckshot" Lane, Wharton; Mary Baker Rockenbaugh, niece of Jules Baker; Mrs. M. O. Baker, wife of nephew of Jules Baker; Mrs. Tom Vaccaro, granddaughter of Jules Baker; Jimmy Wade of Fulshear; Mrs. Lucy Spoede; Mrs. John D. Redfield; Mrs. Dorothy Ransom, wife of

Jonathan Ransom; Mrs. Grover Hillbolt, the former Charlotte Berthelemy; Alvin Grossman, PhD, author, publisher; and Frank Vandiver, PhD, author, historian, university president, Coy U. Spawn, Attorney, Houston.

ACKNOWLEDGEMENTS

The author is grateful for the invaluable assistance from the following: Tony Black, Archivist of the Archives and Information Services Division of the Texas State Library; Dennis G. Hair, Founder and Curator, the Houston Police Museum and Instructor, Houston Police Academy; Tom Burks, Curator and Janice Reece, Librarian, Texas Ranger Hall of Fame and Museum of Waco, Texas; Leland Hillingoss, Genealogy Department of the St. Louis, Missouri, Library; Marge Coombes, Baker Industries-Wells Fargo; and the Texas Pioneers-Trail Drivers of Texas-Texas Rangers Memorial Hall Archives, San Antonio, and Coy U. Spawn of Houston.

Newspapers include "The Houston Post," "The Houston Daily Post," "The Houston Chronicle," "The Sweetwater Daily Reporter," and "The Houston Press," from 1890's through 1918, and the "Austin American Statesman," and "The Daily Texan" (University of Texas).

My thanks go to the County Clerks and their assistants in the following counties of Texas: Austin, Mitchell, Fort Bend, Washington, Harris, Galveston, Colorado, Brazoria, Bexar, Liberty, Waller, Chambers, Travis, Nolan and Tyler.

The staffs at these museums gave me valuable assistance, for which I am grateful: The Texas Ranger and Pioneer Museum in San Antonio, The Texas Ranger Hall of Fame and Museum of Waco, The Fort Bend County Museum at Richmond, The Houston Police Museum, and The Brookshire Museum.

The librarians and their assistants kindly came to my aid at these: the Texas Room of the Julia Ideson Library, Houston; the Clayton Genealogical Library, Houston; the Rosenberg Library, Galveston; the George R. Brown Library, Richmond; the Sam Houston Library at Liberty; the Sterling Library, Baytown; the Hempstead Public Library; the Bellville Public Library; the St. Louis Public Library's Genealogy Department; the Daughters of the Republic of Texas Library, San Antonio; and the Carrizo Springs Library.

Most helpful were the Eugene C. Barker Texas History Center, University of Texas, Austin, Texas General Land Office, and the Archives and Information Services Division with the Genealogy Department, both of the Texas State Library, Austin. Extra thanks to Gaylen Greaser and Tony Black.

The latter graciously permitted the perusal and inclusion of copies of letters and wires received by and sent from the Adjutant General's office.

Reference for the above: General Correspondence, 1846-1943, Adjutant General's Records (RG 401), Archives and Information Services Division – Texas State Library.

My thanks and gratitude go to Joyce Cutler, good friend and expert on her computer, who put this on a disk for me.

Most important, my heartfelt gratitude goes to my late dear husband, Bill, for not only his patience when the dishes stacked up in the sink, but for his editing expertise and knowledge of firearms.

INTRODUCTION

As a small child I heard colorful stories about my grandfather from my mother and grandmother. I was beginning to scribble little stories myself.

"When I grow up I'm going to write a book about him myself," I announced to them. I did and here it is.

Known as one of "the Great Captains" this unsung hero has not been written about before nor has been the era in which he served. Too, Captain Henry Lee Ransom must have been typical of the Texas Rangers described as being "as talkative as an oyster."

Over a dozen years ago while researching another subject at the Texas State Archives, I discovered even more information about him. On inquiring, I found older folks to interview who either had known him or had heard about him. Now most of them are deceased. I am grateful to some who gave me the rare photographs included in this book.

Many of his records were missing or changed. For two summers every scrap of the Adjutant Generals' Correspondence of the State Archives in Austin was examined. All other official papers and booklets available were carefully checked.

Finally after finding only vague reports about the Spanish-American War, details of Lt. Gilmore's famous rescue were located in Boston's Brattle Book Store. Ransom had participated in the eight months of grueling conflict and search. (All history buffs/bookaholics should travel to Brattle's!) Ransom, a be-medaled hero in that war, served in the U. S. Army twice in the Philippines as a Volunteer.

In 1905 he first joined the Texas Rangers. He was in the Ranger Force also a second and third time, as Captain of his companies. He was Chief of Police in Houston having, as the newspaper stated, a "short but spectacular career" during some of that city's wicked "short pants days." Just before being appointed chief, he was in a shoot-out downtown with the man reputed to be the attorney for the underground. Follows a big famous trial.

The Rangers kept in constant touch with the Adjutant General, who was in charge of them. Excerpts from their colorful letters and telegrams are included. Descriptions in their own words of the activities give the unvarnished facts, sometimes exciting, humorous, poignant, showing their human side and how they coped with difficulties of the times.

Ransom was assassinated at age 44, although his death was claimed to be an accident. Ample clues are in the Archives. And the book.

The kingpin of political bosses, Archie Parr, had control of several counties, politics-wise. A letter to the Governor from an election judge is re-printed in this book. He reports that Parr and the sheriff took a ballot box from him. It was rumored that high public officials were involved in plotting Ransom's assassination. He knew too much and was about to reveal it, "they" said.

Apparently Archie trained his son, George, in the "family business." Much later in the 1960's, long after Ransom's time, facts pointed out the junior Parr figuring in the famous "election" of Lyndon Johnson to the Senate by the votes of resurrected occupants of a cemetery.

Research about the Rangers during this era (before the Force was transferred to the Department of Public Service and soon after Ransom's death) reveals the inner workings of this world-famous organization. Readers will learn about the strict regulations proudly adhered to by the men and how one who abused his authority or even took one alcoholic drink would be immediately expelled. Few know they carried secretarial supplies along with the bedrolls in their wagons of camping equipment.

The Adjutant Generals insisted that any complaints about the Rangers were put openly on the table in court. Also they saw to it that some Mexicans were always on the jury. This helped control any falsehoods spread by the criminal element to discredit the Rangers, as is their wont at times.

Law enforcement groups in other countries have patterned their organizations after the Texas Rangers, who are known and admired all over the world.

Readers may find ancestors' names in the handy index. The author would appreciate hearing from those who do.

Direct descendants from the Texas Rangers, including those first appointed by Stephen F. Austin to protect the earliest settlers and called by another name, are eligible to join the Former Texas Rangers and Their Descendants, who meet annually.

Those without a Texas Ranger in their family tree may join The Texas Ranger Foundation to support the group and participate in the events. For more information their contact information is;

Phone numbers: 888-766-4055; 830-895-2262;
fax 830-895-2090
Address: 222 Sidney Baker South, Suite 610,
Kerrville, TX 78029-0229

Pat Goodrich, Author

TABLE OF CONTENTS

    ...fierce blue norther catches Captain Henry Ransom, Texas
    Ranger, and his horse at nightfall...they camp in thick brush,
    buffeted by the wind-blown icy rain...huddles under his
    slicker, horse standing near...drowsy, he finally dreams of early
    childhood with an aunt and uncle...their quiet country living
    ideal for an orphan...

    ...he helps with farm...becomes good marksman, hunts...
    dances on railroad docks with other teens...referees
    squabbles...goes to Brenham for more schooling...loving sister
    regiments him...

    ...a planter, then deputy sheriff...marries childhood sweet-
    heart...baby girls born...wife worries about demands, dangers
    of law enforcement career...divorce...

    ...volunteers U. S. Army...Spanish-American War...shipped
    to the Philippines...hardships...jungle fighting...rescued
    his captain...honorable discharge...returns home to see his
    daughters...younger one dies...he re-enlists...

company this time...Bee in college...they correspond frequently...World War II...Germans dealing with Mexico, at backdoor...years of bandit crimes at the Border worsen...real turmoil...adjutant general wrote Ransom to clean it up or he would send someone who could which spurred Henry on...it was said later if winning Border War could be attributed to one man, it should be Ransom...

...colorful letters and wires from Rangers to headquarters (now in State Archives) reproduced give accurate picture of the times in the words of those who were there, the ideal way to get the facts...few Rangers...vast open spaces...Rangers did the impossible...

... Harry Scullin, steel magnate of St. Louis, permitted to "join" Rangers for a month...chose Ransom's company...courtly gentleman gloried in the action...never flinched at the blood and bullets...returned next year ...

...ranchers, merchants all with families call for help... murdered, robbed, raped...bandits stealing livestock, equipment, food... Germany working with Mexico...Governor Ferguson impeached...Ransom his bodyguard...cryptology expanded... invaluable at wartime...

...head of Rangers Hutchings, good friend of Ransom's...replaced by new Governor Hobby's friend, James Harley, defeated in a re-election effort earlier. (Hobby, as Lieutenant Governor, stepped up as Governor Ferguson was impeached)...Hobby used Rangers to campaign for him when election time came up, which was against the law...Ransom started getting mysterious letters, unsigned...his company would be disbanded...he was sent to Sweetwater ostensibly to investigate a murder...

Home of Henry Ransom's Uncle Hamilton and Aunt Kate

CHAPTER I

The long curl of an angry blue-black cloud sweeping low on the horizon tore across Southwest Texas blotting out the sinking sun. A typical "norther" was slamming through miles of the thick brush the natives dubbed "shinnery."

Blasts of high winds stirred up whirling dust devils of sand and twigs that spun just ahead of the advancing sheets of cold rain that plummeted the temperature within minutes.

It was 1915, Christmas Eve, but no other creature within miles cared except Captain Henry Lee Ransom, Texas Ranger. Being in the middle of nowhere so far from his family at this time was getting to be a habit he did not like. However, a Ranger on duty must ignore the calendar.

And the capricious weather.

Just before the high winds hit, he had tied on his horse's nose-bag of corn. He washed down cold pocket food with a few swigs of water from his canteen, hurriedly preparing to weather the fast approaching storm.

The Captain hunkered down on a thicket-choked slope above a shallow arroyo, the handiest refuge from the searching winds that were blowing slanted shafts of water as the lowering clouds opened up.

His gray horse stood nearby in the small clearing, head down, dappled hips against the wind, his body drawn up to catch as little as possible of the near-freezing rain.

With a blanket around his shoulders, the Ranger huddled under the tent made by the wide-spread slicker buttoned at his neck. A horseman always kept one rolled and tied tightly behind the cantle of his saddle.

His cartridge belt with holstered pistols and lever-action Winchester rifle were tucked under the yellow slicker, cold against his body.

He chuckled to himself, remembering an incident of the previous day.

One of the pistols had spoken with its usual authority—and accuracy—to cause an escaping criminal to freeze in his tracks, turn pale, and grab his ear that spurted a stream of blood.

"I heard you could do this," the miscreant had stammered, "but I didn't believe it…"

"Next time it will be your heart," the Ranger had answered quietly.

Ransom had been trailing cattle thieves that had raided the Garcia Ranch, figuring he was getting fairly close to their camp when the norther blew in. No need to keep watch tonight. They, too, would be busy trying to keep warm and dry.

Rain pelted his hat, cold rivulets cascading over the brim on down his coat. The relentless torrent seemed to isolate his small dry island from the rest of the world.

Captain Ransom and his horse had put a long, hard day behind them and the fatigue he had ignored for hours began to sit heavily on his bones. His eyelids felt like lead. With eyes half closed, he reviewed in his mind where he had stationed several men in the company to watch for the outlaws on the other trails. They would meet him the next day with more supplies.

As he began drifting into a fitful sleep, his thoughts turned to his family in Hempstead. Knowing he would be needed back in the "Valley" at this time, he had ridden a train home a few days before to leave gifts for Anna, the infant Jonathan, and toddler Ruby Lee.

The oldest daughter, Beatrice, out of school for the holidays, was in Brenham with her Aunt Vickie, his favorite sister.

When Captain Ransom was close to Ruby Lee's age, he had lost both parents. Now memories of later times were fading, his thoughts drifting back to an earlier time, to the day of his mother's funeral, held not long after his father was buried.

He, little Will, and his three older sisters were split up to live with five different families of aunts and uncles.

At that time he was a small boy of six or seven, of slight build, with a mop of brown hair, face freckled like a turkey egg, and electric blue eyes visible to others across a large room.

He often remembered the knot that tied his stomach in a hard ball. It had felt big enough to choke Uncle Hamilton Ransom's spotted milk cow. A long drink of water or one of Aunt Kate's mile-high biscuits would not have helped. He had tried that before they left for the funeral.

Thoughts of his mother's funeral brought back memories of his father's burial service a couple of years earlier.

Henry recalled the sight of the uncles and friends in dark Sunday suits, the tearful ladies in long black outfits with skirts that made swishing sounds when they walked.

The lower half of the adults was almost all he had seen that day. Small Will, he thought, must have been on eye-level with a lot of black-clad knees and long skirts blocking his view.

He had been glad they had not put a dove down in the grave on top of the casket. Some folks said if the dove squatted down, refusing to fly up to the sky, it meant the dead person's soul did not go to Heaven but to the Other Place. Henry figured with everyone staring down at the bewildered bird, it would be afraid to fly up anyhow. Grownups seemed rather foolish at times, he had concluded.

And now his mother was gone, too.

The days ahead, what did they hold for a little boy like him?

A gust of loneliness had swept over him like a sudden icy wind making him shiver. All five, now orphaned, had hugged each other before the preacher got started, then they backed off to size up how much each had grown since the last time they were together. Henry did not know when he would see Will and his sisters again. He missed his younger brother especially, but Hamilton and Kate could take in only one more, with their own growing yard trotters and house young'n as their father loved to call them.

After hugs and goodbyes, Hamilton called his brood together, helped them scramble in his horse-drawn wagon. The church and its graveyard were only an hour or so away from Ham's farm.

When the horses reached home, they took the path across open fields to stop by the front porch of the small house of unpainted clap-boards.

The fan of the nearby windmill was squeaking as it turned, impatient milk cows by the barn began lowing, and the dogs were barking a welcome as the family climbed out of the wagon.

Hamilton unhitched the horses. Kate herded the children in, but Henry sat down on the porch, chin in hands, his uncle's favorite hunting dog trailing after him to sprawl close by, nose on paws, silently offering sympathy. He sensed Henry's despair as only a member of the canine community can.

Hamilton changed clothes, let the back door slam as he rushed out to the barn. Aunt Kate began banging pots and pans in the kitchen. getting supper. In a few minutes Henry rose to go help with the chores, the dog tagging along.

Dogs were important to families in the 1800's. As farm dogs, they rounded up the cattle in the evenings, chased errant hogs out of the brush back into their pens, ran snakes out of the yard. They warned of Indians and other strangers approaching, monitored the children's activities, and went fishing with the family. A most important function was to assist in keeping fresh game on the table.

Being a conscientious family dog was a serious duty in those days. Hamilton's dogs appeared to take pride in always being where the action was, with tails wagging eagerly. Henry enjoyed their companionship.

His mother had been unable to support her children. A dog would have been an added burden. Relatives said that in the upheaval caused by her husband's death she could not find the receipts proving their 500 acres had been completely paid for, so it was sold in parcels to pay debts she did not feel she owed. The stress was hard on her. Eliza Creed Ransom had no land to farm on shares and no other way to feed five children.

The land was in the Dime Box area, notorious for its rocky terrain and stubbornly rooted and twisted trees that some said had been screwed in the ground by the Devil himself. Kinfolks claimed that E. B. Ransom, Eliza's husband, had literally chopped his heart out trying to clear the unyielding land in time to put in some crops. Ironically, many years later the legendary black gold would spout high in the sky one day, bring in a major oil field to enrich other families. Also some said their cistern had water contaminated by paint, which poisoned the drinking water. Who knows.

Possibly Eliza was in poor health also, which would explain her early death. The children were better off with sympathetic kin.

While in Hamilton's home, Henry became acquainted with the Coles "down the road a piece." They lived on land granted Gabriel, the patriarch of the family, by the Mexican government in the 1820's.

Officials below the Rio Grande were eager to settle the broad prairies and hills as a buffer between the hostile Indians and their country. Also they desired to get it before the French or Spanish, who also had their eyes on the area.

Stephen F. Austin promised the Mexican government to colonize it with only families of good repute. He kept his promise. Most of the early Texas pioneers were honorable people who never hesitated when duty called. This pioneer generation had been reared close to nature, breathing the air of freedom, influenced by forebears active during the American Revolution era.

The distant horizons that appeared to stretch forever under a limitless ceiling of open skies expanded the human spirit to fit the space, not unlike goldfish enabled to grow larger when living in bigger tanks.

Petty thoughts and actions had no place in the struggle for daily food and a roof over one's head, all gained in the wilderness only by exercise of muscle and mind. Such a legacy of respect for hard work and cooperation with one's fellowmen engendered lasting characteristics that saw them through whatever obstacles fate dropped in their paths.

The early Texas families had in common a lot of important traits. Being kind and helpful to each other meant a lot.

Henry was treated like a brother by the lively juveniles in the rollicking Austin Cole household, where a new one joined the flock every other year. The two oldest were Annie and John, followed by Casper, named after the maternal grandfather, Casper Habermacher, then Matthew, James, and Richard, nearer Henry's age, the latter three and Henry collaborating in their fun and mischief. Youngest was little sister, Martha Ella, until the last, Minnie, came on the scene.

Henry, lonesome for Will, who had been his shadow, was quick to look after the child. Pretty Ella of the laughing blue eyes, dark curls, and dancing feet was happy to be under his wing. Many years later she recounted riding to school with him, when he carried her books and boosted her up on her pony.

As the Cole children rode by to the one room Hartsville School each weekday morning, Henry joined them on one of Uncle Hamilton's horses, carrying with his books a shiny syrup bucket. It held his lunch of leftover breakfast biscuit with sausage or venison.

When Ella reached school age, she took along her own syrup bucket, as did the older siblings. She rode sidesaddle like her sisters, wearing a little split skirt. Lady-like in appearance, it must have been difficult to manage with her small hands. She clung to the saddle while her body was twisted at an angle, one leg crooked over the pommel.

Ella loved school, especially her books, and diligently pored over her lessons in the evenings by lamplight. She committed to memory her favorite poem in a McGuffey Reader, remembering it all her life. Its appeal to her perhaps reflected thoughts or dreams beginning to stir in the child's mind. "The Violet" by Jane Taylor expressed the poet's wish to "grow in sweet humility" as that attributed to the modest flower content to blossom, hidden from sight.

Before the Cole children came by each morning, Henry hauled in more wood to make his aunt's huge black stove roar, especially needed when wintry winds howled across the prairie and slammed against the house. Sometimes the kitchen water barrel was empty, or the big wash tub, so he carried in buckets of water from the well.

The schoolhouse, a small whitewashed building of plain design, boasted a covered porch to protect from the rain. Its grounds were worn partially bare of grass by the racing feet of pupils determined to get all the mileage possible out of the short time allotted for "recess." When the tardy bell was swung by the relentless teacher, they skidded through the sand to the door under the porch roof.

Grades from one through eight shared the one room, with younger children sometimes perched on the laps of older ones for reading lessons. Then the little fellows could recite at home what they heard the older ones say, and learned to read earlier than their older seatmates.

At the time Henry Ransom began attending, its door was open only five months of the year. Soon the time lengthened to seven months. Families needed children home to help in the fields, but by early 1900's Hartsville remained open for nine-month sessions. The teacher's salary came from fees paid by parents.

One day when a reluctant pupil was sent to the well in the back to replenish the school's drinking water supply, he hid behind a bush, urinated in the bucket and set it on the rim of the well to abandon forever the environs of learning. This shocking finale to his scholarly efforts rocked the community for weeks. Lest his descendants by embarrassed, he shall remain nameless.

Always springtime was eagerly awaited by the school children. Long johns and shoes would be discarded, with toes freed up to wiggle in ecstasy in new shoots of grass.

The open prairie, with patches of dark, foreboding woods, fairly sang with opportunities for exciting adventures on an eye-ball level with nature itself, a wholesome life for Henry and his schoolmates.

An important activity, one he especially liked, was berry picking, when visions of cobblers spurred the youngsters on to take their syrup buckets after school to patches along the fence lines and abandoned areas where the thorny bushes prospered.

They competed with the birds and quite a few beasts for the succulent fruit, sun-ripened to a sweet delicacy. Even shy box turtles would be discovered among the prickly plants with telltale berry stains on their small faces.

Henry developed a life-long love for blackberry cobbler, his favorite dessert. Aunt Kate baked layers of juicy berries sprinkled with sugar, interspersed with criss-crossed strips of melt-in-your-mouth pastry. The concoction would like indolently in the long, slow heat of Kate's oven to become an almost candied confection. No water or milk was added, with only the berries and sugar combining to make an unforgettable taste. Sometimes she served it hot, topped with cold "hard sauce" of butter and sugar whipped together.

Another popular rite of spring the school children enjoyed, little monsters that they were, was to pick handfuls of the wild pink primroses, known locally as "buttercups". They chased each other to smash blossoms on noses, painting them bright yellow with the pollen. Smashees usually sneezed quite a bit, gratifying to the smashers, who had the compliments returned if they could be caught.

Henry and his friends concentrated on making racket by holding blades of grass between their thumbs and blowing through them, hoping to annoy the girls with the rude noises that resulted...Also they searched for patches of needle grass to throw at each other. The vicious little shafts penetrated clothing and worked through to the skin, with tiny fish-hook barbs gripping tightly whatever they touched, difficult to remove from tender skin.

Sometimes the boys did join the girls when cutting thistles that became soft powder puffs for the ladies and shaving brushes for the fellows who had hopes of sprouting something some day worth the notice.

The school children were skilled at improvising amusement with whatever was at hand, even if it was nothing more than staring at each other to see whose eyes would water first.

After school the Cole children and Henry livened things by making saddle horses out of the family milk cows and stout yearlings that heartily resented being pressed into such service. The young daredevils found themselves dragged or tossed through the muck of the barnyards. Henry was tossed and rolled in the dirt with the rest of them.

One Cole cousin, a mischievous girl, invented her entertainment by defying convention. She "caused talk" by donning men's pants, in itself shocking enough, then rode any beast with hair on it.

She set the community on its ear and gloried in taming down the wildest livestock. When rocking-chair bound, her memories of those wicked ways enlivened her old ladyhood. The risks and the "talk," she reckoned, had been worth it, every bit of it.

Thus the orphan, Henry, enjoyed a somewhat normal boyhood, and at an interesting time when the countryside still retained vestiges of the early frontier.

Marksmanship was important to those families yet on the fringe of pioneer days. As each child became strong enough to shoulder a rifle or aim a pistol, it was taught the proper handling of firearms and likely became a good shot, girls as well as boys.

Folks in the Austin and Fort Bend County areas frequently had wild game on the table, with bear meat among the plentiful supply that included javelina, turkey, and pheasant.

Some of the hunting occurred at night, when the darkened wilderness closed in on the scattered farm houses. At times the air was rent with howls of wolves and coyotes. On nights lit by a Comanche moon, the children would be awakened by whoops of marauding "hostiles" and the thundering hoofbeats of their horses as the Indians raced over the prairies.

Henry, with Dick and Matt Cole following plows, found arrowheads and other artifacts in the fields. They spotted uniform buttons and spoons dropped by Mexican soldiers who had camped there some decades earlier.

Discovery of a rusty musket caused excited discussion around the supper table. It was leaning against a tree in a remote part of the Cole farm of several thousand acres.

For years deep ruts remained hardened in the trails widened by numerous tracks, a reminder of the many families frantically fleeing from their homes with only what they could carry or haul in wagons and make-shift carts, desperate to get out of the path of Santa Anna as he swept through with his armies in 1836 on the way to San Jacinto. He vowed to burn and kill his way across Texas.

One day Dick Cole's missing pet goat was found trapped in a deep hole in the ground on the edge of the property. After the goat was lifted free, marks of the three legs of a large iron pot were visible in the freshly exposed dirt.

Then the Coles recalled seeing several strange Mexicans lurking about a few days earlier. Santa Anna, who had carried gold and silver to pay his troops, must have buried some as he traveled through the countryside. Someone had been told by a participant where to dig. The Mexicans with long memories had come to get it many decades later.

The youth during Henry's boyhood certainly grew up with vibrant, living Texas history in their backyards. Also some of the effects of the Reconstruction Era on the land were still painfully visible.

At mealtime riveting tales were told by family members and frequent guests about forefathers whose lungs had been full of battle smoke since the early days of the American colonists who defied the British.

When Hamilton, his friends, and kin gathered, fresh memories of monumental events were trotted out in the evenings around the fireplace and battles were refought with enthusiasm by the old warhorses present. Of course, the young folk were all ears.

Whenever men's arguments had deteriorated into conflicts that later appeared in the annals of history, the Ransom men would leap up, strap on their guns, kiss their womenfolk goodbye, and patriots that they were, ride off to fight for their freedoms.

Their ancestral flesh and bone joined that of other pioneers to chase off the Redcoats, to forge the Colonies into an independent entity, to add weight to the War of 1812. They fought in Indian skirmishes, and assisted in the struggle of early Texans to set up a republic in spite of the despotic Santa Anna who broke all earlier agreements with the colonists.

Young Henry's great uncle, John Smith Davenport Byrom, had put his life on the line with the rest of the signers of the Texas Declaration of Independence. Then in 1860 Ransoms helped uphold states' rights beliefs of the Confederacy with every able-bodied male unhesitatingly joining the armies of General Lee.

Henry's grandfather, Reuben Ransom was reputed to have at least ten sons and nephews enlisted.

Hamilton's brother Henry had a leg blown off at Fort Sumter in contradiction to historians' erroneous reports that no one was injured. From then on he bore the nickname of "Pegleg Henry." The orphaned boy was named after him.

During this time the South continued to reel from the devastation from the War Between the States in the 1860's after General Lee tendered his sword in surrender to General Grant. It was farther leveled by deliberate actions calculated to cause more hardship and mistreatment.

Corrupt individuals had been put in offices and given unbridled authority to continue the ravaging of the defeated, encouraging injustices to be exacted against persons of both colors. Diaries and journals by those who were there related soul-searing experiences suffered by the conquered long after all hostilities had ceased officially.

Young Henry had fallen heir to intrepid ancestors with courage and loyalty to duty. Genes surged through his being that would influence his character, his interests, his profession.

What would he, an orphan, do with them? Little did he dream of what the future held: a brilliant career in law enforcement that included his becoming one of the great captains of the Texas Rangers, a dedicated Chief of Police in Houston, a be-medaled hero of the Spanish-American War, and tragically, a victim of what was claimed to be an accidental shooting.

Or was it an assassination because he knew too much?

The Little S.A.A.P. Train

CHAPTER II

Others in the scattered community with children who visited the Cole and Ransom families were Casper Habermacher and wife, Eliza Jane Coates, whose parents came from England. Their daughter, Susan Artemicia, was the wife of Austin Bryan Cole. In the 1830's the Habermachers had come from Alsace-Loraine to Pennsylvania, then Texas.

Henry's association with the high-spirited Cole boys continued to brighten his days. The boys hid in the barn for forbidden card games, to their Baptist mother's consternation. They good-naturedly tweaked her apron strings when she pretended to flog them with her bonnet. "Just love taps!" the sisters would scoff.

Known for their ready wit and daredevil tactics, quotes and tales of the boys' escapades were handed down through several generations, as they got into hilarious and memorable scrapes. All were crack marksmen.

Henry became acquainted with firearms as a young boy with the rest of them. They were good hunters, not wasting ammunition.

Being adept with a gun was not always necessary. Some unique occasions required another kind of sudden action to avoid grave disaster.

With the summer heat, doors and windows without screens were left open. Wild creatures sometimes dropped in unannounced. On such a day an adult skunk, thick furry stripes rippling across his back, casually strolled through the house from the dog trot. When the skunk sauntered up to join Henry and the Cole boys, all four leaped off the front porch, not over the banister but through it, taking every board and nail ahead of them.

As they sailed through the air, Dick hollered "Why are you running, Matt?"

"Because I can't fly!" Matt yelled back, as a large section of the railing crashed along in front of him.

They survived their pranks, some rather frightening, including one which electrified the countryside. One day Matt, miffed at the local sheriff, waited for the man to drive his horse and buggy past him. Then he drew a careful bead and shot the spokes out of the man's wheels.

The locals whooped over this, none of whom with the nerve to pull such a stunt themselves. Matt was not the only one who disliked the sheriff. Something dire probably befell the boy for his naughtiness, but no one remembered a thing about that.

An account of Matt's mischief must have flashed via post cards all over several counties, for families, even without much to say, kept in touch by the prodigious use of the mails. Now they had more to tell than simply short greetings.

The golden age of post cards was close to the turn of the century to about 1910 when telephones with party lines took over, but nothing replaced a long, gossipy letter. Stationery for writing was somewhat limited to the small ruled tablets on the "linen finish" sheets of ecru or eggshell tints found on the school supply shelf in grocery stores, near stacks of Big Chief tablets.

Ladies also continued the custom of leaving printed calling cards, those in town making regular visits by horse and buggy.

So much were the colorful post cards valued, with their flowery sentiments and Victorian designs for all occasions, that families mounted them in thick albums. They were kept handy in the parlor on the table that held the lamp with the fringed shade. When company came they were pored over, along with the "tintypes" and photographs in sepia and hand tints. Such albums were destined to become eagerly sought collectibles.

Shades in the summer were kept drawn in the parlor to retain cooler morning air as long as possible, ready for the comfort of any callers. Family members would use the parlor only on special occasions, children allowed to sit quietly looking at the albums, a treat.

Henry was familiar with albums in the neighboring homes. A faithful correspondent with those he loved, he too kept in touch by mail, especially during his courtship days a bit later.

Activities in general were bustling in the countryside that included the towns of San Felipe, Bellville, Richmond, Sealy, and Wallis, with the community of El Pleasant equidistant between the latter two.

Farm work shifted with the seasons. Woodsy smells of fall ushered in the harvest time called "Indian summer," with the smoke of fireplaces and wood stoves permeating the frosty air. The crop of purple and yellow wildflowers brightened the roadsides, with leaves from the shade trees dropping to the ground in their final red and orange glory.

The country folks' thoughts turned to the first good freeze that brought hog killing time. The families helped each other with the butchering, sausage grinding, fat rendering, while the children played ball with pig bladders gingerly inflated by some brave soul.

Mouth watering odors of pumpkin pies, roasting turkeys with tasty stuffing, and other holiday cooking drifted over the crisp air on frosty mornings.

In the evenings families basked in the warmth of roaring fires while heating up sad irons to take to bed with them. Youngsters were bundled in a nest of featherbeds to doze off with small feet curled around warm bricks.

The capricious coastal weather regulated the lives of the farmer, rancher, housewife, those who depended on it. They wrestled and railed against its idiosyncrasies. It dictated when fields would be ready to plow, when to plant, to butcher the hogs, to round up and brand the cattle, when to hang out the clothes to dry. Then the housewife had to rush out to beat the torrents of rain and high winds that would twist through suddenly, threatening to rip everything off the lines.

Henry learned from practical experience the ways of those wresting a living from the land. He benefited from joining in the activities of the closely knit families of the communities.

About this time before the railroads came in, Austin Cole drove cattle down the old Chisholm Trail several times, and once all the way to the Dakotas. He proved this by having a photograph of himself taken in a studio there. Sometimes he and Jacob Hill, a good friend, rode together. Jake had come to Texas as a teenager in 1833 from Kentucky, with his siblings and courageous mother. His father, John, had died in Arkansas on the way.

Austin always returned from these trips with gifts of books and prints, once with a fine music box. Many of the same families in El Pleasant turned up with copies of the same pictures as he brought items to the others as well. Such interests contributed to the refining influence of the worthwhile, cultural things. Some of the gifts he brought endured through the years to be treasured by his descendants.

Those who had come to Texas earlier in covered wagons had brought necessities for starting homes in the new land, plus extras they could find space for, such as a favorite rosebush, books, and a musical instrument. A few pianos made the trip, but must have sounded like a host of tin pans on arrival after all the jostling.

Some families thought of something else. They did not want to risk cousins marrying cousins. The solution was to travel two weeks apart so the young ones would not be together. Parents feared close association on the trip might trigger romance.

After the early struggles hacking out homes, settlers began to turn to the finer things. They trotted out customs of refinement and education remembered from days in the Eastern United States. Folks began erecting churches to serve in lieu of brush arbors, hosts to ambitious insects and lizards that made pests of themselves. Schools and orphanages were founded. In time universities were established over the foundations of the earlier schools.

Music teachers were hired. Eventually entertainments were devised that included balls that rivaled the cotillions of other states. Before long many towns boasted about their own ornately gilded opera houses.

Gradually the rough edges of frontier life were being smoothed. Log cabins were replaced or covered by houses of clapboard that signified the occupants were going up in the world. More flocked to towns, founding businesses that were needed, such as lumber yards, mercantile establishments handling dry goods, and farming supplies.

The families in the El Pleasant area found time during slow seasons on their farms and ranches to hitch up buggies and wagons for occasional gatherings.

They frolicked at dances in different homes on Saturday nights. Pump organs were popular as well as some music boxes that played large discs of waltzes, arias of favorite operas, hymns, and popular hits of the time. Some of these were followed later by player pianos.

Every family seemed to produce at least one musician. Most of the Coles entertained with varied instruments that included violins, guitars, flutes, and an organ or piano.

Years later the older folks, too stiff to get out of their rocking chairs, continued to recall the Saturday night parties and dances, remarking on the three Cole boys who furnished most of the violin music.

"I'll always remember them," said Orville Stuessel of Elm Creek, near Bastrop, almost 90 years later. "They were musicians of the first water and played my favorite kind of music."

With her brothers in great demand for playing for dances, Ella managed to attend at an early age. Henry had to be light of foot to keep up with the little girl who loved to dance. Even later during her grandmothering days, the mere hint of a tune would inspire her slippered feet to begin a gay shuffle, sometimes leading to an impromptu buck and wing, her eyes sparkling at the memories.

The farmers and ranchers, well aware of how they came by their prosperity, wasted nothing and "put on no airs." When automobiles replaced the horses and buggies, they acquired cars, but many drove the same ones until only rust seemed to hold them together. All of them could afford new ones, but impressing others was of no interest.

These were a special kind of honorable folks, whose handshakes were as good as written agreements. Most of high character and integrity, they were helpful and considerate with their neighbors.

One of the Habermachers, when asked why he continued wearing his old, dilapidated boots to church instead of some new ones he had, replied that he did not want to embarrass others who had no new ones. He did not add he was sure God would understand, but would have had he thought of it.

He was one of the many local men who could pinch hit on Sundays for an absent minister. Extemporizing a hard-hitting sermon about avoiding sin that gave food for a week's worth of thought, these men could also lead the congregation in singing hymns, often slightly off key. God probably understood about that, too.

By the late 1800's families of the area collaborated to help bring in the railroads so that driving cattle for months through rough terrain and uncertain weather came to an end.

More interest was generated in Austin and Fort Bend Counties when the San Antonio and Aransas Pass Railroad became an important part of that area, its first tracks being laid out in 1884 by Uriah Lott on a shoestring budget.

Henry would have many occasions to hop aboard later.

The "Sap" was greatly responsible for the development of the virgin land into some of the richest in the world, according to John W. Hedge and Geoffrey S. Dawson in their rare book, THE S.A.A.P. RAILWAY. Lott had been successful in first establishing the Corpus Christi, San Diego, and Rio Grande Narrow Gauge Railroad.

A Mr. Crawford from a northern state spotted opportunity and built a depot, arranging for a train to come for the ample crops of produce that flourished in the soil enriched by the overflow of the Colorado, San Bernard, and Brazos Rivers.

Vegetables such as beans, corn, melons, and pumpkins grew alongside feed for livestock, sugarcane, and sorghum, molasses being made from the latter. Harnessed mules circled a grinder that extracted the juice to be cooked in huge pots to a syrupy consistency. The Ransom, Cole, Habermacher, and Weaver farms contributed a large percentage of the produce shipped to states up north.

The young people congregated on the loading docks at El Pleasant to wait for the train that sometimes came at night and as often as every other evening. They mustered the strength after working in the fields picking beans for $1.50 a bushel to party and dance away the night. As usual the Cole boys and their violins furnished the infectious foot-stomping music.

Henry attended the festivities at the loading docks with the others. He became known to assume the role of peacemaker at these gatherings of teenagers. If arguments were beginning, he was the arbiter, talking his peers into being reasonable, a harbinger perhaps of his future career in law enforcement.

The little S.A.A.P. became an important part of the lives of those on the Texas coast in the late 1800's through the early 1900's. Whistles and toots could be heard as it rattled along, stopping at each town and settlement to change riders. Its engine usually pulled a couple of silvery passenger cars and sometimes a baggage car that hauled light freight and mail. Springtime brought perforated boxes of baby chicks cheeping loudly as they traveled from out-of-state hatcheries.

Passengers' destinations were written on small cardboards that men stuck in their hatbands to expedite their getting off at the correct stops.

The train's schedules regulated the daily routine of those on the route, with folks pulling out watches to see if it was on time when its whistles rent the air.

A movable hub of society, the little train added a touch of "uptown glamour," keeping remote areas in touch with the world. Picturesque depots, with charming architectural details, were built along its route, but one could board it anywhere. It would stop for a person standing in the middle of the track, at a distance, waving a handkerchief or newspaper. The engineer would respond with a whistle, then brake it to a squealing stop.

Some left horse and buggy near a depot, caught the train for a day's round trip, to return that evening to collect the patient horse and drive back home.

Travel on it was an exciting adventure, with friends visiting and eating fried chicken from shoeboxes as it clacked along its tracks, the whistle greeting every little town, and startling occasional runaway cows grazing perilously close to the tracks. A sort of metal "bumper" attached to the lower part of the engine's front was called a "cow catcher" for a reason!

The train traveled through Bellville, which boasted a railroad "roundhouse" for turning about. Sealy was said to have its own turnaround, making the area quite a bustling railroad center.

Then the natives discovered another interest, a different use for their horses. Polo.

For certain Henry Ransom was an avid observer and probably a participant as his older uncles were. Fierce rivalry soon existed between the towns, each with its own team pawing the ground to whip the others. Always there were crowds of loyal boosters to egg them on. At the end of the 1800's the South Texas prairies resounded on Saturdays with the hearty chock of a polo mallet smacking against the regulation ball.

Horses were important in many ways to those settler families, good ones highly prized. Back in the "old days" a horse thief could quickly find himself wearing a rope "necktie."

Frequently the well-cared-for saddle horses were raced, because of man's uncontrollable desire to prove his horseflesh was veritable greased lightning.

But the curried, pampered, highly trained polo "ponies" were a breed apart. Some were a mix of thorough-bred or saddle-bred and a quarter-horse type, those that could cover a short distance at an unbelievable speed.

High-strung, they could be dangerous around anyone ignorant of what might trigger their fine-tuned reflexes. Children, for their own safety, were cautioned to stay clear of these spirited animals.

Ten-year old Abby, daughter of Austin Cole's brother, John, headed for the stables one day to encounter trouble even before getting near a horse. The last person using a pair of heavy clippers for roaching manes had failed to put them back in place. Small Abby casually picked them up. They slipped through her fingers. The clippers slid down her leg, opening a deep gash nearly all the way to her shoe. Her mother, hearing her screams, came running.

Ola Self Cole was used to handling emergencies. When she saw the gushing blood, she called the other children to come hold Abby down within sewing distance.

She then poked sturdy thread through her needle's eye, and with no deadening agent handy, calmly stitched her daughter's leg whole again, ignoring the screeches of her patient. Abby carried the long scar the rest of her life, a souvenir of the polo period, and a reminder to stay away from the horse barn.

The advent of the automobile gave the dedicated polo fanciers engines and sparkplugs to tinker with and became another thrilling mode of travel. However, their leisure time was soon filled with another exciting activity. Golf.

The craze leaped the ocean from Scotland to spread like wildfire over America, infecting even the hinterlands. The small towns turned their cow pasture polo grounds into manicured golf courses. Men walked instead of riding to swat balls with sticks. Henry Ransom apparently never abandoned a horse for a golf club, however.

A few ladies became golfers, but some of their other enter-tainments exposed unique hazards. Henry's Aunt Kate was a loyal member of the local ladies crochet club.

Once a week they struck out in their buggies for a different hostess' house. News was exchanged while their fingers flew. One time they were speculating on who would be the first to use the new doctor in town.

The medic was such a fascinating subject they spent most of one meeting discussing him.

Fanny Patillo, one of the most vociferous about being the first to use him, went one time too many to the buffet for refills supplied by the hostess. Plate in hand, she sat down without looking back, landing on her crochet needle. Consequently she did have the honor of being the first patient, getting the long needle removed from her backside.

Other doctors began practicing in the area. With prosperity more folks were moving in, young ones were growing up, and the elderly were dying off, especially during the severe winter weather.

The kin bathed, dressed, and put on display the corpses. Each end of a coffin was set up on a chair, to expedite the "viewing" ceremony of the wake. They used flowers from their own yards, but in winter the only ones available were the narcissus blossoms in every yard. The concentration of their pungent odor about the coffins almost overwhelmed the nostrils of the mourners.

One elderly survivor who had attended all her peers' funerals announced she was sick of the flowers' odor that always reminded her of all the corpses she had bidden goodbye. Reputedly she quit attending, no matter who passed on.

Henry's formative years were spent among characters who were honest and ethical, with members of the closely-knit families attending each others' weddings, christenings, and funerals. This prepared him with a solid foundation of values and ethics to carry him through his perilous future on the cutting edge of danger.

Before his adulthood, however, his life took an important turn.

Pistol in holster

CHAPTER III

Henry's oldest sister, Victoria, just married, sent for him as soon as he finished the eighth grade at the Hartsville School. He and his brother were reunited as she wanted both boys to live with her to complete school in Brenham. Her new husband, John Davis of the postal service, welcomed the boys as well.

Vickie was a stickler for good habits, clean living, getting a good education. Organized and business like, she immediately bought the boys a new suit apiece, enrolled them in school, took them to church that first Sunday. Then she documented their new lives for posterity by having their pictures taken.

The studio photograph depicted a solemn, be-suited, and stiff-collared teenaged Henry, whose expression betrayed the fact he was not there willingly. His mind appeared to be miles away while the photographer fussed with equipment.

Probably his ears were cleaner than most, being regularly inspected by strict Victoria who took seriously her responsibility of getting her little brothers educated and socialized. She herself might have substituted the work "civilized." Henry must have longed for his comrades just down the road from Hamilton's place, and missed the pranks and wide-open space of country life.

As it was, he caught the Baptist upbringing on both ends of the line, with Vickie carrying on what Ham and Kate had started at the school house which on Sundays was used for church services.

However, Henry greatly appreciated what she did for him and Will. She always remained his favorite sister. The rest of his life he visited her and her family as often as he could.

Post cards came in handy for him, as he maintained contact with his aunt and uncle, the Coles, and other families at El Pleasant. Ella was some years younger than he was, but the two kept up a long-distance friendship that began to blossom. Marriage plans would be in the future, once he completed schooling and made some nest-egg money.

The prosperous larger town of Brenham was situated in the lovely rolling hills of Washington County, not far from Cole's Settlement, named after Judge John P. Cole, brother of Gabriel Cole. Later called Independence, it was originally "laid out" by Gabriel, a civil engineer as well as attorney.

With a large population of German settlers, who could be depended on to locate the best farmland, Brenham was clean, tidy, with charming, well-kept Victorian homes, several churches, and schools where German was taught as well as English. Quite early each spring the hillsides were blanketed with bright fragrant blue-bonnets that attracted tourists.

In Brenham, Henry and Will attended what was the first free public high school in Texas, established under the Landmark School Law of 1875. Nine grades were offered, including classical literature and science courses. In those days high school requirements included four years of Latin. The school sessions there, too, were shortened so that the young people could help at harvest time.

In 1883 a new building for the high school was erected, with 15″ thick walls, cedar beams, and plaster mixed with cow hair. Located at 606 Alamo, it boasted windows and doors with marble arches and sills that held up well under the students' traffic.

When Henry went to Brenham, the Cole boys were sent to school in Austin during winters. When it was out, their father hired a music teacher who spent the summer with the family so the boys could continue their lessons. Occasionally Henry visited them during the summer.

Matt and Dick would settle on the front porch for their instruction, but the other brother who marched to his own drummer refused to join them. Instead he would wet his fishing line in the nearby river, pretending no interest in the progress on the porch. However his ears were tuned to what transpired, for after the lesson, he would get his violin out to sit alone somewhere else to play everything he had heard.

A facet of Matt's talent manifested itself in his rhyming ability, for reams of poetry poured out of him like cane syrup out of a jug. Those few allowed to hear it rated it "quite good."

Dick appeared to be his family's leading comedian, who also had the uncanny ability to train his dogs and horses to do unusual things. All three brothers became much more in demand for playing for dances, with state-wide engagements.

The boys' joyful outlook on living was exactly what the orphaned Henry needed as he headed into the teens.

Their rugged individualism shaped them as the town that livened the scene for all who knew them.

Once Matt was offered a salary, sizable for the times, to play regularly on one of Houston's daily radio shows. He could not accept the job, he said, because he did not want to leave his animals at home. Later he called off his wedding to a local lady when at the last minute she told him he could keep his horses but had to get rid of his hunting dogs.

He quietly packed away his wedding suit, found folded in an old dusty trunk by a niece sorting his belongings after his death. From the day he put it away, he never uttered another word about the incident and never married.

Henry missed his childhood playmates, but in Brenham he was growing beyond the carefree days of the grammar school set. On graduation from the school there, he began work as a planter.

Before long, to no one's surprise, he returned to El Pleasant to claim for his bride Martha Ella, his childhood sweetheart. She was 17, he 21.

On January 6. 1892, the wedding, with A. S. Poindexter, minister of the gospel officiating, took place at her parents' home, near what was called Burrough's Switch.

All the kin and friends flocked over to help the happy pair celebrate with a party that lasted until the wee hours. They made a handsome couple, pretty Ella with the laughing eyes and dancing feet and her attentive groom, liked and respected by everyone for his manners and ambition.

Vickie, always proper and correct, had instilled in Henry the social graces which probably accounted in part for his gentlemanly conduct around the ladies. His chivalrous manner was even remarked upon by one lady whose compliments about his courtly demeanor were quoted in a book published many years later.

Ella's parents let the young couple move into one of their rent houses on another parcel of the land in a remote, wooded area. Relatives and friends contributed several pieces of essential furniture and other gifts for their new household.

To provide for his new wife, Henry continued work as a planter for awhile, then accepted a job as a sheriff's deputy in Austin County. His boyhood experience with riding and marksmanship gave him confidence and skill needed for this work.

Ella had been rather shy as a child, and loved to play with her cousins. She married so young that she still was inclined to have fun with them whenever they visited. Sometimes Henry would come home to find her playing with others, even joining in when climbing trees.

He laughed when he found her standing on a box to reach the clothesline. Cutting a pole, he showed her how to use it to raise and lower the line, something he had seen Kate and Vickie do.

Ella worked hard at housekeeping. She had learned early at home how to "sew a fine seam," calling it "sewing on my fingers."

She wrestled daily with the cumbersome, cranky wood stove. When inspired, she could produce a minor miracle with freshly shelled black-eyed peas or a "mess of wild greens." She knew which plants growing wild were edible, having learned from her mother and pioneer grandmother.

Ella worked her sorcery with the old stove, its firewood stacked in a nearby wood box. Water for cooking and washing dishes was hauled in, kept handy in a barrel in one corner of the room.

Memories of the wood smoke odors combined with smells of tall, fluffy biscuits and chicken with dumplings bubbling in a big pot were never forgotten by the fortunates who visited her kitchen.

Years after, along with Ella's cooking odors, any fragrances resembling the "grandmother smells" brought back memories of the sweet perfumes of her face powder and soap at her mirrored dressing table. Over the years even the taste lingered of the pink peppermints she always carried in her purse for the grandchildren. But back to Henry's time…

He was kind and generous. Ella described how he acted if he noticed her wearing a house dress with a hole or tear in it. Playfully he would poke her through the hole, then reach in his pocket to give her a handful of bills, saying, "Go buy some new clothes, Ella!"

Another tale that delighted the grandchildren was about the time Henry came home from work and noticed her leaning on a post of the front porch of their home. She was waiting for him to come into the yard. He stopped at the little gate in the fence.

"Hold still, Ella!" he called, taking one of his six shooters out of its holster. "I'm going to shoot through that knot on your head!"

A crack marksman, he was almost religious about staying in practice. His life depended on hitting what he aimed at, so his reputation eventually preceded him as he traveled over the State.

"Tell us more! What then?" the grandchildren would urge her. Ella, employing a dramatic pause, had the youngsters hanging onto every word. Although they had heard the story before, they loved to marvel at it again. All of her recollections of Henry's deeds provided riveting material.

"Well," Ella would continue, "I stood still and he did. He shot right through my chignon on top of my head." She always hesitated in order to pat the very spot. "That bullet just skimmed right over the top of my scalp."

"Weren't you afraid?" she would be asked.

"No," she always assured them. "He was a good shot. If I moved, he might hit me. I knew I was perfectly safe if I didn't move."

She remembered him fondly, recalling little endearing things about him, speaking of his favorite breakfast being soft-scrambled eggs and a tender broiled steak, of his penchant for blackberry cobbler, and of the only piece of jewelry he wore, a large black opal set in a heavy gold ring.

Ella recalled two things that irritated him most was when someone else would assume in advance what he would do or say, or what his opinion would be about something. She also pointed out that he did not like leftovers at mealtime!

Henry decided for certain that he was cut out for working in law enforcement when he became a deputy, working in Fort Bend County.

He and Ella had moved to Richmond, the county seat, to live on the Box P. Ranch that belonged to his father's cousin, Robert J. Ransom. Their firstborn, a girl, died at birth. The second, a daughter they named Beatrice, was born December 20. 1894, only a few days before the wife of a close Mexican friend gave birth to a little girl also. The father thought so much of Henry that he named his infant Beatrice also. The two babies played together as long as the Ransoms stayed there.

Robert Ransom branded a colt and two calves for his tiny great niece, the custom of the time.

Henry and Ella doted on their child, excited when she sprouted teeth, began to talk and to toddle about. However, Ella was apprehensive about being alone many nights with "Bee" while Henry was on duty.

As his work became more intense, Henry's hours off duty were more uncertain. He made great effort to reach home while Beatrice was still awake.

He loved to be the one to tuck in bed the little child he adored. He was known to love children and enjoyed every minute with one of his own.

His wife, hardly more than a child herself, would stand in the doorway, smiling at the usual bedtime ritual, knowing how precious this sweet interval was to him.

He enjoyed putting the little one to bed in the evenings just to hear again her usual response to his last words. The slight young man would lean over, gently unclasp the toddler's arms from around his neck, and put her down on the small bed. She always smiled up at him as he carefully pulled the quilts up to her small chin.

Then he would look down at Beatrice and say, "Good night, little Bee!"

With her blue eyes sparkling in the pale lamplight like twin stars on a cold, clear night, she never failed to pipe in her tiny voice, "Good night, little Papa!"

Henry's hours at home became more erratic. Now when he came it was usually after dark. Many times he did not remain at home all night.

He did not mention much about his work, but moved his family to a more remote area to protect them from criminals that became enemies because of his apprehending them.

They might retaliate, hurting him more by harming his family.

From all accounts he was fair, thorough, and exact, treating all lawbreakers alike, no matter how prominent or wealthy. During his career he would be known to step on the toes of public officials in high offices in upholding the law. Sometimes this caused obstacles to be put in his path by the political sector, but he never wavered in doing his duty.

Ella was well aware of the dangers to her family, made more apparent to her when she observed the precautions he took when returning home. It was told that one morning his pillows had marks of bullets going through them.

Suspecting trouble, he had placed them under the covers to appear like a body in his bed, while he slept on the floor by the wall directly under the window, a habit he had acquired for safety. At any time, day or night, wherever he sat or stood, he always chose a corner and kept his back to the wall, with visibility clear to all windows and doors. Relatives he visited agreed he took the same precautions at their homes as well.

Whatever his kin knew about his activities they kept to themselves, knowing that an innocent comment could be dangerous to him or his family. Although they loved and deeply respected him, sometimes they wished he had settled on a different occupation.

When Bee was three, her little sister, Mary Ella, was born. Bee was ecstatic about having a live "baby doll" to tend, and Henry welcomed his second daughter with open arms. He longed to have more time to spend with his children.

And Ella worried more about being alone so much.

She even had to shoot her own hawks.

She kept a shotgun by the back door. When a hen in the chicken yard squawked for help, she would snatch it up quickly, run out and blow the feathers off the marauder.

One day a large hawk flew up high with one of her prize laying hens, a "Dominecker" or "Rhode Island Red," and she filled the hawk with heavy shot. He dropped her hen to the ground before flapping off lopsidedly.

Schooled in home remedies of the pioneers, Ella knew exactly what to do. She brought the hen in the kitchen, and while toddler Bee watched, cracked open an egg. Removing the membrane just under the shell, she stretched it for a patch over the large tear under the chicken's wing. In a few days the fowl was out with the others, busily chasing grasshoppers in Ella's kitchen garden.

She was a true Cole. All family members, known to be marksmen, were well able to defend themselves. They were peaceful, not starting anything, but capable of finishing it.

Ella's cousin Abby was alone in her home one day when a sheriff's deputy was going about warning people that an armed and desperate convict had escaped from the prison farm near Richmond and was believed to be in the vicinity.

When Abby answered her door, he warned her, then asked, "Do you have a gun? Can you shoot it?"

Being one of the few short Coles in the family, she drew herself to full height, looked him in the eye, and said simply, "I am a Cole."

"Oh," he said, and left without another word.

Once when Ella's brother Dick came to see her, he walked in with a brace of fat squirrels over his shoulder. He carried nothing else but a small suitcase.

Later when he opened it, his pistol was seen lying on top of his folded clothes. Each squirrel had been shot through the eye.

Ella enjoyed his visit and hearing about the larger world beyond her own. When he departed the next day, though, she felt lonelier than ever, watching him disappear down the path, whistling with every step.

At this time she was feeling quite defenseless, with not only a runabout toddler to care for but an infant as well. She was unnerved about potential danger because of demands of Henry's work. And what if the little girls became ill, living out in the middle of nowhere? There were no close neighbors to call in an emergency. What would she do?

Her increasing fears multiplied when an old man knocked loudly on her door late one night when Henry was not home. This man had lived not far from the Coles when she was a child. When she refused to open the door, he began to threaten her, using abusive language.

Terrified, she stood with her shotgun aimed at the door. Finally he left after she convinced him she would shoot if he broke open the door.

The next morning, after a sleepless night, the troublesome thoughts she was entertaining must have grieved her sorely. Henry had been her childhood sweetheart, was now her loving husband, albeit a high spirited and frolicsome one at times.

They divorced at her instigation, according to relatives, although neither ever said a word to anyone else about the real reason for the break-up. However, her family understood her worries and knew that she could no longer cope with the dangers and uncertainties inherent in her husband's work as a lawman.

Henry must have been terribly torn to leave Ella, whom he still loved, and the little girls he adored. All the Coles thought a lot of him and continued to consider him one of them.

He moved Ella and their daughters to where the now-widowed grandmother, Susan, was living with her married son, John, and his family. Ella and the girls were greeted joyfully by their cousins, Artie and Abby. Ella's siblings who were still single lived there also. She was relieved to be back in the security of her big, loving family.

While the toddler trotted beside her, Grandmother Susan taught eager Bee the alphabet and multiplication tables on the way to the well or to the henhouse to gather eggs. She was reading shortly, her active mind absorbing literature like a thirsty blotter soaking up puddles of spilled ink.

Many years later, when in her nineties, Bee's memory of riddles, legends, poetry remained fresh. No one else could rattle the alphabet off backwards at breakneck speed. She astounded her grandchildren by reeling off reams of classical literature she had learned "by heart" in those early days. At age 90 she reviewed updated books on higher math, calculus, and trigonometry just for fun and could still race backward through the alphabet.

But this is ahead of Henry Ransom's story.

With his own home broken up, he could use a distraction at this time. He found one.

A war was going on.

Americans in the Philippines

CHAPTER IV

Shortly after the divorce Henry enlisted in May 1898 in the U. S. Cavalry, reputedly the only volunteer from Fort Bend County. After a brief training period he was shipped to the Philippines in the Spanish-American War. A Ransom never flinched before the possibility of hot lead and gun smoke.

The conflict in Cuba would soon be resolved, with troops needed at other islands held by the Spanish.

Problems with Cuba had been fermenting for some time, with discontent and discord building up because of the cruel treatment by Spain. The United States was interested because of trade with Cuba, investments in the island itself, and also because of its proximity to America's own shores.

After several U. S. Congressmen had been urging that the U. S. recognize the independence of Cuba, newspapers started reporting atrocities committed there by the Spanish. When a letter from Enrique Dupuy de Lome, an official on the Spanish delegation to Washington, D.C., was discovered and published, it was found to be insulting to President McKinley.

Americans became greatly upset.

All protests and demands were met with the evasive, shifting policy which had always characterized Spain's dealings with American interests.

Open breach of "international law" occurred in Cuba with imprisonment of Americans for no reason, some being held incommunicado. One American was arrested and tortured, it was published, because he had a Cuban stamp in his collection.

Then on February 15, 1898, the United States was shocked when the U.S. Battleship, "Maine," docked in Havana, was blown up. Various negotiations with Spain failed. War against Spain was declared on April 19, 1998.

American troops were sent to Cuba to fight under the severe tropical conditions of extreme heat, frequent torrential rains, and rampant disease, including malaria. It was transmitted by the clouds of mosquitoes constantly harassing the soldiers.

The Spaniards would have preferred the Cuban operations of the United States to be during the rainy season, so difficulties would increase for the offensive forces, and decrease and improve for the defenders. The Americans would rather wait before landing soldiers there until after the malaria season was over.

Theodore Roosevelt and his Rough Riders gained fame with their heroic efforts alongside the other courageous troops fighting against almost insurmountable obstacles. All American forces remained cheerful and uncomplaining during these trying times.

Commodore George Dewey, with his squadron docked in Hong Kong, received a cable with orders to destroy or capture the Spanish fleet in Manila.

On May 1, 1898, the same month that Henry Ransom volunteered for service, Dewey's ships ploughed into the harbor, flags flying and guns blazing, ignoring danger from torpedoes, mines, and enemy fire. He blew the Spanish vessels out of the water all in one day, losing not a single American sailor.

During the battle Dewey refused to stay behind a special protective barrier on his ship, but stood up high, within the enemy's sight. He could better observe the action, he explained later.

Then he set about rescuing the terrified Spaniards bobbing about in the bay, taking them for medical treatment at specially set-up facilities within his line. He sent 200 more sick and wounded to a hospital on shore. Also Dewey protected the city of Manila against looters who began swarming into the area.

The Spanish fleet in Manila Bay was destroyed completely by Dewey and the U.S. Navy, which had been well prepared by Teddy Roosevelt, Assistant Secretary to the Navy.

Dewey was a hero overnight, America proud of his incredible feat. Parades, flags, and wild cheers broke out everywhere. And many a baby boy born in months to come was named Dewey. Sharp eyes these days may yet spot at antique auctions weathered whirligigs in the shape of a sailor boy painted to represent the nation's hero.

The Commodore kept rigid control of the bay, its beautiful, heavily wooded banks a picture post card with backdrop of mountain scenery.

To arrive soon would be troop ships of soldiers, including Henry Ransom, to advance on land to dislodge the enemy from its trenches and other fortifications.

The official dispatch from Dewey at Manila, dated May 1, 1898, announced the victory: "The squadron arrived at Manila at daybreak this morning. Immediately engaged the enemy and destroyed the following vessels: 'Reina Christina,' "Castillia,' "Don Antonio de Ulloa,' 'Isla de Luzon,' 'Velasco,' the transport 'Isla de Mindanao,' and one other vessel, and water battery at Cavite. Squadron is uninjured.

"Only a few men slightly wounded. The only means of telegraphing is to the American consul at Hong Kong. I shall communicate with him." The following was telegraphed from Cavite on May 4: "I have taken possession of naval station at Cavite, Philippine Islands, and destroyed fortification at the bay entrance, patrolling the garrison. I control the bay completely and can take the city at any time. The Squadron is in excellent health and spirits. The Spanish loss is not fully known, but very heavy, 150 killed, including Captain on 'Reina Christina' alone. I am assisting in protecting the Spanish sick and wounded in hospital within the line. Much excitement at Manila. Will protect foreign residents. Dewey."

Dewey's fleet that won the Battle of Manila Bay included the gunboat, "Petral," the protected cruiser, "The Baltimore," the gunboat, "Concord," and the "McCulloch," a revenue cutter.

Dewey was noted with pride by his associates to be a "heroic character of few words, but a doer of brave deeds."

He received this dispatch from Secretary Long: "The President, in the name of the American people, thanks you and your officers and men for your splendid achievement and overwhelming victory. In recognition he has appointed you Acting Admiral, and will recommend a vote of thanks to you by Congress as a foundation for further promotion."

He had run past mined harbors and land fortifications to follow orders 9,000 miles away from a home base of supplies.

Spain had held the Philippines in her iron grip for three hundred years. During the previous 60 years, 17 rebellions against Spain had occurred, as the idea of Philippine nationality was gradually taking hold. With a "Young Filipino Party" formed earlier, and another organization, this time Tagalog, founded by

1891, called Katipunan, it was not surprising that insurrection had broken out several times.

When hostilities were beginning between the U.S. and Spain, the Filipinos declared their independence on June 12, 1898. Emilio Aguinaldo was elected their permanent president, with the capitol set up at Malolos.

Constant unrest was fomented by corrupt politics and the repressive treatment of the ordinary citizens by Spanish officials and soldiers.

The Philippines, with over 1200 islands, were home to a diverse assortment of natives of varied origins and religious beliefs that collided in many instances. Customs ranged from those of civilized groups to tribes living in primitive conditions who were determined to remain so.

The islands had been conquered by the Spanish in the 1600's. They came not to help the natives but to squeeze out everything that could benefit themselves and their mother country. The Filipinos were unfairly regulated, held firmly in the grip of the military and politicians stationed there.

Incredibly, almost every move was taxed in some way. Often when a person wanted to butcher his own hog he was compelled to pay a tax. Anyone trying to avoid this, including a woman who concealed a sale of home-made goods, was fined and sometimes severely punished or imprisoned. With countless tax collectors, each was assigned to about 60 people only, in order to hound them enough to bring them to their knees.

When Henry Ransom volunteered, he was unaware that he would learn more about this faraway land than he ever read in his geography and history classes.

When he enlisted, he gave the name of a cousin, Miss Mable Ransom of Richmond, Texas, as next of living kin to be notified, if need be, of his fate as a soldier.

His physical description included height of 5'8", weight 140 pounds, hair brown, complexion fair, and eyes blue. His age was about 28.

He had no military training but possessed valuable assets that saved his life many times: his talent of incredible marksmanship, his cool head and courage in dangerous situations.

After living on transport ships for several weeks, he and the other American soldiers must have been happy to set foot on solid ground again. They had arrived at the land of monsoons, typhoons, volcanoes, and earthquakes.

The islands were unstable geographically and weatherwise, paralleling the upheaval and turmoil of the varied races of people there.

The ordinary citizens, after harsh treatment for several centuries, were braced for any other foreigners coming on their islands to act accordingly.

To their amazement and gratitude, the American soldiers were kind and helpful, not acting like conquerors at all. This had been undreamed of by the wary natives, who were happy to welcome the affable soldiers.

The children, not knowing otherwise, were completely uninhibited in offering friendship, which pleased the Americans, who were lonely and homesick for their own families back home.

Generally speaking, the Filipinos appeared to the servicemen to be a happy-go-lucky people described by some as preferring to dance, play, and loaf, the tropical nature of the islands making life easy. However, the frequent clash of traditions and cultures festered until pockets of violence would break out.

Certain groups had a veritable contempt for death. With the hotbed of intrigue always present, they could be incited to violence by corrupt persons who knew how to use the natives' volatile emotions for their own purposes.

The Americans had to exercise care in their dealings with the natives, but one of the most important matters to the soldiers was "Mail Call." Letters from home were treasured, and the soldiers answered them during spare minutes.

Henry missed his little girls, writing cheery letters to Bee in his flowing Spencerian hand by lantern light at night between duties. Memories that he conjured up in his mind of his lively toddler helped him through the stress and horrors of war. He kept a small Bible to give her on his return home. She valued this token of his devotion all her life.

When he wrote to his brother, Will, he spoke of how homesick he felt, 5,000 miles away. He commented about having bouts of malaria, adding that when someone brought him a baked chicken, the doctors refused to let him have it.

He probably reported to Will that the .38 double action revolvers which were supposed to be an improvement for the

Army did not knock down the enemy after all. When the Army was convinced that nothing less than the .45 single action revolvers would do the job, their new .38's were traded back for the old ones.

The Americans were interested in this land so different from their own and wrote home about their observations made during scarce breaks in routine.

They were amazed at the plentiful supply of the fast-growing bamboo that had so many uses.

Homes and municipal buildings were constructed of bamboo, wood, and stone, reflecting the natives' ingenuity as well as the influence of their conquerors' architectural styles.

Most families, naturally musical, entertained themselves with instruments of their own contrivance, using bamboo. The abundance of the bamboo with horns and flutes of all sizes and shapes was noted by all visitors. Frequently the air was filled with haunting melodies of a lonely flute's birdlike song in a distant area.

A band of natives just out for pleasure marching down the road might appear at any time, all joyfully playing on whatever they had constructed. Such charming intervals were happy surprises, a welcome contrast to the turmoil of war.

A Spanish cathedral in Luzon boasted a huge pipe organ made entirely of bamboo that, according to one American, produced the sweetest sounds he had ever heard pour out of an organ.

More mundane uses for the prolific bamboo included storage for food, piping for water, and construction of furnishing and bridges.

Bamboo was not the only plant that prospered in the tropical atmosphere. The lush jungle, so thick the eye could not penetrate it, seemed to grow back within hours after the men chopped their way through it, a slow and depressing project.

The land was laced with countless streams and rivers, some running wildly downhill in the uneven terrain. Crowded mangrove trees prospered along banks of waterways, their knobby roots and trunks hideaways for lurking crocodiles.

Hot and steamy in the daytime, the jungle, although cooler at night, afforded excellent breeding places for insects, especially the swarms of malaria-carrying mosquitoes. Henry and his companions would smear themselves with mud to protect their skin. When really maddened by the relentless hordes, they simply jumped in water that was almost always nearby to wash away their pesky tormentors.

After dipping in the streams, however, they usually had to pluck loose from their bodies the leeches that flourished in the water and smeared mud or tobacco juice on the red welts. Some caused eyes to water excessively as well, almost blinding the hapless victims.

Having leeches crawl into their noses and on into their sinuses was the risk for those lying unconscious on the ground or attempting to rest. How the medics coped with such misery was never explained.

The dangers waiting in the vast jungle were de-emphasized somewhat by the incredible wonders of nature growing unrestrained.

Huge leaves glowed at night with phosphorescence, even when rains came, which was often. The dense vines and dripping foliage ornamented with large, trumpet shaped orchids would have been considered botanical treasures by the men had they not been preoccupied with looking out for the snipers concealed in the thick leafy boughs high over their heads.

Host to immense humming insects that seemed to get louder at night, the jungle harbored huge fireflies and giant bats that flew into the men as they struggled through in the darkness.

Sudden storms would blow up, with howling winds and drenching rains causing the numerous streams to rise rapidly, becoming impassable. Trails were narrow, if visible at all, and the land beneath the verdant growth was hilly, making penetrating the density more difficult.

In open areas away from the jungle a kind of grass 8' to 10' tall flourished. It could cut a man's arm off as efficiently as a razor blade. This was another favorite hiding and breeding place for mosquitoes.

Malaria felled many of the soldiers. Ransom fought in numerous battles and skirmishes, in between what seemed like constant sick leave with the fever and chills of the disease. For some years after his days in the Philippines he had recurring bouts. Other than that he came out of the service with only a bruised knee.

The enemy was fierce. When worked into a frenzy, some of the tribes fought like fiends, adhering to radical religious beliefs.

Life was miserable for this segment and considered cheap. They gladly killed for the sake of killing, taking great risks after being promised they would have life in paradise with all their desires granted, once they lost theirs on earth.

Treacherous and cruel, they brandished the big cane knives called bolos, their favored weapons for beheading their victims. They fought a war of terror, determined to weaken the spirit of the Americans.

The unfamiliar ways of the tropics, the unknown dangers hidden in the jungle, the invisible snipers clinging to treetops drawing a bead on anything that moved, were more than enough to shatter the morale of the most intrepid of soldiers.

However, the Americans maintained the reputation of being courageous fighters. Their morale remained high.

Will Kincheloe of Wharton, Texas in 1937 met another member of Henry's family.

"What tales I heard when Henry Ransom and his commanding officer were reminiscing about the days in the Philippines together!" he exclaimed.

In the early 1900's he had met Henry in the lobby of a Houston hotel where they sat down for a visit when along came the major under whom Ransom had served. This unexpected reunion produced tales of the hair-raising experiences they had shared in the jungles of those islands.

Kincheloe remembered Henry telling about his commander asking for a volunteer to cross a river to distract a group of the enemy that was peppering his men with gunfire from a high cliff.

Immediately Ransom jumped forward, cut a slender reed to breathe through and slid silently underwater, crossing downstream to climb the bluff further away in order to circle behind the snipers to surprise them. This distraction gave his companions a chance to cross without being shot in midstream.

He had to swim noiselessly beneath the surface of the leach-infested water. The ploy worked so well that all the others crossed safely. This was because the enemy came after Henry, all of them.

He described being on the run the rest of the day and on into the night, with his pursuers after dark being within five or six feet of him many times. He had to stand stock-still awhile, he said, then move cautiously only a few feet, then stand still again for fear of discovery. This went on all night long, run and freeze in his tracks, run and freeze again, until finally by daylight he managed to evade them and return to his company.

An incident of Spanish rule depicting their brand of cruelty involved Dr. Jose Rizal, martyr, considered the foremost poet, novelist, political essayist, and historian of the time, a man who had many friends and loyal admirers. An intelligent person e ducated in France and Spain, he had helped organize the Young Filipino Party that opposed the Spanish rule.

Also he had written a book about Spanish oppression of the Philippines and was exiled to the Island of Dapitan.

There he met, fell in love with, and became engaged to a young lady of Irish descent. However, on some pretext, he was brought back to Manila, sent to Madrid to be tried, and then returned to serve as an example. The Spanish did not trust this learned patriot.

His fiancée related events of his shocking fate: "Everyone knew that Dr. Rizal was innocent. All that could be brought against him was the publication of his book, and Spanish officials who tried him had never even read it. Nevertheless he was condemned to death. I then asked permission to be married to him, and they granted my request, thinking to add to the horror of his martyrdom. The marriage was celebrated by a friar the same day on which he was sentenced. I passed the whole night on my knees in prayer before the prison door, which shut my husband from me.

"When morning dawned the Doctor came out, surrounded by soldiers, his hands tied behind his back! They took him to the Luneta, the fashionable promenade of the city, where all the military executions take place. The lieutenant in command of the firing party asked where he would prefer to be shot. He replied, 'Through my heart.' 'Impossible,' said the lieutenant. 'Such a favor is granted only men of rank. You will be shot in the back." A moment later my husband was dead. The soldiers shouted, 'Hurrah for Spain!' and I 'Hurrah for the Philippines and Death to Spain!' I asked for the body. It was refused me. Then I swore to avenge his death. I secured a revolver and dagger and joined the rebels. They gave me a Mauser rifle, and the Philippines will be free."

Dr. Rizal wrote a beautiful poem titled "My Last thoughts" the night before his execution that has been translated into heart breaking and lovely English prose. What control over his mental faculties he must have had, under such circumstances!

The Armistice between Spain and America was signed August 12, 1898, the peace treaty signed December 19, 1898 in Paris, France, with the U.S. agreeing to pay $20,000,000 for the Philippines, which would receive independence in 1946. By 1901-1902, the Filipinos were pronounced citizens of their islands, no longer under the control of the Spanish.

At the end of the war with Spain, some of the American soldiers, including Henry Ransom, were sent back to the U.S. and discharged. Henry was mustered out on November 14, 1898, and returned to Richmond to work again as a deputy sheriff. He lived near the home of good friends, the Kegans. A bayou was named later for the prominent family.

Ella packed up toddler "Mamie" and runabout Beatrice to catch the local train to Richmond for several days' stay with their long-time friends so Henry could visit with his daughters. The little girls had a grand adventure riding the "Sap" with its initials, S.A.A.P. painted on the sides of its several passenger cars. Flashing by as the train rattled along were fields that had already been harvested of the fall's crops of cotton and corn. A few flocks of placid cows grazed without looking up at the passing train.

The girls were fascinated with the wicker seats, the moveable windows, the rhythmic clickety-clack of the wheels, the wheezy whistle that sounded far up ahead as they were coming to crossings.

The novelty of drinking water from the big bottle with a spigot, and using pointed paper cups that could not be set down gave them something to do.

Most interesting was the conductor, who solemnly punched holes in everyone's ticket, and the "butcher" who carried a basket of intriguing wares as he swayed down the aisles. Candy, jaw breakers of rainbow colors, gum, apples, and bananas were piled high. Most desirable of all were the small hollow glass dogs, horns, pistols, and dolls stoppered and filled with tiny hard candies of red and green. Ella's own treat was a sack of pink mints.

When someone flagged down the train between stations, those on board craned their necks out the windows to see the newcomers that climbed aboard, using the little stool the conductor set on the ground for them. Then he would take their money and hand them tickets, duly punched, all done quite efficiently.

The exciting trip thrilled Bee and Mamie, to be climaxed by their adoring father waiting for them at the station in Richmond.

But it was a happy trip that ended in tragedy.

During the visit of several days, the three-year-old became ill with pneumonia and died. She was interred in the family burial ground on the Kegans' ranch. Both parents and their families were devastated.

Henry could bring dangerous outlaws to justice with his courage and pair of six shooters, but was helpless and defeated by Death's claiming so young and tender a loved one.

In a letter dated August 9, 1899 to Corine Cole, Ella's sister, Viola Kegans wrote the following about the ordeal of the parents.

"My dear friend, I suppose you have heard of your sister's trouble. Little Mamie was interred here as it was impossible for her to be taken to Wallis as she died of congestion Monday night at 10:08 o'clock.

"She was the sweetest corpse I ever saw. She was dressed in a beautiful white organdy dress trimmed with white lace and ribbon with fine underclothing. I could not get white slippers but I got white stockings and tied white baby ribbon around the ankle and made a bow in front so it looked like she had on slippers.

"I made a small bouquet of two white roses and white verbena tied with white ribbon to place in her little hands. Also made a white wreath and placed it on her coffin.

"The coffin was white and certainly a lovely one, also fine. It had a silver flower in the center of the lid and was lined with white satin. The motto was on a large silver plate with "Our Darling Girl" on it.

"We had a preacher here to hold service...She had a nice funeral and those around were all both parents' true friends. Poor, poor little darling, she was too sweet and smart to live but God took her to a place where she knows peace and happiness.

"It looks like she came to her father to die, and he certainly took it hard. It looked like he could not be away from her before she took sick...

"Mrs. Ransom is almost prostrate with grief and wants to come home Saturday, and says if you get this in time to come and go back with her as it seems hard for her to go alone.

"She says if you can't come, ask Delia Higgs or Daisy Allen to come...Do all you can to console her in her grief.

"...It was God's work to send her here where her father was...she seemed to love him so much...he never spared any expense in putting her away nice...Ever your friend..."

Her touching letter reveals the loving attention people gave each other during traumatic times.

Nine days after Mamie's death, on August 15, 1899, when volunteers were called for once more, this time to put down the Insurrection, Henry Ransom re-enlisted in what became the famous 33rd Infantry, to return to the Philippines.

The Filipinos had revolted against Spain, but a certain segment of them, after Spain was defeated by the American forces, turned against the United States, which had to put down their insurrection.

However, much furious life-threatening activity that affected Henry Ransom took place before the "insurrectos" were defeated.

Most of the natives, amazingly happy-go-lucky, open-hearted, and hospitable, were used to enduring pain and suffering, their stoicism compared by the U.S. soldiers to that of the American Indians.

They had faith in their leaders, sometimes simply blind faith, which explains how they could be swayed and manipulated by someone like Emilio Aguinaldo, who, clever and ambitious, had convinced much of the populace to trust and follow him.

Spain had been their common enemy, and anyone who promised to free them from her harsh rule found followers. Now Aguinald; appealing to those already in emotional turmoil, formed troops of fanatics to oppose the Americans. Don Emilio Aguinaldo Faury, "President of the Revolutionary Government of the Philippines and General-Chief of Its Army" had been a servant boy for a Jesuit priest, with whom he acquired a good education. His native wit, combined with his extreme ambition empowered him to climb cleverly to the present position of leader of the Filipinos. Shrewd schemer that he was, he knew how to profit from and use the traits of the natives, conniving, deceiving, and even murdering to get what he wanted.

A young man of slight build, he had an incredible hold on the natives, partly from fear, as those who dared to oppose him were sometimes exiled or simply "disappeared."

After the Philippines were freed from Spain, Aguinaldo, intending to be dictator, tried to convince the Americans he was friendly. At the same time he shrewdly tried to manipulate events so that the U.S. would not recognize his plans and interfere with him.

This was like a deadly game of chess to him, with the prize being the beautiful islands that he intended to loot. He cared not for the future of his country, planning only for personal gain, according to his intents and actions. The American troops attempted to stabilize and clean up the land by helping the natives organize their own government, activate their commerce, and learn to better handle their new-found freedom.

Aguinaldo became less and less cooperative and friendly. He and his followers continued to deal in treachery, causing all the difficulties they could for the Americans.

With the islands under the U.S. military occupation, American officers issued orders for natives to help clean up streets, bury the dead, assist in creating sanitation systems.

To thwart them, Aguinaldo ordered that the wheels be removed from all available carts and wagons needed to accomplish such tasks. After much searching, the Americans found all of them hidden in a particular house and promptly replaced the wheels so the clean-up work could be continued.

Ransom Volunteers a Second Time

CHAPTER V

On his second trip to the Philippines, Henry Ransom joined Co. D of the 33rd Infantry, U.S. Volunteers, under the command of Captain John A. Hulen. Emilio Aguinaldo had taken over the leadership of the Katipunan in 1896, and when a friend, one Bonifacio objected, he was another one who disappeared, believed to have been murdered. Then Aguinaldo declared all Filipinos would be considered members of the Katipunan whether they desired to be or not. The peaceful people lived in fear of what had become a radical and violent group.

Aguinaldo became angry when the U.S. Congress refused to recognize the representative he had sent to Washington, D.C. He did not want to lose his "prize," the Philippines, so decided to wage war against the United States.

From traders he acquired 10,000 Mauser and Remington rifles, a huge supply of ammunition, two 20-pounder Krupp guns, and several pieces of field artillery to arm his 20,000 troops. This man was able to incite the natives against the Americans even after peace was made with Spain.

The insurrectos' harassment of the American soldiers escalated into actual fighting that began on February 4, 1899. The Americans defeated them soundly, capturing Malolos. Then the Filipinos moved northward to begin fierce guerrilla warfare.

All but invisible in the treetops, they were sniping at the troops, determined to drive out or kill the men who were ambushed constantly in the thick jungle cover.

The Americans could hardly see through the vegetation in order to shoot back at them. The enemy set traps that were pits dug 4' deep and 2' wide, with poisoned spearheads sticking up from the bottom.

When Henry was struggling through the thickets, did he ever have a moment to stop and think of the tiny girl he had left behind? Imagine her soft little hand almost lost in his, and her saying, "Good night, little Papa" the way he loved to hear it?

His memories of her must have brought him some moments of sunshine now and then, giving him hope and the will to survive in order to see her again one day…but the war calls…

The insurgents were volatile, unspeakably treacherous. They would hold up white flags as if surrendering or wanting a truce. When the Americans approached them, most of the time they would open fire on the soldiers. It appeared that the more they smiled and were "polite," putting on an act of respect, the less they could be trusted.

In one instance the Americans foiled a plot by some of the cut-throats to exterminate all foreigners, including women and children.

The insurrectos capitalized on the psychology of fear, hacking their victims to death with the long cane knives, decapitating and mutilating, shooting over and over the corpses of those they killed.

On a number of occasions, according to historical reports, older and cooler heads among the Filipinos, grieving over the appalling violence and devastation, would approach the insurrecto officers, begging them to put down arms and consider peaceful negotiations. The poor fellows would be shot down in cold blood to show that even attempting to achieve conciliation or agreement was the farthest from the officers' minds.

Filipino entrenchments were almost impregnable, concealed in the jungle and almost impassable swamps, but they could not withstand the impetuous rush of the U.S. troops who kept on pressing forward "with the precision of machinery" even in the face of fire. "The relentless sweep of Americans carried everything before them," reported one account.

General King realized it was useless to call them back. He smiled proudly to his staff on one such occasion. "There goes the American soldier and all hell couldn't stop him!" he commented.

They jumped the insurrectos out of their trenches, killing scores of them without losing a man. Had they made the cautious advance that was expected, many would have suffered severely, probably.

It was explained that the volunteers displayed more eagerness to fight because that was why they enlisted in the first place. The well-loved "Bantam General," General Frederick Funston, also known as the intrepid volunteer officer, and the other officers inspired their men with their own courage and daring.

The officers generally admitted that the volunteers were well-seasoned troops, certainly equal to the regulars for all purposes.

Some of the regulars themselves said, on seeing some of the action of the volunteers, "Just look at those men! They don't seem to fear anything!"

Life for the soldiers was not easy, being what seemed like one endless hike after another through steaming jungles, flooded fields, and swollen streams. Much of the time their clothing was wet and clinging to them. Also frequent gunfire from the insurrectos unexpectedly crackled through the thickets and undergrowth.

At any time they could look for a sudden charge by a group of fanatics shouting and swinging their bolos. Once Captain Hulen was attacked by a knife-wielder but was saved by Ransom's quick thinking. He shot the enemy a split second before the man could reach the officer.

The Americans had at best poor communication with their scattered groups and small garrisons, a major problem they dealt with as best they could.

Newspapers in the United States flashed headlines each day about the conflict thousands of miles away. Citizens eagerly read of the progress of "our boys" overseas.

The May 13, 1898 issue of the Houston Daily Post commented on "the end of Cuba."

Next day's issue stated, "Rear Admiral Barker is of the opinion that not enough soldiers have been sent to the Philippines."

Among the war news was another headline about Carrie Nation being jailed after busily smashing saloons. She had been offered her freedom if she would quit.

The Monday, August 16, 1900 Houston Daily Post shouted, "A Filipino command surrendered near Taguy!"

On Thursday, August 16, 1900 General Arthur MacArthur, Jr. cabled that 5,129 of the soldiers were sick, which was 8.47% of the total there.

The Houston Daily Post of August 28, 1900 described the extreme cruelty of the Filipinos, as told by men returning. Twenty-two Americans were attacked by 250 insurrectos.

The fight lasted an hour and 45 minutes and survivors had to leave the dead. When the Americans returned, they found clothes had been stripped from the bodies, and corpses had been stabbed and shot repeatedly, with fires built on top of their chests.

The November 21 issue stated, "The acuteness of the situation in the Philippines is admitted by high officials in Washington; no soldiers will be allowed to leave the islands before July 1, 1901."

On Christmas Day, 1900, the Houston Daily Post announced, "Volunteers will be kept there until others are sent out to take their places. The Administration will keep an army of 60,000 men in the Philippines,"

While fighting was hot and heavy in the islands, another island closer to home was battling a record-making hurricane.

Henry Ransom no doubt heard after the fact about the deadly hurricane that struck Galveston in September the same year, affecting the Texas coast far beyond its coastal area.

No newspapers were delivered in the deep jungle; Ransom was too busy to read one anyway. He and other volunteers were searching for Lieutenant Gilmore and his men who had been spirited away by the enemy.

Had Henry heard of the devastation, he would have worried about the safety of Bee and Ella.

For some time the Houston papers carried updated particulars of the gigantic storm that nearly wiped Galveston Island off the map. Just fifty or so miles south of Houston, its connection to the mainland was completely destroyed.

The Texas Mecca for sun worshippers, for those addicted to playing on its long stretches of beaches, for the avid fishermen and sailors, is a narrow strip of land on the Gulf, accessible by a "causeway" paralleled by elevated railroad tracks. At this time each had a short section, a draw-bridge that would tilt up to let water traffic go across.

After crossing on the causeway, a person is on Broadway that cuts straight across to the beaches, with its wide esplanade covered with rampant tropical greenery such as flowering oleanders and stately palms. Picturesque Victorian homes rub shoulders on their narrow lots, their roofs encircled by dainty iron grill widows' walks, all nestled in overgrown abundant plant life. These houses compete for attention with numerous mansions of unique design by noted architects of yesteryear.

An outstanding port, the island's wharves were alive with activity, with small crafts bobbing alongside large ships from far-away places.

In the paper's first story about the huge hurricane, 1,000 persons were reported drowned or missing, with 4,000 buildings destroyed. Figures jumped sky-high in the next day's issue: 6,000 dead, countless residences torn up as far inland as Brookshire, Hempstead, and Brenham. Houses were reported to have "walked" to the smaller town of Wallis. Activity along the railway going from Galveston through Houston and on to Katy included the "Katy Flyer" train that "went into a ditch."

A man who made a raft to float about investigating damage described the horror of the scene, saying he had counted 200 bodies hanging in fences, and saw feet of corpses everywhere.

For days lists were published of people who were missing. Headlines were "Anxious Inquiries For These People," along with the names of the known dead. Lists of survivors were given also, but those were pitifully short.

News of the fighting in the Philippines took a back seat for some time. Heart-rending accounts by survivors of the ordeal leaped off the front pages in big, black type.

Units of the National Guard came to make some semblance of order out of the chaos, with orders to shoot "safe looters" and other two-legged predators taking advantage of the grieving unfortunates, as they had to be treated in the great Chicago fire everyone remembered.

Shortly the Houston newspaper began featuring large front-page advertisements about impending flood sales.

Four days before the storm hit Galveston, Isaac Cline, the weather man, heard from the U.S. Weather Bureau in Washington, D.D. about a "tropical storm disturbance moving north over Cuba..."

In those days of much less sophisticated weather instruments, he had no way of knowing the unusual size and the terrible consequences it could bring, but he flew the storm warning flag above the Levy Building in Downtown Galveston.

The winds arrived on that Saturday afternoon, hurling huge waves of the Gulf over the island. By 8 p.m. low parts of the city had water 15 feet deep, with 10-12 feet in the downtown area. Thousands died before the next morning.

Called the worst natural disaster to hit in the history of the continent, it killed more than 6,000 people and demolished two-thirds of the buildings, nearly destroying the entire city.

Henry could have done nothing but worry. Blissfully ignorant of the disaster, he kept slogging through the forbidding jungle, dodging the enemy, defying death himself.

Bee and her mother were still living with Ella's family near El Pleasant and the Hartsville School, between Wallis and Sealy. They were in the vicinity of Allen's Creek and the railroad frequented by the "Sap" and other trains.

The Cole family was riding out the storm together. Those that were at home, that is.

John Cole, Austin's oldest son, had been parked at the entrance of the causeway when the record-setting storm hit the island. He had arrived to find that no one was allowed to come across the bay to Galveston. He was forced to remain right there and battle the storm.

Miraculously he survived but his fifteen freight car loads of cattle to be shipped were all drowned. He was unable to return home for some time, as all survivors nearby were required to stay and help bury the dead.

Grandmother Cole, Susan, almost blind with cataracts, received a blow-by-blow description of damage by the winds as it occurred. Her mischievous teenage sons, watching out the windows gave graphic descriptions, enjoying the privilege of broadcasting the action.

Beatrice heard it all and could quote their remarks for years afterward when describing the hurricane's battering of the community. Her endearing habit of seeing the funny side of things probably helped keep the scene, dialogue and all, in her memory. She could never repeat the story without laughing.

"Well, there went the windmill!" one boy announced loudly. "Now the water tower is gone, too!"

"Aw, hush up!" his mother hollered back at him over the racket of the winds bending the yard-trees to the ground and ripping the shutters off the house.

"That big old shed in the back is not there any more!" exclaimed another boy.

"You hush up, too!" she yelled, shrewdly sensing her boys were getting a bit of pleasure in alarming her.

Had they looked out the window in another direction at the debris filling the air, they could have described something even more astounding, a report that would have brought her straight up out of her chair.

The wind whipped an unattached freight car from the railroad "yards" at Sealy down the track all the way to Wallis more than twelve miles away.

What stopped it?

It rammed into a house that sat squarely across the tracks. A small blurb about this freakish occurrence appeared in the center of the front page of a Houston newspaper.

A few miles away in San Felipe, a grandson of Jacob Hill, little Justus, celebrated his birthday during the storm. He grew up to marry Beatrice, the love of his life...his grandfather and her grandfather had driven cattle together down the Chisholm Trail...but this gets ahead of our story.

Gradually the storm news receded to back pages of the papers, to be supplanted by later news of the American boys slogging through the jungles of the Philippines.

Henry Ransom's most grueling ordeal began in the middle of April, 1900 and lasted over six months of horror.

Lieutenant J. C. Gilmore, with 43 of his men, was sent to the east coast of Luzon on reconnaissance in mid-April 1899. Leaving the boat that brought them, they walked up a slope along a stream, searching for signs of the enemy. Suddenly they were surprised and captured by a large group of Tagalogs, who killed a majority of the men. The Lieutenant and the other survivors were whisked away, disappearing as if they had fallen off the planet.

For a long time no news of their fate reached the other Americans. Eventually, somehow, word of their capture came to General MacArthur, who sent Colonel Luther Hare with a group of picked men from his famous 33rd Regiment of volunteers to locate and free any survivors.

Of course, Henry Ransom was one of the Colonel's group. During his visit with Will, after his return to the States, Henry, who was never very talkative except with close friends and family, described in detail the dangerous months of search and rescue.

Will's little son, Henry's namesake, was always rooted to the floor at the feet of his beloved uncle at such times. The small boy soaked up every word Henry uttered, pigeonholing the tales in his memory for the rest of his life.

Ransom described to Will how the group led by Colonel Hare struggled through the thick vegetation of the steaming jungle, fighting off hordes of mosquitoes, where hardly any sunlight filtered through the dense growth. Huge trees grew close together, vying with each other for space, twisting and turning to catch any slim shafts of light.

The jungle floor, entangled with thick vines, tripped up the men as they pushed through, the undergrowth crowding high into the upper stories of the forest. At night it was pitch black, the kind of darkness so intense, Henry stated, looking solemnly at his little nephew, that if you stuck your finger in your eye, you could not see how to take it out!

Some of the time the Americans had to lie low during days, traveling more at night, with hours of groping their way along, without food and rest. Unable to use much lantern light for fear of exposing their position, they crept blindly, desperate to make no noise.

Finally after months of "patient search and vigorous pursuit," they located and stole away the captives.

The alerted enemy, accustomed to coping with the impossible conditions of the terrain, was hot on their heels, skillfully silent.

Henry said the men of his group scattered apart, creeping only a step at a time, freezing in position, hardly daring to breathe, knowing that many times an enemy lurked only several feet away. The Americans kept up their nerve-wracking escape methods for days, weeks.

The outside world anxiously scanned newspapers and listened for reports by phone or cable for news of the courageous volunteers.

After many months of no news the men were given up for dead. No one felt it was possible for them to survive any longer in the unforgiving jungle, even if they could have located the prisoners and escaped their relentless captors.

Finally one day more than six months after this almost hopeless rescue operation began, Colonel Hare and his men, with the erstwhile prisoners, stumbled out into a clearing where a small group of other Americans were camped. Staggering from sheer exhaustion, they were starving and nearly naked with most of their clothes torn off their bodies, their nerves frayed from the almost interminable ordeal.

Later when Ransom returned home, he brought with him a medal for bravery and was a corporal.

For the Americans, an occasional respite from the daily mayhem was a visit from another veteran of the uprising in the Philippines. That was Jerry, the Army mule who led Pack Train No. 17.

Jerry applied his mulish resolve to the job, never failing to get his train to camps on time. Many a weary and hungry soldier was thrilled to hear his welcome bray as he approached with rations and other needed supplies.

He and his fellow mules came into their own when they took the place of heavy trucks that could not cope with the impassable pathways. He plodded through tangled forests and treacherous streams, never losing the correct direction.

The soldiers took great pride in his prowess. Undoubtedly Jerry and Ransom crossed paths during their time in the islands. All soldiers heard of the mule as his fame spread through the ranks.

The four-legged veteran was accorded a warm welcome when he and his train were brought back from their travels abroad to be stationed, and eventually retired, in Marfa, Texas.

Evelyn Brogan recounted in her book, *Famous Horses of American History*, that the sturdy little fellow was a veteran of not only action in the Philippines, but the Spanish-American War in Cuba. She wrote that he also accompanied General Pershing's expedition into Mexico chasing after Pancho Villa.

More headlines and notes from Houston newspapers kept Henry Ransom's folks apprised of activities so far away.

On January 14, 1901 newspapers reported that "a number of Filipinos alleged to have committed murder and other crimes have been sentenced to hang. They were murdering peaceful and unoffending persons."

General MacArthur was quoted as saying they "were cowardly and secret assassins with inhuman methods. They attacked and burned, using bolos against defenseless persons. Some represented themselves as policemen to gain entrance, then gagged, bound, beat, and robbed innocent families."

Saturday, March 30, 1901 brought news of Aguinaldo's capture and discussion at a Cabinet meeting of the reward of General Frederick Funston.

The General had been assisted by some unusual and able natives. The Macabebes, "a brave little tribe" of only a few thousand, lived on a narrow strip of land between the powerful Tagalogs and Pampangas, defying both tribes many times.

Always they had hated their neighbors on each side, and although conflicts lasted over three centuries, the indefatigable Macabebes of unusually small stature managed to flourish. They were considered the best troops in the Philippines.

When the Americans first arrived, they had flocked to offer assistance. "Little brown men though they are, each Macabebe is today worth ten of any other natives of the islands. Our men in khaki treat them as brothers," remarked one military official.

In March 1901, General Funston hatched and executed successfully a bold plan to capture Emilio Aguinaldo, with 78 Macabebes accompanying him and four of his officers to set a trap for the wily dictator. The Americans were dressed as prisoners, with the "little brown men" acting as their captors.

After sending letters to bait the trap, the group arrived at Aguinaldo's quarters where he had a household guard of 50 troops.

When he appeared, the order, "Go for them!" was yelled out. The Macabees did just that, with enthusiasm grand to see.

One of them grabbed Aguinaldo, who found himself suddenly surrounded. General Funston had drawn his pistol, taking command and helped tie up their prisoner.

This did not bring the insurrection to a sudden halt, but the last surrender, that of General Miguel Malvar on April 16, 1902, did end the fighting.

Under the wings of a benevolent United States, free trade was begun with the Philippines. America began extensive assistance in numerous ways, such as rebuilding roads and bridges, improving education, updating their agricultural methods, and solving the health and sanitation problems of the populace.

After the smoke of battle cleared, General John A. Hulen, at the request for information from Colonel Wortham, wrote about interesting details of the "second expedition" of American troops in the Philippines. As an active participant, he certainly possessed first-hand knowledge of the action. Hulen submitted the capsuled information that follows:

The 33rd Infantry, known as the "Texas Regiment," was organized at San Antonio, Texas, during July and August, 1899. The men were to put down the Philippine insurrection. Officers included Colonel Luther B. Hare, Lieutenant Colonel Bereton, and Majors Marcus D. Cronin, Peyton C. March, and John A. Logan. Other Texans appointed were Captains G. R. Fowler, John F. Green, John Hulen, and Lieutenants Lee Hall, ex-Captain of the Texas Rangers, and Rucker. Hulen said the regiment trained in San Antonio and Fort Clark for a few weeks, then moved to San Francisco to be sent to Manila in early October. They arrived the latter part of the month.

For a short while they were on outpost duty not far from Manila, relieving some of the men of the first expedition under General Merritt. Then they sailed with General Wheaton on his expedition to northern Luzon about November 4 to cut off the retreat of Aguinaldo's army.

Bombardment by warships, including the Battleship Oregon of Admiral Watson's fleet, preceded the landing of the American troops. Entrenched insurgents, 1,200 of them, were defeated, with 2,000 more dislodged from the town of San Jacinto, and some minor engagements occurred before the insurrectos were put down.

Hulen described what were to him the three most interesting incidents of his Philippine service.

One was the month of intensive target practice at Fort Clark. He remarked that it resulted in developing the most excellent marksmanship of virtually every man in the 33rd, to which he attributed the "remarkable success" of that regiment in all its engagements in the Philippines.

The second was the first fighting at Magaldan Bridge, the Bridge of San Jacinto, where according to Hulen "in each case the good judgment, fine marksmanship, and bravery of the men took exceedingly heavy tolls and routed far greater forces of the enemy. It not only brought most important victories to our forces but developed in each officer and man in our regiment the feeling of confidence and superiority that carried them through all other engagements, expeditions, and all kinds of hardships with the will to conquer."

He considered remarkable a march of two days to San Jose, when he and his men covered approximately 60 miles in 26 hours' marching time. This was the beginning of the Gilmore Expedition in which Henry Ransom participated, and was, at the start of the march, nearly the entire regiment.

When General John Hulen returned to the United States, he brought along an adopted son, a small Filipino youngster. Hulen was to become later the Texas Adjutant General, in charge of the Texas Rangers as well as the State's National Guard.

A touching letter found in the files of the Adjutant General of the Texas Rangers was from Hulen's son a number of years later. He asked permission to join his father in his current endeavor. The young man stated he was a "third year man" at the Rice Institute, later termed Rice University, of Houston.

The Spanish, unconcerned about wiping out illiteracy, had done little to educate the natives. The Americans built numerous permanent school buildings of concrete. Teachers from the States flocked to the islands to raise the literacy rate of the eager Filipinos in record time.

By 1945 the Philippine Archipelago would be an independent republic, no longer downtrodden and heavily taxed.

The March 30, 1901 issue of Houston newspapers front-paged the thrilling news: "The 33rd has arrived. Texas Regiment reached San Francisco on the Transport Logan on March 29…25 days from Manila and 19 days from Nagasaki. She had on board the 33rd and 34th Infantry and 80 cabin passengers. There were no deaths during the voyage of the Logan and she brought no bodies from the Philippines."

Corporal Henry Ransom, who was honorably discharged June 30, 1901 from his second enlistment, had participated in a total of approximately 19 battles and skirmishes, two expeditions, and three operations. Also, in 1900 he assisted in the rescue of Lieutenant J. C .Gilmore and his men. Ransom's war records list the specific engagements.

His captain's report was: "Wounds received in service: None.

Remarks: Character, Excellent. Service, Honest and Faithful"

Ransom had suffered frequent attacks of malaria, as did a large percentage of the troops, being sick for several days, up for a fight, sick again, up again, on and on. His military medical records reflected these bouts, but also stated that his health in general was good. The severe fever and chills continued to recur for some time after he returned to civilian life.

Henry's troopship docked on the West coast to a wild reception of bands playing, flags snapping in the wind, and huge crowds of shouting people laughing and crying at the same time. He headed home by way of the nearest railway station but not before he, in dress uniform, had his photograph taken for his little Beatrice.

Traveler, a Gift from Beatrice's Great-Uncle

CHAPTER VI

When Henry Ransom returned unscathed from the fighting in the Philippines, one of the first things he did was bring to Beatrice the horse that had been given to her as a colt by his Uncle Robert Ransom when she was born. Henry presented her with a complete riding outfit and a small "over and under" .410 shotgun. Bee and Ella were still living with the Coles.

Delighted, Bee promptly named her steed "Traveler" after the famous horse belonging to the South's General Lee. However, one of her young uncles "borrowed" the horse several times, leaving him tied near a tavern, to Grandmother Susan's dismay.

She did not want Beatrice's horse seen tied by a saloon. She ordered her son to stop riding it, and becoming irate, simply sold it. At this time her husband, Austin, had passed away, and she, going blind, had a difficult time keeping up with and disciplining her teenaged boys who were "feeling their oats."

Henry next visited Vickie and her family in Brenham. They were assembled in her living room when a niece entered the room to announce that dinner was served. She walked up behind him, touching him on the shoulder to get his attention.

With lightning reaction, he leaped up involuntarily and flung her across the room against the wall. When he realized what he had done, he grabbed her up to determine if she had been hurt, and began to cry. His nerves were still jagged from the stress of battles just weeks before.

Being re-united with Beatrice helped soothe his nervous system more than anything else could have done. Thoughts of her while battling the enemy had helped him cope with the stress. Now when he actually held her on his knee and shared in her laughter, he could feel the tension begin to fade.

Each morning on awaking to discover he really was back in Texas, he became more relaxed. Memories of the horrors of war that had been like a raw wound would recede eventually, being replaced by thoughts of each new day's activities. Seeing his daughter helped him return to normal life.

Bee was especially elated when allowed to take trips on the train with her "little Papa." Such travels, although short, were high points of her childhood. Not only did he buy her little treats from the candy butcher going up and down the aisle, but he made her feel like such a lady, discussing with her how acting with dignity and good manners was important, and other grown-up subjects.

When walking beside him she would stretch to her fullest height and step with toes pointed straight ahead, not sloppily out to the side like a wobbly duck. Back on her Grandmother Susan's front verandah she had practiced walking with feet straight by following cracks between the boards. When on the train she was careful not to stare at anyone else or turn around, craning her neck to peer at people behind her. She wanted Papa to be proud of her.

Beatrice realized she came from families of mannerly, wholesome people, well-respected in their communities. They were considered solid citizens but with a twinkle in the eye, which accounts for some of the younger ones' tomfoolery. They worked hard, did their duty, helped their fellowmen, and also made life fun, some on purpose, some just through their own idiosyncrasies.

Always Beatrice stood straight as a ramrod, head high, Aunt Vickie all over. "Walk with pride and purpose," she would say. To the last of her long life, she retained the stately posture instilled in her at an early age, and was the epitome of a lady. She too had a permanent twinkle in her eye. No matter how difficult a situation could be, she usually could find a funny side to point out.

Bee and her father rode the little "Dinky," another fond name for the "Sap" train so she could spend the night with him in the sheriff's living quarters in the Fort Bend County jail in Richmond.

On alighting, she skipped proudly beside him, swinging tightly on his hand. It was only a short distance from the small depot with the flaring roof line and angled, scalloped eaves to the new showpiece of the area.

The stone and brick building was the biggest, most elaborate edifice Bee had ever laid eyes upon. An imposing three stories with basement, it sported carvings and cornices of contrasting stone, and more embellishments that included a cupola.

The pride of an inspired architect, with tall turrets surging to the sky, it was resplendent with stony frills and lacy curlicues that could be appreciated mostly by the fat pigeons cooing high on the rooftop.

Some of the taxpayers had complained, saying it was too fine a building for its purpose — and occupants.

During these times architects and builders went from county to county designing and erecting jails and courthouses that, although a bit different, still resembled each other in the popular "birthday cake" mode that retained vestiges of the Victorian style.

Not only an impressive architectural accomplishment, the jail was one of the most secure and escape-proof in Texas. Anyone caged there must have had second thoughts about continuing a career of crime after doing time there during the torrid, humid summers with heat waves bouncing off the metal sheeting between the cells. It was perforated with small holes in a neat pattern for ventilation.

The sturdy building's impenetrable facade was scarcely appreciated by the "guests," but most of the townspeople took great pride in showing it to visitors. The very sight of it reflected stability and officialdom.

Earlier jails frequently consisted of sheds with chained or locked doors. Prisoners' comfort was not a major concern. Reasonable thought was that if not comfortable, perhaps those incarcerated would reform, once free again.

Accustomed to the comfortable farmhouse of her grandmother, Bee was awestruck by the huge building's formal appearance.

On one corner, with separate entrance from that where the prisoners were brought in, was the monstrous door. Bee noticed that these rooms had high ceilings and tall windows, with wood wainscoting. The quarters included a large kitchen with many cabinets and storage closets far better than the average person's house. The living room had a large fireplace with carved mantle buried under thick coats of white paint.

The only clue about the proximity of criminal inhabitants was the thick steel door, impregnable with heavy locks, which led to the prisoners' area.

The child was not given a tour through the entire building, or she would have remembered the grisly sight of the scaffold with narrow steps leading to it, the deadly trapdoor that stood waiting in silence near the high third floor ceiling, ready to drop out from under a convicted murderer. Allegedly during all the years of the building's use, it had been used only once.

Bee was impressed most with the kind-hearted Negro cook who made a special breakfast of fluffy scrambled eggs, Bee's favorite, for the little girl.

On returning home, she described the county jail in minute detail to her grandmother.

Shortly after, Ella spoke to her family about re-marrying. Susan pleaded with her daughter to let Bee remain with her. She knew the cotton farmer who always went to remote areas in the river bottoms where the soil was made more fertile by frequent overflowing. The Coles were concerned about the well-being of both Ella and Bee and about Bee's education in particular.

They had some education themselves and an appreciation for the finer things. Their forebears in Virginia and South Carolina had held responsible positions in their communities. In the wilderness of Texas, the early ones helped establish settlements, schools, and other evidences of civilization.

Ella's new husband moved his family near a river, as predicted, where the topsoil and fresh nutrients would be washed over the prairie for miles by raging waters surging through, eating at the cliffs, gnawing wider channels, uprooting massive trees, taking houses off their blocks. This best farm land was always used at great risk.

True, Ella would not be alone so much, but she soon realized that she might have preferred solitude, according to what she said after being married only a few days. Bee came skipping along, chanting "Now I have another daddy!"

"Hush! It's pure hell," muttered the poor woman bitterly. She had never before resorted to using a curse word of any kind. To her dying day she refrained from explaining more, even to her own daughter.

Docile Ella obediently worked as a field hand which was expected of her, kept up with the cooking, baking, and other household chores, patiently submitting to the hard life of a tenant farmer's wife.

They moved frequently, having some good crop years, but also the usual failures because of floods and droughts.

During this time Henry Ransom did not have much contact with his daughter. He wrote letters to her and had news of her from the Coles when he saw them. His work kept him occupied over the State many miles away.

Being isolated was a hardship for Ella and Beatrice, with roads frequently impassable because of the rains of the coastal country. Sometimes when the stepfather traveled alone to the nearest town for supplies, he not only bought food but several yards of "piece goods" for Ella to use making clothes for herself and the child. Bee said later that he brought home new shoes for them which, of course, never fit, and sometimes were painful to wear.

"But we wore them anyway," she said, adding, "It was that or nothing."

The man, although domineering in his ways, showed a kindness at times, too. In many cases, ignorance was to blame for his treatment of Ella, along with thoughtlessness, and the belief that women as the weaker sex existed to be dominated and used.

Some other people in those times appeared to have this outlook. A formal education was not always considered to be important for women. He cared not a whit that Bee was not in school.

Always eager to learn, the little girl had been exposed to books and the much-played pump organ in her grandmother's house. She drew piano keys on a long, narrow board which she tied to the lower part of the fence separating the yard from the fields.

By sitting on the ground, she could slide her legs under it and sit in a position so she could race her fingers up and down her "keyboard." In the evenings she sat alone, playing silent "pretend" scales and chords, composing little melodies heard only in her head.

In the spring, alongside the adults Bee helped chop weeds out of long rows of cotton and corn. Her step-father expected his new family to work in the fields with the hired help. He fashioned a small hoe to fit the child's hand.

In the fall she dragged a long sack behind her, picking fluffy cotton from the spent bushes. Slight and small-boned, dark-haired Bee had a fair, alabaster complexion that suffered in the harsh Texas sunlight.

She described vividly the hot hours in the sun and how welcome was the cool shade under the wagon where, at noontime, she could crawl near the family hounds that lay panting by the water jugs. The dogs refreshed themselves by licking off the condensation with their long tongues.

Because of the step-father's loud, coarse manner, Bee feared physical abuse, keeping her distance as much as possible. Although she felt the man realized that her father would wreak terrible revenge if one hair on her head came to harm, she was wary.

Not believing in school for girls, he threatened to take away the books that Ella's family always brought her when they visited, which was not often.

The only open defiance she dared was to put a warning inside the cover of her spelling book, written under stress in childish scrawl: "Nobody better don't take this book." The speller was later found in the effects of her aunt after Bee herself had passed away at age 91. The pathetic little threat, still legible, brought home to her family the fear and desperation she as a child must have felt. It hit her children hard.

Her early handwriting was cramped, stifled, but later became free-flowing and consistent, denoting the happier time in her life.

Henry, oblivious of the danger for Beatrice, was on special Ranger duty far away. Later when apprised of her situation, he was galvanized into action. But first Bee was to suffer through a natural disaster.

One day John and Ola Cole brought in their wagon a new pump organ to their niece. With an ornate high shelf and carved top, it had an ivory keyboard surrounded by bright red felting with a mirror above. An adjustable stool with claw feet matched its elegant appearance. Bee's joy knew no bounds.

John had heard about Bee's piano "keys" she had drawn on the plank.

That spring an angry Brazos River again burst over its banks. Red muddy water rose rapidly, rushing through the river bottom, fields and woods alike, ruthlessly sweeping away everything in its path for miles over the flat prairie. Beatrice's recollections of this flood were seared in her memory for the rest of her life: the muddy water rising so relentlessly, so rapidly that livestock was trapped and drowned, the sickening smells of death after the water receded, and the heart-break of losing her beloved organ.

Her step-father's brother rode to warn them about the rampaging river and to help in a last-ditch effort to save what they could.

The men chopped holes in the ceiling while Bee and Ella dragged piles of clothes, food, and jugs of drinking water to be stored in the attic space.

Hurriedly they stuffed chunks of cornbread in their pockets, and at the mercy of the rising water, climbed on the roof to escape drowning. Soon the house was lifted off its blocks, an awkward vessel that wobbled uncertainly in the red, swirling sea.

Helpless, they watched as boxes, buckets, parts of chicken coops floated along. The ladder-back chairs and rockers were washed off the front porch. The brother, lying on his stomach on the roof, clutched at his horse's bridle reins as the poor creature swam alongside the house.

Probably no one said anything about what they would do if the house came apart under the stress. Had it been closer to the river it would have been swept into the midstream. In past floods, houses washed into the raging water were carried downriver only to burst open when they struck a big bridge crossing it.

The horse, eyes white and rolling with fear, stayed close to the swaying house, its master desperately holding his head above water. Finally completely exhausted, it sank beneath the surface. The man had to let go or be pulled under himself. The grief-stricken fellow burst into tears. Bee shrank back in horror, tears streaming down her small face.

After many fearful hours, when receding water left vegetation flattened, only to be scalded once the sun blazed down, the weary and disheartened foursome crawled down off the roof, grateful to be alive.

They were almost overpowered by the sickly odor of death and dying, the rot and mildew of the fields. The few outbuildings were sprawled, falling apart.

Half-buried cans and bottles and bodies of dead fowls dotted the spongy ground.

Clean-up meant lots of hot water and soap for scrubbing. Bee's job was to keep a fire burning under the big black wash pot near the house sitting crookedly in the field where surging flood-waters had carried it.

A tearful Bee found her organ in pieces, half covered in the red mud. With its bellows and pipes waterlogged beyond recognition and repair, no more sweet tones would pour from its reedy throat.

She was chopping it up for kindling when suddenly she darted to a loose board to rip off the remains of the manufacturer's label that had been on the inside, out of sight. This last angular scrap was all that was intact. She quietly put it aside. Years after her death it was found among her things in an old trunk.

Now, what of her father, Henry Ransom, at this point?

Bee and Her Little Papa Going to the Sheriff's Quarters

CHAPTER VII

In 1905 when Ella remarried, Henry had joined the Texas Rangers, becoming a private in Company A and stationed in Colorado City in Mitchell County. First in charge was Captain J. W. Brooks, then Captain Bill McDonald. These two men personified the fearless, quick-thinking Rangers. McDonald was said to be the man who "would charge Hell with a bucket of water."

Henry took the oath of service, was required to swear that since the adoption of the Constitution of Texas that he had not participated in a duel or assisted anyone else in such activity. Also he swore he had not paid or contributed money "or valuable thing" to secure his appointment in the Rangers.

Shortly however, Henry was dismayed to learn from the Coles that Beatrice was not in school. He obtained emergency leave to confer with Ella on their daughter's future.

The mother agreed with Henry that Bee must have a good education to be independent, to avoid being trapped in the same way Ella was, now unable to support herself.

Vickie, his sister in Brenham, wanted to keep Beatrice with her family to attend school there, just as she had helped him and Will earlier.

Bee was ecstatic when informed she would leave in a few weeks.

She pored over her books even more, determined to be prepared enough to be put in a grade with other children her age, in spite of having missed out on the first elementary grades.

Her step-father dared not contradict Henry, but continued threatening to take away her books.

The little girl sat up late each night, waiting until he and her mother fell asleep.

Fearing discovery, she carefully lit a kerosene lantern to pull it under the quilts so no light could be seen by the others. Hiding under the bed clothes, she studied her lessons.

Poised to blow out the flame quickly should someone wake and walk about, she kept an ear cocked for footsteps. Miraculously she did not set herself on fire.

Ella made the sacrifice, sending off the only bright spot in her life, to be gone during school terms. How bereft the mother must have felt when the sound of Bee's footsteps faded from the house! Her last glimpse of Bee for months to come was a small hand waving from a window of a train.

Her days seemed unending with working in the fields and cooking for the hired hands. Living on an isolated farm in a river bottom, she regretted her unhappy second marriage from the first but stoically endured it.

Ella cherished every letter Beatrice sent her, describing the wonders of school, her studies, the friends she made. During summers when classes recessed, she planned to return to her "Muzzy" and would work in the fields again to make a little money. Little Bee already had college in mind.

She loved the sleepy little town of Brenham, with its streets and few sidewalks that rose and fell like gentle roller coasters. The air was crisp in the fall, crackly with frost in the winter months. The spring would arrive to blanket hillsides with beautiful blue-bonnets of a brilliance that put the blue Texas sky to shame.

Vickie and her family lived in a neat white frame house on a quiet, tree-shaded street, several blocks from the main road going through town, their church just down the block.

Her philosophy in a nutshell was to be a good person, be thorough in whatever one does, take responsibility for one's own actions. Every tub should stand on its own bottom, she preached.

When Beatrice arrived, her aunt showed her pretty printed material for two new dresses. Vickie sat up late that night sewing so Bee would have something new to wear on her first day in school.

Before leaving for school each morning, Bee sat on a stool for Vickie to braid her long dark hair into two fat pigtails.

"She pulled so tight to get my hair smooth, my eyes were bugged out all day!" she exclaimed, laughing. "I have to stand up straight and always be a good soldier!"

Beatrice missed her mother, but she loved her pretty aunt, who stood straight as a poker herself even years later when she was quite elderly, a cloud of wispy white hair framing her face.

An eager student, Beatrice advanced rapidly in school, making all A's in every subject. In those days that meant not having to take final exams. Even in college later, she never had to bone up for finals.

Her father, proud of her progress, could concentrate on doing his Ranger duty, knowing Vickie was at the helm of Bee's future.

Acquaintance with the regulations and conditions under which the Texas Rangers were required to operate gives a better understanding of this important law enforcement organization.

The Adjutant General of the State of Texas was in charge of the Rangers, answering only to the Governor, who had appointed him. He submitted to the Governor an annual report in detail concerning the year's activities, accomplishments, and related information. The following summaries distilled from some of these reports through 1918 indicate the changes and progress of the force during that period.

Before Ransom's enlistment in 1905, Adjutant General A. P. Wozencraft, serving from 1897-1898, had recommended a raise to $40 a month for privates, adding that the "so-called Frontier Battalion" consisted of only four small detachments.

He wrote that reports to his office indicated that the men, "while fearless and prompt in performance of their duty, have always acted with discretion and in the most orderly manner."

The men were ordered to keep within the bounds of discretion and the law under all circumstances, adding that "any who might make unreasonable display of authority or use abusive language or unnecessarily harsh treatment of those with whom they come in contract in their line of duty, or who are not courageous, discreet, honest, or of temperate habits, will be promptly discharged and new men enlisted."

An important addition was that "officers and men of the Frontier Battalion will in no manner take part in elections of any kind otherwise than to vote." Later on this was not adhered to, with some politicians arranging for a few unprincipled men to campaign behind the scenes.

His report also listed officers in the 33rd U. S. Volunteer Infantry "on duty in the Philippine Islands." Made up almost entirely of men from Texas, the 33rd "has done most gallant service," including one of the most trying marches on record "to rescue

Lieutenant Gilmore and his party." This refers to the action that Henry Ransom participated in that won him a medal for bravery.

In the report for 1903 and 1904, the correct size of the Ranger organization was given: four officers and 28 men. All officers had each seen over thirteen years of service, those being the famous Captains J. A. Brooks, W. A. McDonald, J. H. Rogers, and John R. Hughes.

The territory Captain Hughes covered when headquartered in El Paso was larger in area than the combined New England states.

The summary of the accomplishments included 768 arrests made, over 150 of them being for the most serious crimes. Rangers assisted 76 times in District Courts, 579 horses and cattle had been recovered, and 275,557 miles were traveled.

On June 3, 1903, Rangers had suppressed a riot of several hundred employees who went on strike against a street car company in Houston. The greatest call for help from the Rangers came from the counties bordering the Rio Grande, to run down cattle thieves, smugglers, and murderers. According to the annual reports, lynching and riots were prevented, feuds suppressed, peace kept in the country, with thieves, robbers, and smugglers being apprehended.

Henry Ransom's Company A was stationed in Southeast Texas oilfields, with some of them sent to Hempstead, then apparently to headquarters in Colorado City.

Private Tom Goff was killed September 13, 1905 in Brewster County by a prisoner in his charge. Ranger Homer White of Captain Johnson's company was killed in Weatherford February 4, 1901 while attempting to arrest a man abusing a woman at the railway station. From Colorado County, White had been a Ranger only two months.

A. P. Wozencraft added that the Texas Rangers had been sent to Galveston after the 1900 hurricane to stop robberies of the dead and articles washed up, houses from being robbed, and the peace kept. The Texas Guard delivered relief supplies.

Contents of the report of 1906-1908 reveal activities occurring while Ransom was in the Rangers the first time. The Force then consisted of four captains, four sergeants, and nineteen privates. J. O. Newton, Adjutant General, said requests for Rangers were too numerous to be granted except in the more serious and urgent cases, adding that there was enough work to keep 100 Rangers busy.

During those two years 1,017 arrests were made, of which 458 were felonies. He urged that more men be hired, that sergeant's pay be raised fro $50 to $75 and that of privates from $40 to $50 to keep experienced men in the service. He added, "The present rate of pay is not sufficient to hold good men without their making personal sacrifices, which they are doing for the love of the service."

Each Ranger furnished his own horse, saddle, other equipment, and clothing. The State would pay for the horse if killed in action, and furnished a carbine and pistol at cost.

The Force was not to exceed four companies of mounted men, with each company to have a captain, one first sergeant, and 20 privates, with one quartermaster for all. The captains and quartermaster were to be appointed by the Governor, and "this force shall always be under the command of the Governor."

Adjutant General Hutchings' report to the Governor for January 23, 1911 to December 31, 1912, was during a time that Ransom was not in the Rangers but on special duty in Houston.

To his report, Hutchings added, "Your Excellency, on taking office, reduced the Ranger Force to two captains, two sergeants, and eight privates." It was re-organized on October 1, 1911: Co. A, Captain John R. Hughes, Co. B, Captain J. J. Sanders, and Co. C, Captain J. M. Fox, with one sergeant and twelve privates in each company. William Smith was made Captain of Co. D and used also as a detective.

The Governor convinced the President of the United States of the value of the Rangers during unsettled conditions on the Border. He recommended that Congress reimburse the State for extra expense involved. The Adjutant General asserted that "the work of the Ranger Force during the Reyes activities at Laredo and later the Orozco activity in El Paso was all that could be desired.

"Scout reports filed monthly by commanding officers show that an immense amount of territory and work is covered by the indefatigable force which has served as a pattern for the State constabulary of many sister States and some foreign lands."

He recommended pay raises.

Mentioned for the first time are pensions to assist surviving State troops or Rangers, or their surviving wives, who served from 1855 to 1860 on the frontier of Texas against Indian marauders.

The Biennial Report of Adjutant General James A. Harley from January 17, 1917 to December 31, 1918 showed the following companies existing in January 1917:

Co. A, Captain J. J. Sanders in Alice, Co. B. Captain J. M. Fox at Marfa, Co. C, Captain E. H. Smith in Austin, and Co. D, Captain Henry L. Ransom succeeding Captain Smith, with headquarters in Harlingen. He had a detachment at Edinburg. Ransom himself was transferred later in August.

Harley reiterated in his report that this force "shall always be under the command of the Governor."

The above information gleaned from official reports reveals that the small Ranger Force, through courage and dedication, covered almost an impossible amount of territory in exercising its duties, many under stressful circumstances.

A Road Runner

CHAPTER VIII

When Henry Ransom first joined the Rangers in 1905, his company was given right away an assignment in southeast Texas. Shortly after that his company was pictured in a photograph showing their camp in a remote area of the western part of the State. They chased criminals who had taken refuge from the law in the sparsely settled brush country, an ideal place for the lawless to hide and ambush those coming for them.

Thick growths of vegetation were made tough and impregnable by the difficult conditions of scant rainfall and rocky soil too poor to produce much nutritious forage for any creature. Trees and shrubs, even the stringy, thin weeds grimly hunkered down, defying destruction by man, beast, or weather, without attaining normal height. The "rain crows" didn't have much dampness to announce and a good bit of the year they had no job.

Armored and sturdy, with long, determined claws, the low-slung, comical appearing armadillo scratched out his living in the forbidding country. In turn, he was a meal for the members of the cat family that easily adapted. Bobcats and their kin flipped over their scaly quarry to rip it wrong side out, the tough plates on its back no protection for the soft underbelly. With the usual cocky expression on its face, the scampering chaparral bird, or roadrunner, sashayed alone and easily through the tangle of brush, as if eager to get off a hot skillet.

A variety of other feathered folk lived and nested in the curious, thorny vegetation. The wildlife blended so well with their matching coloration that one had to look quickly at their fluttering, spot them by their songs or squawks, or else miss the sights altogether. The pygmy owls that lived in the ends of hollow limbs of the stunted trees lent their soft, gentle hoots to the night sounds.

Once "in a blue moon," sudden or seasonal frog stranglers unexpectedly roared downhill out of swollen creeks and canyons to sweep unsuspecting riders and their horses off their feet. However, most of the time animals, plants, and humans were thirsty.

Sometimes the brush-riding Rangers tracking lawbreakers in remote, inaccessible territory were accompanied by a chuck wagon carrying food, water, and bedrolls, driven by the most appreciated person on the tour, the cook. His personal interest was making certain any firewood, as they came across it on the trails, was tossed in the cowhide slung under the wagon.

Often the men traveled alone, searching for outlaws holed up in the mesquite or huisache thickets full of thorns that led a treacherous life of their own. They appeared to reach out and grab passersby, refusing to let go, even if it thundered!

A Ranger wore chaps and other outer garments of leather to keep his clothes from being torn away and his skin peeled. Most important was muffling material, such as pieces of jute or burlap, to wrap around his horse's feet. Usually in rocky country the horses' feet were shod for protection. The burlap wrappings stifled giveaway noises as hooves struck rocks. All parts of the bridle and saddle equipment were silenced by being tied rigid with strips of leather or bits of wire.

Also needed in extreme situations were straps and muffles for tying a mount's jaws to prevent a "nicker" at strange horses when the rider desired complete silence.

Neatsfoot oil on the saddle leather not only lengthened its life but silenced the unwelcome squeaks caused by simple motion of the horse as he walked.

At the same time the Ranger would have to be wary of traps and being ambushed himself. His own silent and stealthy approach made it more possible for him to hear the crack of a breaking branch, the ring of horseshoe on rock, or the soft whinny of another mount hidden in thick brush.

Detecting faint campfire smoke, estimating the age of burned-out coals, spotting elusive tracks and bent twigs called on tracking ability that a man's life depended on. Constantly working over equipment and firearms and inspecting for potential problems took up a man's spare minutes, if any, around the campfire. If there was one. At times there was not a chance for a cheery fire or food, even cold.

However, care for his horse came first with the Ranger: water, nose-bag of feed, rub-down, stake-out nearby for the night.

Many had their mounts trained to be "tied to the breeze" to crop grass at the equines' discretion, and faithfully remain handy. At times a man had to leap astride after flinging on the saddle that had pillowed the Ranger's head a few moments before.

One Ranger picked up his saddle after a good night's sleep to find a rattlesnake coiled up where it had been.

"I let him go,"the fellow admitted. "He could have killed me but he didn't."

Times were rough but the Rangers took pride in doing their jobs well. Those not sincere in this, any who were pre-occupied with self-aggrandizement or abusing the authority that was theirs, did not last long in the Force.

The outlaws were deadly, hiding out in gangs, ravaging the countryside, stealing, murdering, raping. They wiped out entire families living on remote ranches. Mexican desperados came across the Border, committed crimes, then hightailed it back to safety on the other side of the muddy Rio Grande, sometimes aided or partnered by white outlaws from the American side.

The criminals had no love or mercy for the lawmen, devising trickery as they went, spreading rumors and lies in an effort to discredit the Texas Rangers and other law enforcement groups.

In those days of poor transportation and communication it was difficult to handle some situations that had involved gunplay. Problems might include wounded men or captives that had to be kept prisoners before they could be taken to a town for the meting out of justice.

Many times the Rangers had to protect their prisoners from mobs equipped with a lynching rope. The Rangers' duty was always to get the culprit in for trial, not allowing the "kangaroo court" of a mob in the woods to take things in its own hands.

Certainly there appeared to be occasions when unwise solutions were implemented but all the Rangers cannot be condemned because of some bully-type activities committed by a handful. The Rangers put their lives on the line every day for the benefit of their fellow citizens.

Plenty of evidence exists about several questionable instances that were investigated thoroughly, resulting in the firing of the guilty men.

A few present day writers about the Rangers, some of them under the illusion they can change history by "re-writing" it, who sit in the safety and comfort of their homes, have little conception of the hardships, dangers, and ordeals the Rangers encountered daily. Some present myths as facts — or facts as myths — about many figures in historical events, perhaps to get more attention for themselves.

In any event, Monday morning quarter-backing does not suffice when documented facts exist.

And they do exist because of the careful daily and monthly reporting and cooperation among the Rangers, their officers, and the Adjutant Generals. Much of this is being preserved in archives and museums in the State.

Furthermore, the old timers worked without benefit of modern science that now contributes to the law enforcement profession. They had no instant communications, no back-up by plane or helicopter, no advanced forensics, no latest techniques of identification, no "Life Flights." Who today could have worked so successfully under such circumstances? Who would have the courage or ability to fill the boots of those admirable old timers?

Think about it. The early Ranger had only his wit, sharp shooting skills, his horse, and his innate fortitude to haul to justice dangerous and sometimes emotionally unstable individuals. Reliable sources say he gladly comforted and assisted the victims when they needed help. He had a job to do and he gave as good as he got, reinforced by plenty more.

Many Texas ranchers of Mexican descent suffered also at the hands of the bandits and eagerly assisted the Rangers. Some actually joined the force. One, had he been Anglo, would have been vilified for his cruelty to the bandits he caught. He spent years wreaking terrible revenge, cold-bloodedly killing them after his wife and daughters were terribly savaged while they were alone in their home. His life was shattered by the horror of finding his innocent family brutally murdered. Who could blame him for going on such a spree?

As a new Ranger, Henry Ransom's time on the Border would come. His good friend, Jules Baker, whom he met when they were young men, would become his partner in law enforcement some time later.

They had a photo made of themselves, obviously in fun, considering their position, attire, and fire power. In a light-hearted moment they dressed the way they figured everyone would expect

them to and took themselves to a photographer's studio to surprise
their families. In their wildest dreams they would not have
thought their photo to be published in a book some day, and probably would have snorted loud and long over the idea.

Another example of dressing the way the public might
expect could be the reason another Ranger, whose career partly
overlapped that of Henry, stated in his autobiography that he
never carried a gun. Perhaps he did not.

But some photos of him show his firmly holstered pistols,
sometimes with other guns visible about his costume. To some, his
accoutrements smacked of a well-armed "drug-store cowboy," featuring fuzzy chaps and other items a regular cowboy would refuse
to be caught dead in. This Ranger was undoubtedly posing with
his men for the fun of it.

Now to get serious: Henry's company was sent to the
Humble area where hoodlums had flocked to the black gold fields
to prey on workers with any nefarious schemes they could hatch.
They terrorized the populace of the nearby small town, and in general bullied their way brawling, drinking, and harassing the innocent citizens who were not safe on their own streets.

The Rangers, whose reputation of no-nonsense handling of
criminals preceded them, found only small pockets of resistance
left that disappeared completely when the Rangers exerted their
authority. The one Ranger, one riot concept was no exaggeration.
After a few testing confrontations, the lawless elements felt it wiser
to vacate the premises.

The Rangers had barely caught their breaths when the
courthouse in Hempstead literally blew up with tempers and lead
equally hot.

The town was called "Six Shooter Junction" for good reason.
Notorious for the number of arguments that had escalated to settlement by firearms, living within its boundaries was known to be
somewhat chaotic. In fact it was said that someone headed that
way would hop aboard a train saying, "I'm going to Hell." And
everyone understood that he was to be let off at the Hempstead
depot. Trouble always seemed to be bubbling just beneath the surface, threatening to spill over. For years Hempstead, in spite of
being known as a hellish place, had billed itself a sort of watermelon
capital, with the required soil, climate, and eager work force at
hand. Then someone came up with the more expansive claim of

being the best in the world, this information quickly dispensed by town boosters. The easy winters, early spring, and black loamy soil combined with warm rains to inspire the seed to shoot green sprouts at the sun to cover the ground quickly. Before long, lush vines and melons basked in early spring sunshine, growing sweeter by the hour.

One April the famous melons were hardly mature when more hot lead began to fly in the Waller County Courthouse. Someone called Adjutant General, now John A. Hulen, head of the Texas Rangers, who ordered Ransom, Randall, Timberlake, and Smith to jump on the next train to Hempstead while he hurried down from Austin. Sheriff Anderson of the Humble–Houston area would appear on the scene, too.

The confrontation occurred at a public meeting during discussion of a petition to the Governor that was circulated that day. It requested him to send Texas Rangers to Hempstead to preserve order, also stating that local officers were not doing their duty.

This was the Waller County Prohibition League meeting, with members gathered to ratify the petition of about 200 names of some of the foremost citizens of the county.

It was largely attended by people of the town, with a great number of ladies present. Ratification of the petition was almost unanimous.

This time the pot had boiled over and bedlam broke loose, the noise terrifying citizens even at a long distance from the courthouse. Those inside flew out for their lives, desperate to avoid the hail of bullets zinging past their ears and ricocheting off the walls of the stately building.

Those outside who dared to halt in their tracks at what they hoped was a safe distance called to others in flight, hoping for an explanation. No one knew for sure. No one had the time to discuss the matter. Bodies were dropping inside, with others dodging and scrambling over anyone and anything in their paths to get out of bullet range.

Newspaper descriptions, vivid and even flowery in spite of the grim subject, failed later to tell the complete story. Everyone, depending on where he or she had been, had different impressions to relate.

Daily the town cripple had sat near the courthouse doors conversing with the folks going about their business in

Hempstead's Square. Ordinarily he navigated about in a slow and painful manner, absolutely agonizing to behold.

After the smoke of the shooting cleared, those who observed his hasty flight reported that he had sped out the door ahead of everyone else, down the steps, across the lawn, and on out of sight. He was not seen again until late the next day. A small spot in the newspaper concerning this remarkable incident added some comic relief to its otherwise shocking report.

The body count afterward was as follows: Dead was Congressman John M. Pinckney, W. D. Pinckney, brother of John, H. M Brown, lawyer, and J. E. Mills, farmer. The wounded were Roland Brown, son of H. M. Brown and R. E. Tompkins, private secretary of Congressman Pinckney.

According to news reports, Mr. Tompkins was speaking for the petition when Captain H. M. Brown made a remark which was answered by Congressman Pinckney. Then when Tompkins was speaking, Brown tried to get his attention, and finally, after being ignored or not seen, clutched at Tompkins coat, allegedly using profanity. Mr. Tompkins was suddenly hit over the head with a six shooter.

"About 20 shots were fired in a general mix-up of about 100 men," stated the newspaper. The ill-fated evening was termed "A Night of Pandemonium" in the Houston Daily Post but the Rangers' arrival restored a shaky tranquility. By their remaining no further trouble was anticipated, according to General Hulen. They were to keep the lid on for some weeks until the boiling pot reduced to a simmer.

Florence Guild Bruce, in her book, *Lillie of Six-Shooter Junction*, commented that several of the handsome Rangers found brides in Hempstead at that time.

Henry Ransom was one of them. Anna Hope Cooke, also descended from early Texas families, would become his second wife.

He and Anna, age 18, were married December 26, 1906. He had been called by his first name by Ella, but the new wife used Lee, his middle name. He continued his term in the Rangers.

During his various duties, Henry kept a vigilant eye out for more opportunities to visit his brother, Will, and his family living in Simonton, not far from Wallis and Sealy. Will's land was near the Brazos River, where Henry was buying a hundred acres himself, with the intent to retire on it one day.

The countryside was lush and green most of the year, the soil made richer by occasional flooding of the river on a rampage. Both sides of the river were heavily forested, which made a fine flyway for colorful migrating birds heading south to more tropical climes.

Ransom's namesake, Will's youngest, especially looked forward to his uncle's visits.

When little Henry was a toddler, his uncle would not come to the door to knock. He merely strolled into the yard, searching the ground, which was grassless as was the custom then and kept swept with a broom.

Ransom would lean over, looking for small footprints. Usually finding tracks of some kind, he would shout suddenly.

"There's a bear's track! I'm going to find that bear!"

He would even drop to his knees to scurry about for more tracks, bellowing that he was really after that bear and was going to catch him.

By this time the entire Will Ransom family, alerted that he had arrived, would be watching out a window. Henry would keep tracking until the occupants of the house hustled through the doorway to meet him. Then the man would rush to the child and snatch him up in a bear hug before looking at the others.

Little Henry would sit on the floor at his uncle's feet for hours at a time, soaking up the stories recounted to his brother by the usually reticent Ranger. Hanging onto every word, the small boy pigeonholed in his memory the fascinating facts, recalling them vividly the rest of his life.

The Ranger described the scene of the Philippines engulfed in the smoke of battle, the terrifying enemy concealed in thick undergrowth in the suffocating darkness of the rotting jungle, snipers firing from the tops of palms, the leach infested streams. He told of the capture of outlaws and of narrow shaves of dangerous kinds in barber shops in Texas, making indelible imprints on the youngster's mind.

Once in the country at his brother's, Ransom's routine activity was to keep up his constant pistol practice. Sometimes his life depended on no one else getting the drop on him. His first shot had to count.

He would hitch his brother's horse to the family buggy to drive it down a lane with barbed wire fences on each side. With the child sticking tight beside him, Ransom would give the reins a couple of turns around the frame of the spring seat.

Then he would take out his two loaded six shooters that were as much a part of him as his shirt and pants. With a click of his tongue, the horse, accustomed to these ways, would obediently break into a long-reaching trot, ignoring the gun shots except for working his sensitive ears back and forth.

The man would rapidly shoot at the barbs to spin them on one side and then on the other, with both hands. Then he would cross his arms, firing the right-hand gun to his left, and the left across to the right. To make the barbs spin, he had to hit the small points sticking up on each one.

When standing in the yard, he also honed his marksman-ship skills by occasionally tossing several coins in the air, shooting a hole in each as it reached its apex.

The little boy would stick his fingers in his ears, to his uncle's feigned disgust.

"Don't be such a sissy!" Ransom would exclaim.

Years later the nephew admitted the loud noise did make his ears ring several hours afterward.

Also, the boy, admirer of his famous uncle and eager to emulate him, could never be termed a sissy in all of his life.

When the one-way steel bridge was built to replace the rickety old wooden one across the Brazos River, near his home, the little fellow made pocket money by catching red-hot rivets in a bucket and tossing them on to a man who seated them, still smoking, in the steel beams of the "modern" bridge with overhead bracing.

When his family moved to Houston, he started quite young working as a caddy at the Houston Country Club. Observing closely the professional golfers, he practiced hard to twice win the World Championship. He held for years the position of golf coach at the Texas A & M University. Taking careful aim with a steady hand seemed to be in the Ransom genes.

The uncle's reputation of being an expert marksman, unbeatable at the draw with his lightning movement, preceded him, convincing many that confronting him was simply not worth the risk. His mere appearance on a disturbing scene would cause action to stop instantly, as if suddenly slashed with a sharp knife, according to numerous witnesses. Ransom was that rarity, an ambidextrous marksman who never missed, a crack shot with either hand, a formidable enemy of the outlaws.

Allegedly, an article about his prowess with firearms appeared in a national gun publication years ago, but clues about when and which one are lost in the obscurity of many years.

Once while in the Texas Rangers, he was sent to the outskirts of Hempstead. Two brothers there with sawed-off shotguns intimidated everyone, were more or less running the place and doing whatever came into their reckless heads. It was said that Rangers were sent two at a time, but the brothers would meet them at the train depot and run them out of town. Someone told that they would not allow the men to get off the train. Several pairs were sent without success, according to townspeople.

Henry Ransom went alone.

As was his usual custom, he went straight to a barber shop to sit in a chair, covered with a sheet, getting a shave. Lady Luck was smiling on him.

It so happened the other two were sitting in the shop when he arrived. They did not recognize him, he who had a habit of dodging news photographers for good reason. The pair had no inkling that a Ranger was in the same room with them.

In fact, at first he was not aware of their identity either.

However, they had to start laughing and bragging about how they had treated Texas Rangers that came after them.

Suddenly Henry tossed aside his sheet, threw open his coat to display the badge pinned to his vest, and said, "I am Captain Ransom with the Texas Rangers! You are under arrest!"

One of them made a move toward his gun but Henry was quicker.

From the hip he shot the other through the ear.

"Next time it will be your heart." He said simply.

He was known to execute the ear shot, always successfully, a number of times. It worked wonders.

He handcuffed the two, took their guns out to a post and beat them to pieces, caught the train and delivered them to the Governor in Austin.

"Here they are," he said. "Do what you want with them."

Trouble had not subsided altogether in Humble where oil and a myriad of opportunities for the lawless were still spouting high.

The citizens were so mistreated by three hoodlums who had moved in, stealing in broad daylight whatever they wanted, that the townspeople appealed to the Governor for help.

The thugs would go into a grocery store, cut down hams and sausages hanging by strings from the rafters, and grab anything else handy. If the storekeeper complained, they simply shot him on the spot. Gamblers as well, they used crooked dice and cards, taking money from men who unwisely joined one of their games

Henry arrived on horseback. The outlaws had heard somehow that he was on the way, and were waiting for him.

They were sitting on a front porch of a house by the road, watching him as he approached. He calmly rode right up where they sat, to their surprise, and pretended to start getting off on the correct side of his horse. In a flash he leaped off on the other side, coming up under the horse's neck with a cocked pistol in each hand.

"You are under arrest!" he shouted at them. They were covered before they realized what was happening.

He held his guns on them while others tied them up, put them on their horses. According to his instructions, their feet were tied together underneath their horses' bellies. Henry, on horseback himself, drove them in this position ahead of him all the way back to the sheriff in Houston.

Dead-serious about his job, he had a twinkle in his eye at times when he joked with friends and occasionally surprised someone with a prank.

Solemn as a church as he rode along behind his crestfallen prisoners, he probably was laughing up his sleeve at the comical sight before him. People fortunate enough to observe the odd procession must have chuckled and talked about it for years. He was known to use this unique solution a number of times.

A Texas Ranger worked under difficult circumstances many times, not always with help, in isolated territory, with no food at times, no doctors or ambulances, jails or undertakers. He had to guard prisoners to prevent their escape; to protect them from would be lynching gangs or other bandits that wanted them silenced. In some of these cases, the Rangers were blamed wrongly for a captive's death.

Prisoners were made to sit down, when camped. Sometimes they were chained to trees while the lawmen prepared food or tried to get some rest. With one eye on a prisoner, a lone Ranger took no chances, not even to put on a clean shirt. If he had one.

Except at these grueling times, Henry was meticulous about his grooming, always well-shaven, with hair neatly trimmed. He looked "scrubbed," folks said. He preferred to wear fresh white shirts, as most of the Rangers did, unless it was important to blend in the landscape or be invisible at night.

Later, with the advent of automobiles and more trains, Rangers used their horses less. When Henry traveled by rail, he wore a smaller brimmed black felt hat and dark suit, looking more like a traveling businessman on the job. The artillery was within easy reach but not obvious. He had a system.

Barber shops were the obvious places to hear the latest of local happenings. Embroidered or not, news circulating throughout an area always accumulated at the barber shops. One wonders why the news editors did not station a reporter within earshot of the barber's chair to pick up the latest while it was still airborne. And hot. Perhaps some did.

Another time Ransom was sent to quell some trouble brewing in Navasota, and, on arrival in that picturesque East Texas town, first went to get the usual shave.

On this occasion when Ransom was lounging under the customary sheet, with the barber giving him the "once-over," a young tough casually strolled in who had actually recognized the Ranger. Ransom might have appeared vulnerable under these particular circumstances.

Swelling out his chest as he reared back on his heels, the newcomer greeted Ransom in a cocky manner, adding, "How about letting me see that six-gun of yours?"

"Here." Ransom quickly pulled it out from under the sheet and handed it to him.

The other man looked at it a moment, then jumping around in front of the Ranger, blurted, "Now what will you do if I decided to blow your head off with it?"

"You won't," answered Ransom calmly, making no move under the sheet. "The other one is aimed at your heart."

The other handed back the six shooter. He couldn't let go of it fast enough, then raced out the door.

He did not realize, or had forgotten, that Captain Ransom always carried two pistols.

No one remembered how the barber reacted to this unusual scenario about a "close shave."

Henry Ransom did carry only six shooters. He refused to risk using automatics as they were in danger of jamming sometimes, which would never occur at a good time. He must have been amused at the newsmen who ignorantly headlined their stories about his feats in some disturbances or outright gun battles, speaking of "Henry Ransom's blazing twin automatics."

How he treated upstarts is illustrated by what happened when he planned to raid a notorious gambling den on Galveston Island where buttons were pushed to warn of the approach of lawmen so gaming tables and other incriminating evidence could be spirited away almost instantly.

He was instructed by the Adjutant General to take along a new quite young Ranger, so Henry confided in him the date, time, and place.

Saying nothing to his captain, the novice Ranger took it on himself to go the day before to raid the place alone.

The risks and insubordination infuriated Ransom, who was bent on correcting the very young man in a way he would always remember. Henry waited for an opportune moment. It came soon.

The "new" Ranger appeared at a gathering at the Rice Hotel that Ransom attended. Numerous prominent Houstonians were present, but the Captain did not hesitate.

He went into the kitchen to borrow from the chefs the largest longest knife they had. He returned, flipped the unsuspecting fellow across his knee and gave him a good spanking with the blade, as one would treat a naughty juvenile, in front of all the others. This, in spite of being a much smaller man. No love was lost between them from then on.

When veteran Ranger Captain A. J. Allee was asked many years later why the young man had taken such initiative, that gentleman simply replied, "To get all the glory himself."

The new Ranger did indeed become a well-known figure in the news media. Ransom stayed out of the news as much as possible. However, he had many admirers who were intrigued by his methods.

Some mysterious occurrences folks remembered and talked about indicated they thought Ransom might have some sort of sixth sense, as he appeared to know what other people were thinking. For certain he was adept at reading body language.

One day another man approached him, saying that he had heard that Henry had some kind of power that enabled him to tell what was on a person's mind and even if that one carried a concealed firearm.

"I don't know about that," Henry replied, "but I guess it's just how I know you've got a gun on you now," at the same time reaching into the man's coat and pulling out his pistol. No lump or other sign had been visible to reveal its presence, asserted a person with him.

Another time when getting a shave in a barber shop, after the barber had lathered his face and picked up a razor, Henry leaped out of the chair, threw down some money, and rushed outside, followed by his friend, Henry Bouchard.

"That man was going to cut my throat!" exclaimed Ransom.

The next day the barber went berserk and slashed the throat of another customer he was shaving.

Later when Henry Ransom arrived in Houston during some of its most evil days, he would cope with some unstable characters along with a concentration of criminals on its streets, including numerous pistol toters.

A Street Car in Houston

CHAPTER IX

He had been city marshal for a year in Colorado City, then in 1908 resigned to manage the huge H. S. Ranch in Mitchell County. Afterward he and Anna returned to Hempstead where he was a deputy sheriff again. Their first child, born September 3, 1908, was named Ruby Lee, after Henry's grandfather, Reuben.

On April 2, 1910, Ransom and his good friend, Jules Baker, were brought in as special officers by Mayor H. Baldwin Rice to clean up the rampant crime in Houston. They were to work on the streets to stop the gun toters. For awhile they stayed at a boarding house until Henry moved his family in the Houston Heights by the White Oak Bayou.

Gunfire in his backyard and nearby on the banks of the bayou frightened the neighborhood ladies until they discovered it was merely Henry Ransom keeping up his daily pistol practice. Then they declared that they felt so much safer, knowing that he lived nearby.

Before Ransom's arrival, when Houston was struggling to become a metropolis as fast as possible, its rough-hewn beginning was typical of frontier times in Texas.

Back in the early 1800s the initial promoters of Houston, the young Allen boys and their sister, staked out the fledgling city on the flat prairie of the Gulf Coast, 50-60 miles north of Galveston Island which was named after the Spanish Governor, Bernardo de Galvez.

It became a brawling, sprawling half-tamed settlement on the fringe of the saltgrass-choked wilderness. In some areas occasional patches of canebrakes spread across the terrain, growing taller than a man mounted on horseback.

Houston in its short pants days was awash with many creeks, gullies, and bayous, with steamboats coming up into the "downtown" section and daring boys bobbing about in swimming holes shaded by trees leaning over the banks. Now and then an alligator lounged about on the land, soaking up the sun, then slid silently into the water, keeping the swimmers alert like nothing else could.

Gradually most of the gullies were filled in, with bridges put over the remaining largest ones. Transportation in Houston in 1868, before Ransom's time, was improved by the Houston City Railroad with its mule-drawn cars. By 1893 electric street cars flourished, scattering their sparks throughout the small business district.

The new "horseless carriage" was paraded elsewhere in 1897, and reputedly the first automobile to clatter and oogah on the Houston scene appeared in April 1903.

In 1903 when a man exceeded the speed limit of six miles an hour, he was the first person, according to records, to get ticketed for endangering lives.

By 1904 with several autos dashing about the city, officials decided some rules had to be made and enforced. Each auto was to have a bell or horn, which the driver was to clang or blow when within 100 feet of an intersection and during the crossing as well.

The number of automobiles in Houston by 1905 increased to about 80, with the city council deciding in 1907 to increase the speed limit to eight miles an hour downtown and fifteen in the country. In every case, no one could argue with any horse on using the road. With the law on his side, he always had the right of way. Later, Houston, yet in its gangly youth, called its sinkholes "streets," gave them names of Texas heroes. Few all-weather roads existed, and even fewer sidewalks, with only rough boards spanning some of the mud holes.

Houston was hell-bent on having her traditional balls, in spite of the uncooperative weather where the cool air from the north met the warmer breezes blowing in from the subtropical south, which spelled frequent downpours, and mud, on the party-goers.

A major improvement was the completion of the Main Street Viaduct across Buffalo Bayou, at that time a wide, beautiful stream bisecting the north and south parts of Houston.

Several streets downtown were paved with bricks, but narrow Washington Avenue had only one side paved, leaving the other mud, where trolley tracks were laid. Creosoted blocks paved Fannin and San Jacinto but they swelled and heaved out of place after torrential rains to trip up men and beasts alike. However, the less elegant "mudshell" was the usual road covering in the early 1900s.

South of McKinney on Main were a number of large, stately homes with well-manicured lawns. In 1913 far out "in the country" at the end of Main the Rice Institute opened its doors across from the 284 acres of thick woods that would be donated in 1914 by George E. Hermann for a park.

For a nickel and, by transferring to other trolleys, travel was easy all over "town." Bellaire, with only a small scattering of homes in the middle of the vast, windswept prairie, considered by the townspeople to be the epitome of the hinterland, was connected to civilization only by the "Shuttle," the smallest trolley of them all. It came out from Fannin and McGowan, passing Rice on the way.

At times during the almost unending rainy seasons, the route was inundated by deep water. Until the drainage problem was solved, which took many years and lots of wading, folks joked that they had all grown webbed feet.

Houston, playfully termed by pundits the "Baghdad on the Bayou," was criss-crossed by picturesquely names streams such as "Chocolate Bayou," with murkish tendencies. "Buffalo Bayou" conjures up visions of thundering herds of the noble beasts coming to drink and frisk on its banks. That romantic notion is dashed by old-timers who insist it was named for the buffalo fish prospering there. No one wanted to catch and eat them because they had more bones than a fish really needed.

The bayous would amble quietly along except during periods of heavy rainfall when they turned mean and muddy, roaring over their banks to cause damage and grief before emptying into the shallow, sluggish bays on the fringes of the salty Gulf.

Mayor Rice had been a commissioner earlier who was a leading figure in the creation of Houston's deep water port. He contributed much to the progress of the city while serving as mayor from 1896-1898 and 1905-1913. While he was commissioner, the first highway in the country was paved.

Houston's growth about the time that Henry and Jules came resembled a bowl of bread dough gone wild, full of fresh yeast that heaved and bubbled, spreading like something alive over the edges of its container.

Commerce flourished with wagons of timber and produce crossing the streets, locomotives whistles renting the air, trolleys rattling along their tracks.

Like a large noisy ant bed the town's streets were working with pedestrians, horse-drawn vehicles, a few puttering autos, and loose livestock wandering casually in and out of the walkways.

Those that wanted to drink were readily accommodated by the saloons almost shoulder to shoulder in some blocks, especially around the town square. These helped the lawmen earn their salaries and kept the jailhouse from standing vacant.

But the stray animals meandering about gave them more trouble than the criminals, according to the sheriffs. However, law-breaking began to escalate in a few years.

Until then, the lawmen kept busy chasing cattle out of the streets or catching errant pigs tearing up someone's turnip patch.

One old-timer related how stray cattle impounded in a pen next to the sheriff's office often peered in at him through the window. He added it was not so embarrassing in those days to rope a cow and drag it through the streets to that pen, but it certainly was when he brought in a hog, resisting loudly every step of the way. A pig's squeals always attracted a jeering crowd with a lot of smart aleck advice, as did squawking chickens.

Horses regularly clip-clopped through neighborhoods as peddlers brought fresh produce for housewives to select at their doors.

Occasionally, Anna rode the streetcar over to "Produce Row," taking small Ruby Lee along. Sometimes the swaying and squeaks of the street car, with sparks hissing off its metal roof, would nauseate the child, but Ann traveled prepared.

When Ruby turned white around the mouth, her mother would wipe her face with a wet cloth she always carried and hold half a lemon for her to lick.

By 1910-1913 a few of the downtown streets were cobble-stone. Many were still paved with blocks of wood. Progress was reflected more in new building. This was the city Henry Ransom and his partner were hired to clean up behind the scenes.

Erected on the northeast corner of Main and Texas in 1901, the first skyscraper was the Binz Building, proudly sporting one elevator. It was followed by other large buildings that included the eight story First National Bank at Main and Franklin, and the 16 story Carter Building at Rusk and Main. It was called "Carter's Folly" by those who feared that bricks stacked that high would fall off on their heads.

The eleven story Scanlan Building joined them, as well as a blacksmith shop and lumber yard at nearby Market Square. A few rickety remnants of frontier days remained within the shadows cast by the tall buildings.

The Rice Hotel was completed in 1913 on the site of the first Capitol of Texas, when Sam Houston was the Republic's president. This hotel became the virtual hub of social activity day and night.

Parks, churches, famous homes of prominent Houstonians continued to spring up like mushrooms under a wet board. With the ever-present saloons were the vaudeville houses such as the Prince Theater, opposite the courthouse, where Will Rogers spun his rope and tales, and Clark Gable thrilled the ladies as the actress, sultry Nazimova, did the men.

East of Produce Row a number of blocks away was a meat packing company, with smaller related businesses nearby. Just inside its entrance gate an artesian well gushed a wondrous column of water several feet high and six or eight inches in diameter. As years passed with more wells tapping into the water table, the pressure weakened, with eventually its musical sound being silenced forever.

Unfortunately, with the progress of growth and disappearance of the frontier characteristics, Houston, struggling to get out of its short pants days, had its evil side increasing. The law-breaking elements, smelling opportunity, flocked to the center of the ant hill of activity to add some underworld turbulence. The term "disorderly conduct" became too mild to describe some of the thugs.

Local police and other law enforcers were hard put to keep the peace and protect the citizens. This was why Ransom and Baker were called in to help.

It should be reiterated at this point exact dialogue is taken from trials in newspaper accounts, from letters and journals, from actual conversation quoted from people who were there or remembered conversation they had earlier. No dialogue is "made up." All spoken or written words are repeated exactly from the extensive research for this book, just as noted in the preceding chapters.

Russell Wolters had remarked that Houston was anything but peaceful and law-abiding. He was the son of General Jake Wolters of the law firm of Lane, Wolters, and Storey. The General was the former Chief Officer of the National Guard.

Russell added that by this time the notorious "Happy Hollow" was closed down but the "Reservation" on San Felipe was the toughest house of ill repute, where in broad daylight women were snatched off the streets and sold into "white slavery." Also word was around that some of the prominent businessmen who got their secretaries pregnant sent them out of sight to the insane asylum near Austin.

Lawmen had been slapped about by toughs and thugs on Congress Avenue, and were shot in the stomach if they indicated they might reach for a gun, Wolters added. He stated also that "burglars operated without hindrance."

Henry Ransom and Jules Baker had their work cut out for them. The two friends lost no time in making conditions extremely warm for the gun toters who had been ruling the streets. Some hauled in court had been escaping punishment with clever attorneys who cast ethics aside in favor of their clients. In the minds of some the lawyers were considered no better than the criminals they defended.

Ransom and Baker were ordered also to investigate the earlier shooting of Police Chief Murphy.

Henry was involved in a number of altercations. On one occasion he was with a number of others at some function of officials in the Rice Hotel. He was standing near Mayor Rice when a man rushed up, knife in hand, with obvious intent to kill the Mayor.

The fellow found himself flying out the window that some said they thought was on the second story. Henry's reflexes, fine-tuned with the Army training and battle experiences in the Philippines, were in good working order. Only 5'8" tall and weighing 140 pounds, he was physically fit and muscular.

One man told Henry Jr., "Your uncle surely did some great work in Houston. With so much crime people were jumpy and did not feel safe in the streets until he came."

A black man told Henry's nephew that he thought Ransom was the greatest and a good, kind man. Owner of a little grocery store, this person said he was threatened with beatings and robbery all the time. Finally he told his tormentors he was going to call for Ransom. That stopped his trouble.

Elderly George Teague, who grew up in Baytown, said when he was a small boy walking along the rails of the old "Interurban," he was attacked by a crowd of black youths throwing rocks at him. Ransom appeared seemingly out of nowhere and made them leave. Teague never forgot the incident.

Another nephew of Ransom's whose father owned a store in Alief, was in Houston at a cattlemen's convention. He had come in on horseback one evening and, feeling his oats, shot out a street light here and there. When he came to the Rice Hotel, he rode his horse right into the covered entrance.

His luck ran out suddenly. Uncle Henry was on the premises and spotted him. Henry walked up and jerked him off his horse. He took the young man's gun away, slapped him, and made him remount.

"Get on home before you get yourself hurt!" he ordered. Ransom treated everyone alike, including kinfolks, when rules were broken.

Late one evening on October 1910, Henry and Jules were in Houston waiting for a streetcar to ride to their homes. J. B. Brockman, known to defend the criminals, crossed the street, coming toward them. When he stepped from the street to the sidewalk by the other two men, neither of them moved.

When Brockman reached them, he suddenly threw his hand to his right side. Ransom, with his usual lightning speed, jerked the pistol on his left side out of its holster to rapidly fire several rounds in the other man's midsection.

Brockman stepped backwards, still attempting to get his pistol out, then staggered to the Crown Saloon across the street where he slumped at the door. Someone there called an ambulance. A pearl-handled dirk and another pistol had fallen out of his clothing where he had been standing.

Holstering his Peacemaker, Henry, with Baker, walked to the freight depot close by to ask a clerk to telephone the sheriff's office.

After being questioned by the sheriff, Henry was released on his own recognizance. The ambulance took the wounded Brockman to hospital where he expired a few hours later.

When a reporter for the "Houston Chronicle" queried Ransom, he replied only, "All I can say at this time is that I regret the circumstances which forced me to shoot Attorney Brockman. I had to kill him or be killed by him."

Their dislike for each other had festered for years, beginning in 1894 when Ransom, in his first contact with Brockman, was the court bailiff in Richmond under Judge Wells Thompson.

Brockman was using insulting language refusing to be quiet and sit down when told to do so by the Judge. Henry was instructed by him to correct Brockman, which he did.

From then on their paths crossed when Henry brought in a lawbreaker who was defended by the attorney said to be the lawyer for the underground.

Any time the two men had seen each other, the air thickened with tension between the man who captured and brought in to justice the lawless and the one who defended them in court, managing to free many of the guilty parties.

Henry Ransom was charged with murder with malice. The trial was held in Houston, beginning April 17, 1911, and lasting about a week. Ransom's character, activities, and records, as well as those of the slain man, were thoroughly detailed by witnesses.

C. W. Robinson was Judge, with Counsel for the State being W. B. Hudson and Judge John C. Williams, partner of J. B. Brockman. The prosecutor was Marsene Johnson. Richard A. Maury was the District Attorney. Counsel for Ransom included James A. Storey, Jonathan Lane, and Jake Wolters.

Many of Henry's past associates traveled great distances to appear as character witnesses for him, friends who had known him in every stage of his career going to great lengths to help. The crowd ranged from bootblacks and janitors, to an adjutant general and other high ranking officers in the U. S. Armed Services and law enforcement groups.

Some evidence of Brockman's activities, spoken of as "most unfavorable," possibly showing his connection with undesirable elements, to state it mildly, was said to be "so vile" that it was written down and shown in silence to the jury.

Out of respect for Brockman's widow, who must have been ignorant of her husband's unsavory dealings, this evidence was not given orally in order to prevent newsmen from splattering the lurid details across the front pages of the print media.

This was a chivalrous and most commendable manner of managing such a matter.

With the huge flood of character witnesses for both Ransom and Brockman, attorneys for both sides agreed to conserve time for the rest of the trial by hearing from only part of the witnesses. How they handled this is shown in the court record quoted here: "The defendant, H. L. Ransom, having offered proof of the general reputation of the deceased, J. B. Brockman, and of specific instances of violence by said Brockman, the State here now admits the following facts to be true: the State here now admits that the deceased, J. B. Brockman, was a man of violent and dangerous character and that he bore the general reputation of being a violent and dangerous man, that he would likely execute threats seriously made; that he habitually carried a pistol and that he was a quarrelsome man and frequently engaged in difficulties upon slight provocation, and often without provocation.

"It is further admitted that the above facts can be established by the defendant by the following witnesses and that the testimony of these witnesses to the above facts is true: Max Keller, H. C. Julian, E. A. Hudson, A. W. Tartar, Clyde Ezelle, Sam Epstein, H. H. Peebles, E. L. Crudge, C. G. Pillot, Joe Free, R. S. Moody, March Beach, D. W. Robinson, Albert Schuller, Earl Cain, Freeman Hill, Lee Wrensky, Miss Ray Blue, Miss Gertie Fowler, H. J. Wagner, C. H. Schultz, George Adams, Mr. Grimmer, E. J. Skidmore, C. G. Wright, C. E. Polk, Joe Stevenson, Mrs. Albert Bush, Miss Hazel Busy, Rufus Howard, H. Duke, Dick Richards, J. F. Townsend, Jake Giles, S. B. Bailey, W. F. Sheldon, George Kiche, Jesse Henry, Mrs. C. Cuthbertson, Miss Cuthbertson, L. A. Veazy, A. D. Spencer, Mr. Hansen, Mrs. Willie Conley, W. G. Taylor, Albert T. Raif, H. Bergman, C. H. Abbott, H. C. Julian, Ed Hussion, E. J. McCullough, George McCullough, Frank Williford, J. E. Lester, John S. Radford, B. B. Gilmer, Sam T. Swinford, John McClellan, S. A. Kincaid, William A. Wilson, N. C. Munger, W. E. Buckley, M. Lyons, H. B. Williamson, J. A. Radford, R. E. Burt, and W. H. Lloyd."

Character witnesses for Henry Ransom included L. L. Johnson and J. W. Johnson, prominent farmers and stockmen, Tom Sproles and Peyton Bland, long-time officers of Austin County, District Judge Wells Thompson of Fort Bend and Waller Counties, W. B. Bertrand, planter, J. C. Flores, lawyer of Fort Bend County, J. H. Stanley, County Superintendent, Mitchell Mayes, merchant and planter, Wes Winner, tax assessor, Albert Cohen, blacksmith, Sheriff C. F. Ryan, Lon C. Hill, lawyer and planter, M. G. Delling, U. S. Deputy Collector of Customs, Levi Davis, peace officer of Cameron County and of Waller County the following: Dr. C. A. Searcy, Sheriff J. Perry, County Judge J. D. Harvey, A. D. Amsler, banker, G. W. Lawrence, farmer and stockman, A. G. Tompkins, bank cashier, Tom F. Dobbs, merchant, John Loggins, family grocery, G. W. Hurd, farmer and deputy sheriff, M. S. Robinson, general merchant, Mr. Osborn, express agent, Mr. Saunders, druggist and Tom Rankin, farmer.

Others were Royal G. Smith, former mayor of Colorado City, Captain W. J. McDonald of the Ranger Force of Texas, General John A. Hulen, who knew Ransom in the Philippines and in the Texas Rangers, E. M. Gordon, Claim Agent for the South Pacific R. R., Duff Voss, Chief of Police of Houston, Dr. Jarrell, physician of Houston, Judge Nick Lambert, Mayor of Humble, and J. R. Montgomery, correspondent for the "Galveston-Dallas News" living in Houston, and who was the bugler of Company B when the defendant was a corporal in Company D in the Philippines.

Brockman had been the defense lawyer for Earl McFarlane, who had allegedly shot and killed Deputy Chief of Police William E. Murphy. He became the highest ranking officer in Houston to be killed in the line of duty. The shooting occurred April 1, 1910, in the Acme Restaurant on Preston Avenue. Later Brockman's partner, Henry E. Kahn, served as McFarlane's counsel because of Brockman's death. McFarlane was acquitted.

Mayor Baldwin Rice stated that he brought former Texas Rangers Ransom and Baker to Houston as special officers to assist the police in keeping order, in apprehending gun toters, and to obtain evidence on perjured witnesses. The two were working on the Murphy murder case.

The mayor asserted on the witness stand of the Brockman murder trial that the two men were not brought to Houston to kill anyone, but to preserve order.

"Ransom," the newspaper also stated, "is well known in South Texas, having been stationed in various places during his service as a Ranger."

On the stand in court Ransom said the following that was quoted in the "Houston Post" on April 18, 1911: he would be 38 on his birthday the following December, and "was born in Lee County near the Washington County line. His father died while he was quite young and his mother followed shortly. He was raised by his uncle, Hamilton Ransom who died in 1885 after moving to Austin County. He has one brother, Will Ransom, who was present in the court yesterday.

"He said he lived in Richmond, was deputy sheriff under Sheriff Pearson, and that he lived in Colorado City where he served as a sheriff first, than was elected city marshal, which position he resigned to accept the management of the HS Ranch in Mitchell County. He later went to Hempstead as a deputy sheriff. On April 20 he came to Houston to begin work for the city as a special officer. He said he enlisted in the U. S. Army and went to the Philippines where he served eighteen months and was promoted from private to corporal."

Henry related that he first met Brockman in 1894 as a witness in a murder case when a deputy Sheriff. He said not long before the killing that he was going into the post office in Houston when Brockman was coming out. The other man said, "I learn that you have been interfering in my business and I advise you now that you had better leave here."

All this is quoted directly from the newspaper.

"I said, 'Judge Brockman, you had better explain what you mean.'

"He said, 'I will explain to you with a pistol,'" Henry told the Court.

Still on the stand, Ransom said one night he and Jules Baker walked along Main Street to Franklin Avenue to San Jacinto and across the street to the freight depot to wait for the next streetcar. Baker sat down on the fence around the depot. Henry stood nearby, leaning with one hand against a telephone pole.

He testified he first saw Brockman on the edge of the sidewalk.

"When he walked up, did he say anything?" Ransom was asked.

"No, sir. He looked me straight in the face, then threw his hands to his right side. I drew my pistol and shot as fast as I could. He continued to go after the pistol and after the third or fourth shot he began to start backwards and all the time I was shooting he was going for his gun."

Ransom said he had been informed of Brockman's habit of carrying a pistol, and had heard of the different assaults he had made with it, so when Brockman threw his hands to his side, Henry said he thought he was going to shoot.

"He said things in the trial of cases that did not please you?"

"Yes, sir."

"You had it in for him?"

"I didn't think he was a good man."

"You were not in love with him?"

"No, sir."

Ransom added that Brockman said things about him in a trial for a motion for change of venues which he did not like and which hurt his feelings.

When he was hired, Ransom said, he was instructed to spend most of his time on Main Street and to pay particular attention to pistol toters.

"You didn't try to arrest Brockman when he tried to pull his gun?"

"No, sir."

"Baker didn't either?"

"No, sir."

"Did you hear him cry murder?"

"No, sir."

"You didn't go to see whether you killed him?"

"No, sir, we went into the depot and asked the clerk to telephone the sheriff."

Ransom stated in court that he lived with his wife and three-year-old daughter on Baker Street in Houston.

The first day of the trial, a group of Henry's Texas Ranger friends planted themselves in the middle of the courtroom, not missing a word of the entire trial that lasted a week.

Each day "the courtroom was taxed to its capacity," with Judge Robinson ordering the balcony opened to accommodate the overflowing crowd of spectators who listened avidly, quietly.

Toward the last of the trial, hundreds of people crowded around the doors and even outside, hoping to get into the courthouse to hear the final arguments. It was stated that this was the most important trial in the State in several years.

The jury was out 23 hours, giving the impression there might be a mistrial. However, later word came that most of the jury had been for acquittal from the very beginning.

"Ransom has remained unperturbable throughout the trial and in the face of the jury's announcement of a disagreement appeared confident and smiling," stated the "Houston Chronicle" on Saturday, April 22.

The Rangers who appeared to be rooted permanently to their seats remained together.

Throughout the trial they kept their eyes glued on the prosecutor, even as they rolled their cigarets to be ready for a quick smoke in the hall during the court's next recess.

Finally the prosecutor became so unnerved by their steady gaze that words would fail him, and he lost track of what he was trying to say. According to witnesses, he was rather rattled near the end of the trial.

"So scared of the Rangers in the courtroom that he was never able to finish his closing argument," said Russell Wolters, who later became district attorney himself. "I can see Captain Ransom yet, sitting there in Judge Robinson's court, a man with piercing blue eyes that never blinked...he was absolutely fearless...and a dead shot."

Sigmund Byrd, in his column years later in the "Houston Chronicle," pointed out again the newspapers never printed the most sensational testimony about Brockman.

"Out of deference to the slain attorney's widow," he wrote, "both sides agreed that testimony about Brockman's connections with Houston's now smashed vice ring should be introduced in the form of affidavits and given to the jury to read. This testimony was unbelievably shocking, Russell Wolters said."

He added, "Dick Maury was D. A. then, but he was a defense witness. Ewing Boyd was an assistant, but he was disqualified because he and Ransom were friends. So Marsene Johnson from Galveston was appointed special prosecutor."

The jury selected included all of the following: George Holbrook, farmer of Pasadena, J. W. Trimble, president of Ineeda Laundry, B. S. Davison of Houston Transfer Co., G. T. Hamrick, contractor and builder, E. G. Garret of E. A. Hudson Furniture Co., G. A. Brandt, James Bute Co., T. A. Havermann, Henke and Pillot, A. L. Brooks of National Packing Co., D. C. Helbert, grocer, Thomas Fitzgerald, Kirby Lumber Co., F. W. Graf, ginner and farmer , and Joe Jones, driver for the American Brewing Association. All but George Holbrook were from Houston.

The "Houston Chronicle" on April 17, 1911, stated that Ransom appeared in court "quiet and complacent. He evidenced keen interest in the examination of the veniremen and talked quietly with counsel during the examination. In outward appearance and through reputation he shares in the three chief characteristics of the typical Texas Ranger: quietness, coolness, and courage."

In some newspaper articles it was noted that occasionally Henry's wife, Anna, and small daughter, Ruby Lee, attended, sitting near him.

When the jury returned with its verdict of acquittal, the Rangers snapped their holsters closed, rising as one to leave the courtroom. Later it was divulged that they had not intended for their good friend to be imprisoned if the jury found him guilty of murder. Among themselves they had decided to take him out of the courtroom at gunpoint, if necessary.

After the verdict of not guilty was given, Henry calmly rose to walk to the jury box where he shook hands with each member of the jury, thanking them all for their decision.

Then he went immediately to send a wire to his adjutant general who had come on an earlier day as a character witness.

A man of few words, Henry's message was simply, "Acquitted."

Sig Byrd's column also included the following: "Curiously a handsome painting of Brockman hangs in a grand jury anteroom in the Criminal Court Building in the 40's and 50"s...I say curiously because Brockman was the attorney for Houston's underworld in its most infamous days, and because there seems to be no publicly-hung portrait of the man who slew him...Captain Henry Ransom, Texas Ranger and all-round peace officer, whom the old-timers call Houston's greatest police chief."

Judge Jonathan Lane, uncle of Wharton County's famed sheriff, "Buckshot" Lane, defended his good friend, Henry Ransom. Later Henry would name his only son "Jonathan."

Henry Ransom always carried two six-shooters

CHAPTER X

In 1912, when Chief of Police Duff Voss resigned to concentrate on running for sheriff of Harris County, the largest county in Texas, Mayor Baldwin Rice took a major step in an effort to remedy once and for all Houston's explosive powder keg atmosphere.

He appointed Henry Ransom the new Chief of Police in February of that leap year. Four policemen resigned one day and three the next.

Preceding Ransom was his reputation as a thorough and incorruptible lawman, with remarkable ambidextrous shooting ability. When word was out a few weeks in advance about his impending appointment, locals said the very leaves rustled with many two-legged "varmints" scrambling for safer ground. Any foolish enough to remain "to play it by ear" would wish later they had not tarried.

It was said when he was seen walking down a street, there were those who would cross to the other side to avoid meeting the steady gaze of his bright blue eyes, startling in their intensity.

Henry could exert more influence as Chief than as a special officer. The local peace officers were relieved for him to become their chief. Those who had not resigned, that is.

To demonstrate the people's confidence in and affection for Ransom, a welcoming banquet was held in his honor, with the entire police force attending. At the same time names of additional lawmen added to the force were announced, along with promotions named for some of the regulars.

The banquet included a formal presentation of badges to the new Chief, to R. R. Smith, new Chief of Detectives, and W.W. Way, night sergeant.

Judge Jonathan Lane "spoke in flattering terms of the officers." He added that the handsome badge given to Henry was a "token of the appreciation of Ransom's many admirers, for his true courage in discharging his duties and his uprightness as a citizen."

The Houston newspaper reported all in detail, including quotes of speaker.

Ransom's successes as a war hero, a Texas Ranger, and as holder of other law enforcement positions were recounted.

His badge, a gold shield with large diamond in the center, had on the front the following lettering: "Henry L. Ransom, Chief of Police, Houston, Texas."

On the back were engraved the words "Presented to Henry L. Ransom, Chief of Police, Houston, Texas April 7, 1912 by his many friends and admirers in recognition of his high character and true merit as a citizen and officer."

An article in a Houston newspaper on the day he was sworn in office gave his background in detail.

"Mr. Ransom is rather modest and retiring. He is a man of very few words and shuns publicity. He is a strict disciplinarian and as an official knows only his duty. He will enforce the law irrespective of persons. At least this is the reputation of the man," stated the article.

The new Chief commented later that his main purpose "would be to conduct a force of officers that may be termed efficient," his main desire being to "maintain a degree of excellency in policing Houston that would be free from criticism and able to meet any emergency of any nature that might arise."

The article stated further, "Mr. Ransom in taking up his duties as Chief of Police will accomplish much."

The modest new Chief avoided as much publicity as possible, preferring to do his duty unheralded, but doubtless the sentiment engraved on his badge was treasured by him. He must have been moved by the outpouring of affection and admiration denoted by this added touch.

Together he and his partner, Jules Baker, would "make it hot," as one person described it, ridding Houston of the undesirable element in an incredibly short time.

However, Ransom told a reporter he would take no action until he had studied the situation thoroughly.

"It is not my purpose to take the place by storm," he said. "I do not wish to take any action whatever until I am sure I am right. After sizing up my work I will endeavor to perform my duty to the best of my ability."

One of his first acts was to assign a special "traffic squad of police" to work at downtown intersections, choosing the most capable men after several weeks of study prior to his appointment.

They included Sam Compton, stationed at Main Street and Texas Avenue, McNutt at Main Street and Preston Avenue, Hilton at Main Street and Congress Avenue, and Yates at Travis Street and Preston. Five new officers were appointed by Chief Ransom, all confirmed by the Mayor. They were Patrolmen Smith, Patton, Cheatham and Wilkins, and Mounted Officer Vickers.

Two smaller notations appeared in the paper about Chief Ransom threatening to take down a fence that extended into the street. Also mentioned was his going to another city to bring back a prisoner alleged to have stolen a Houstonian's horse and buggy, both being minor problems indeed, when compared to bigger things beginning to liven up the scene.

More explosive news soon hit the front pages. "LID GOES ON NEXT SUNDAY" headed one news story, adding "Chief of Police Ransom Issues Manifesto." He ordered all places of business to close at 9 o'clock Sunday mornings except general utilities.

His order, dated April 15, 1912: "The law provides that merchants, grocers, dealers in wares or merchandise or traders in any business whatsoever shall not ply their usual vocations on Sunday, with the following exceptions: that dealers in provisions may sell same before 9 o'clock a.m. This statute does not apply in the sale of burial or shrouding materials, newspapers, ice, ice cream, milk, telegraph and telephone offices, drug stores, hotels, boarding houses, restaurants, livery stables, bath houses, which places of business may remain open throughout Sunday."

"Kindly arrange to close your place of business at 9 o'clock next Sunday morning and each Sunday morning succeeding hereafter."

In a few days an article printed in the "Houston Daily Post" described a police officer charged with using abusive language when apprehending a man, which the court had decided he had not. He had accosted a man who was making himself a nuisance to a couple in their home. They had called the police for help.

The man resented the officer's order to move along and an argument and scuffle ensued with the officer finally punching the man in the jaw. Then the man demanded to know the officer's number, "which was refused."

On investigating the case, the Chief decided both men were in the wrong and found the officer had been drinking. Ransom fired him. Later the man's case was dismissed.

When questioned by a reporter, Ransom explained what had occurred, adding that the other man should not have been abusive to the officer and that his badge was in full view. Also he commented that the officer "could have acted in a more gentlemanly manner" when he approached the other person to ask him to move out of the way.

Concerning the officer's hitting the other man in the jaw with his fist, Henry said he thought the policeman was right, as "the other person was simply trying to create more trouble."

He added that the Assistant Attorney General witnessed most of the fracas and he did not see the officer do anything "out of the way."

In answer to the question about a policeman being required to give his number if demanded by a citizen, Ransom pointed out there was no such rule, adding that an officer certainly did not have to comply with such a demand when it was made "in a mad or insolent manner."

"If a citizen asked a Houston policeman in a gentlemanly way for his number, he would be told. I haven't an officer on the force that wouldn't tell him," said Chief Ransom. He also remarked that not another person had talked to him about this incident. The officer he discharged was a member of the police force when Ransom became Chief. "I didn't employ him," he pointed out.

From the latter part of the same article: "The question was put to Chief Ransom whether, when a person calls an officer a vile name, the officer is warranted in striking the citizen, with either fist or club, instead of arresting him.

"No good citizen," Ransom replied, "Would abuse an officer in the proper performance of his duty. But I don't expect my officers to take insulting names any more than I would expect a private individual to. I am to employ only gentlemen on this police force and I don't expect them to take anything a gentleman wouldn't take. If a citizen called me the same name, I would hit him."

"With your fist, Chief? Or with your club?"

"With any damn thing I had to hit him with," Chief Ransom replied. "That is unless the man was drunk, in which case he wouldn't be responsible, and it wouldn't count. In that case, I wouldn't hit him at all."

Henry gave the reporters plenty to chew on. A lot of print and space were used in more than one issue, going on and on about what he supposedly said.

This foreshadows what appears to be the beginning of a vendetta in print against the Chief. News clippings in chronological order vividly reveal the rapid build-up as it gathered momentum toward a vicious climax. One wonders who could be against a man appointed to make the city safe for law-abiding citizens, a man of Ransom's reputation who is doing his duty? And why?

More quotations from the newspapers: "Replying to the question, 'Is it true that since you took charge of the Houston police department there have been added to the force men known as gun men, professional bad men, men with notches on their guns? Have you employed such men as police officers in Houston?'"

"The Chief said, 'I have no men on the force known as gun men, or bad men or killers. I have not employed any men with notches on their guns. I have neither insolent men nor professional bad men in the department. The statements to that effect are lies and too trivial to notice. I don't employ that kind of men.'

"Chief Ransom branded as false the published charge that his attitude toward the Houston public is insolent and arrogant. He said, 'I have no occasion to change my attitude toward the Houston public and I don't care a snap of the finger for the opinions of a certain element of the city's population. I know all the good and law abiding citizens of Houston are with me and I am with them.'

"'I won't permit my officers to bully anyone or be insolent but neither will I allow the roughnecks and the tough element of the city to bully my police force.'

"In conclusion, the Chief said, 'It is not true I am going to resign. I have no idea of resigning. There is no foundation in the reports in the press to that effect. My resignation has not been broached to me by Mayor Rice, Governor Colquitt, or anyone else. It's false.'"

The above article clearly reveals the news media's apparent intentions to manipulate and enlarge upon any assumed wrongdoings that can be trumped up by insinuation or assumption to use to vilify the Chief. Obviously there were those that wanted

Ransom out of Houston and who opposed the Mayor's appointing him Chief in the first place.

The paper began routinely mentioning there were "complaints against the police department by prominent citizens," but never revealed specifics about the complaints or the names of the "prominent citizens."

It reported that at a council meeting "complaints against members of the police department were discussed," and that a thorough investigation by the Mayor and council would be done. "Much comment has been caused by the statement of Chief Ransom" that he, if in the identical situation, also would have hit the other man. The vague "much comment" was never qualified by names or lesser clues.

The article continued: "Men familiar with duties of an officer insist that an officer while in the performance of his duties has no right personally to resent a violation of the law," adding that he has no right to act as a citizen. Many officers do not agree with this, the article continued, adding it was not surprising when the Chief himself said he would strike the other party.

The newspaper on June 12 spoke of the mayor investigating the charges against the police. He said if rumors were true the men responsible should be discharged, adding that he wanted to hear all sides of the matter. Here he pointed out that no one had taken any complaints up with him. Rumors of clashes between the police and citizens had just then reached him, he said. He promised a "searching investigation."

On June 17, the "Houston Post" said "Police Probe Begins Today—Thorough Investigation Is Welcomed By Police—Interest Centered In Probable Outcome and Many Predictions Are Being Made—Large Crowd Expected To Be Present."

Mayor Rice announced that the council would sit as an investigation body and that no stone would be left unturned until the grievances against all members of the department had been sifted thoroughly and the true conditions brought to light.

"Chief Ransom, representing the department, has stated that the police welcome the investigation," the newspaper said.

Mayor Rice emphasized both police and public would be dealt with alike, with equal privileges. He said no complaints would be received in an indirect way, adding the complaining citizens should appear before the council.

Witnesses would be summoned and the investigation would be conducted as in court, with all evidence submitted before any action would be taken. All citizens with complaints were urged to come. The proceedings, open to the public, were expected to draw a large crowd.

Mayor Rice and Commissioners Kennedy, Jones, Pastoriza, and Kohlhauf announced the inquiry would be held each after-noon from 2-4 p.m. until everyone in Houston who had a complaint would be heard.

"Furthermore," the Mayor continued, "I want to state that the newspapers have been having a great many interviews with prominent citizens and plain and common people without giving their names. I want to ask those newspapers to give us assistance by furnishing the names of those persons to us so that we can summon them here and do justice to the police force and the city."

Only five witnesses appeared: two white men, two black men, and one white woman.

The first to speak was the proprietor of a pool hall frequented by Negroes. He complained of losing business because of the attitude of the police toward those men hanging around his establishment.

Later another person testified that folks were glad to see order restored outside the pool hall as those idling on the sidewalk had caused great disturbance. He added that after Ransom was in charge ladies could walk by unhampered, and it was appreciated by all good people in the vicinity.

Other cases presented had been dismissed in court. The woman complaining finally had to admit her son had been a law-breaker for years, and was at the time whiling away the hours in the penitentiary.

The morning paper of June 19 carried the news that "Proceedings Are Beginning To Lag."

The next day's paper told of the first charges being made against Chief Ransom's "official actions." A man appeared who had been in recent trouble. He said he wanted to "develop" the fact that Ransom's past record showed that his method of handling offenders "was brutal, inhuman, and criminal." He criticized the Mayor for appointing Ransom, claiming Rice did not investigate his record, and acted unwisely. On Attorney John Green's query-ing the man about his own background, he refused to reveal where he was during a ten-year period in his life, replying he had answered enough questions. End of his testimony.

Then two voluntary witnesses for the police testified: D. D. Burns and J. M. Ludtke. Burns was witness to the fact that a former complainant was not mistreated as he claimed, and Ludtke praised Detectives Robinson and Cain for how they handled establishing order at the pool hall in question earlier.

Later Dr. J. J. Thomas testified also about the Odin Avenue pool hall.

"A nuisance to the neighborhood," he called it, adding that as he was driving by one day, a billiard ball thrown at a man inside came out into the street and hit his car. So many loitered outside, he said, because there was not enough room inside for all of them.

According to the newspaper the next day of the public hearings, the Mayor and council concluded to end the investigation. Rice said he did not want it to become a farce.

"We have tried hard," he said, "to induce some of those prominent merchants and business men who appeared in print with interviews against the police department to appear before the investigation body and tell what they knew but our efforts were futile. Besides extending an invitation to them through the press to appear and make known their complaints, we had an officer call upon a number of them and request that they respond, which resulted in only one prominent citizen putting in his appearance."

Yet the newspapers cannot desist, speaking of "a consensus of opinion around city hall," a nebulous group in previous articles, but never named. This "group" is credited with wondering just what kind of measures the "city officials will decide upon to remedy the conditions that have been developed by the present agitation…wholly a matter of speculation."

Just who was to blame for the "agitation" was not mentioned or admitted, nor what was meant by the word.

The one "prominent" person who did show up in answer to the summons was a banker, whose complaint turned out to be hearsay. He had called Chief Ransom at his home at 11:30 p.m. wanting to make bond for a young man being held in jail, but Ransom refused, saying the prisoner had been marked "hold" for the detectives.

The complainant said he called the man's mother then called Ransom back again but was still told he could not make bond. He said he was "sore" about it, and mentioned it to friends and he figured that was how it made the newspaper.

The "Houston Daily Post" printed a new bone to chew on, titled "Police Chief Used Stick."

A brick mason entered Ransom's office the previous day to file charges against a Mexican laborer working on the new Rice Hotel building.

Ransom told the man the complaint could not be taken at the police station, directing him to go to the office of Judge J. H. Crooker.

The man left only to return later saying that office was closed, and demanding again that his complaint be taken. Chief Ransom explained once more this did not come under the jurisdiction of the police department. Ransom also said he had already instructed detectives to try to locate and arrest the Mexican to answer the charge.

Others in Ransom's office witnessed the ensuing altercation when the bricklayer accused the Chief of not being properly interested and began using abusive language about him and the police department.

Ransom advised him to stop, and reminded him he would have to wait for the Judge to return. The man again insisted his complaint be taken, saying he was a citizen and was demanding his rights.

"It was then the difficulty occurred, in which Chief Ransom was said to have used the walking stick," said a reporter.

"It is claimed," he continued, "that the wounds received…are serious because of the fact that he (the bricklayer) was struck twice on the head where a silver plate had been inserted to heal a previous skull fracture. The man stated afterward that he was "ejected from Chief Ransom's office and made his way to Paul's Pharmacy from which place he was conveyed to his home in a carriage."

On the following Monday the paper announced Chief Ransom was indicted for an assault in his office on the bricklayer. He had appeared at the sheriff's office offering to surrender himself but was told all the paperwork had not been completed, so he was unable to give bond for his appearance. Judge Robinson fixed

Ransom's at $200., which the Chief furnished immediately after the necessary papers arrived at the sheriff's office.

During this period, few mastheads or other listing of names of publisher, editors, reporters, and other writers for the newspapers were found. Apparently this was true for most of them.

"CHIEF OF POLICE H. L. RANSOM HAS RESIGNED HIS POSITION" with subhead "Resignation Becomes Effective July 1— Mayor Rice Has Not Named His Successor" headlined the "Houston Daily Post" in a few days.

"Coming as a climax to the recent agitation against the police department of Houston, Chief of Police Henry L. Ransom…tendered his resignation." The article added that he would continue as a special officer.

Published was the full text of his letter of resignation, addressed to Mayor Rice and dated June 28, 1912: "Dear Sir, Several months ago when a vacancy occurred in the office of chief of police you appointed me to that position. From that time I have given about eighteen hours a day to my department, striving to systematize the work and bettering conditions generally in police matters and I am conscious of the fact that Houston suffers less today from the lawless elements than for many years, and I can state with some pride that any good woman can walk the streets of Houston without being insulted by 'roughnecks.' Conscientiously I have tried to do my duty to the people and work for their best interests.

"For several weeks the newspapers have editorially and otherwise taken offense to remarks purported to come from me, some of which were true and many untrue, and a feeling has arisen in this community concerning particularly myself and some of the police force which should not exist for the peace for the community. I have waited patiently for some time to see if any charges of brutality or any overt act could be charged personally to me before I deemed it proper to act as to myself.

"Many of the best people of this city have come to me during the past two weeks and requested me to retain my present position, stating that the city of Houston is in a better moral condition free from lawlessness than for many years. On the other hand, a great many who do not know me think otherwise. Therefore, after weighing the matter carefully, I have concluded to resign from the office of chief of police. Conscious of having done my duty, I am conscious of the fact that no one man should ever be the cause of discontent in a community. I shall remain in Houston and expect to live here, and will always be found on the side of law and order and respectability.

"I have no feeling against any good citizen who thinks I am not the man for Chief of Police, and everyone knows my contempt for the cowardly 'gun toter' and the lawless element.

"I have no idea who will be my successor, but whoever he may be, I suggest to the good people to give him their earnest support. It is no child's play to be at the head of the police department in a railroad center and rapidly growing city like Houston. Officers of the law who perform their duties are seldom liked and never popular.

"With best wishes for the continued prosperity of our city, I remain respectfully, Henry L. Ransom."

The "Houston Post" Friday morning, July 5, 1912, published a letter of appreciation to Chief Henry Ransom written and signed by almost the entire police department: "We, the undersigned members of the police department, who have been associated with you during your administration as chief, take this means of expressing to you our appreciation of your helpfulness in the way of instruction and advice in matters pertaining to our duties as policemen. We desire to express our appreciation of the efficient manner in which you have enforced the observance of law and repressed lawlessness.

"In your retirement we desire to assure you of our best wishes for your future success. Respectfully submitted: Pat O'Leary, Pete McGrath, C. A. Lomax, I. D. Raney, G. H. Hilton, M. J. Hatchel, R. E. Radey, H. Reagan, G. L. Murphy, T. J. Bass, W. A. Bunyard, T. I. Neyland, J. B. McNutt, M. P. Monroe, J. M. Edison, V T. Matthews, G. W. Gibbs, H. W. Woods, J. H. Veale, F. C. Rathke, F. R. Jones, H. P. Kelly, W. W. Way, R. L. Martin, Arch Spradley, J. H. Holland, T. C. Goodson, Frank Smith, George Ratliff, George Iams, H. J. Meinke, T. S. Bishop, D. E. Drennan, Tom Shelly, R. R. Smith, chief of detectives, T. N. Reneau, H. B. Smith, V. B. Cooper, E. Bemer, B. C. Veale, H. McGee, V. S. Randle, D. E. Patton, T. S. Lubbock, W. C. Wilson, R. J. Baker, W. E. Jones, George Peyton, Tice Wilkins, J. E. Dunman, L. P. Bishop, W. D. Williford, F. W. Mitchell, Jake Haas, H. W. Depenbrock, George Mitchell, C. W. Laybun, T. A. Binford, J. K. Irwin, W. H. Campbell, W. C. Williams, S. P. Stone, D. R. Cheatham, W. A. Goodson, B. O.

Yates, H. C. Moody, H. Earlywine, E. B. Shelton, C. M. Wilson, Yancy Brizendine, J. E. Fife, J. D. White, D. W. Robinson, Charlie Cain, F. L. Rexer, C. W. Heck, deputy chief."

"Henry Ransom had a brief but spectacular career as Houston's Chief of Police," was one of the final comments in the "Houston Daily Post."

Captain Ransom's Texas Ranger Badge

CHAPTER XI

On October 23, 1913, the same newspaper, which sometimes called itself the "Post" without the "Daily" — or it seemed that way — reported a shooting at the police station following the arrest of former Chief of Police Henry Ransom for assaulting R. A. Higgins, a reporter for an afternoon Houston newspaper.

Ransom, who was accompanied by his friend, Jules Baker, was registered by the acting night clerk, Horton. Henry handed him $20, assuring his appearance in Corporate Court. Night Desk Sergeant W. C. Wilson had gone out of the station a short time earlier.

Ransom started walking out of the station, refusing to return when the clerk called him back to be properly recorded on the police blotter. Henry, already outdoors, called back that he was not going anywhere but the clerk followed him.

Horton later said he saw Ransom reach toward his hip pocket so he pulled out his own gun and covered the former chief with it. Later he admitted he did not see Ransom with a gun.

This was when Baker fired a shot at Horton, who received a slight wound in his neck and powder burns in his face. Had Ransom been going for his gun, probably Horton would not have had time to "cover" him with his own pistol, Henry being famous for his lightning-like draw.

Several other officers witnessed the incident, but did not interfere although Horton said he called for them.

Preceding this, about midnight others had witnessed Higgins heading for the Colby Restaurant for something to eat. Apparently Henry Ransom appeared but no one reported seeing who started the fracas. The reporter ran into the Dudley Brothers Restaurant nearby on Main Street, followed by Ransom. Henry chased him all the way down the counter where several others were eating and back to the front, where he cornered Higgins and cuffed him several times. Officer Lynch rushed in and arrested the former chief "before trouble grew serious", as he explained.

Police Chief Davison, members of the Police Commission, and Mayor Ben Campbell conferred, with the Chief deciding to suspend several officers who were in the station at the time of the shooting by Baker until further investigation.

Ransom entered a plea of guilty at Corporate Court, paid a fine of $12 for his own defense. Baker employed the firm of Lane, Wolters, and Storey.

When asked for a statement, Colonel Jake Wolters said, "A full judicial investigation disclosing all the facts will absolutely exonerate Baker and Ransom for any misconduct or wrongdoing at the police station. It will also disclose the only police officer guilty of wrongdoing or official misconduct was the man who was shot."

District Attorney Richard G. Maury was quoted in the October 25th "Houston Daily Post" about the right of police to search a person for a pistol, wondering why Ransom had not been searched before being taken to the station. Various city officials were quoted as they discussed at length the situation. What they said was augmented by remarks from visiting Waco Chief of Police and a telegram from the Dallas Press Club, seizing an opportunity to chip in their two cents' worth.

Maury railed against gun toters, speaking of laws prohibiting such.

Considerable interest arose in the hearing of Jules Baker on charges of assault to murder, with many spectators predicted to crowd Judge McDonald's court.

News followed complaints filed against the former police chief for aggravated assault and carrying a pistol. The reporter, Higgins, said Ransom beat him with a steel instrument and also carried a pistol.

Chief Davison instructed his officers to search every person suspected of unlawfully carrying a gun. He added they would have to rely on their own judgment or "upon information given them by reputable citizens." Every person attending the Jules Baker hearing would be searched for weapons to prevent further trouble.

A later news article stated that the mayor urged the district attorney to prosecute Baker if he had aided Ransom in attacking Higgins.

Officer Lynch explained an arrested person would be taken to the police station, then searched there later, when the prisoner goes along quietly. Also records are kept there of items taken from the arrested person. He added he felt any rule permitting arresting officers to search prisoners "would only bring criticism…of officers abuse of such authority."

Henry Ransom's bond was fixed at $200 for each of the two charges.

Baker's bond was $500 for the assault to murder charge, and $200 for aiding a prisoner to escape.

Bondsmen for Ransom were W. E. Carter and John Lovejoy. Jules Baker's were Ben Cohen, J. H. Gorman, Isaac S. Fox, J. B. DeMoss, B. W. Whisenant, J. J. Settegast, and T. Cleveland. Both men would be tried the same day, Friday, October 31.

Later it was stated that people would be permitted to enter the courtroom without being searched, as assurances had since been given that no one planned to come armed. Even the officers attending as witnesses would carry no firearms.

The jury consisted of W. C. Perkins, agent of Pierce-Fordyce Oil Co., W. C. Steger, agent of Magnolia Park Land Co., A. J. Gainey, Hurlburt-Still Electric Co., W. H. Journeay, agent, Sunset-Central Co., H. Fisher, clerk of F. W. Heitmann Co., and M. H. Anderson, salesman of Magnolia Park Land Co.

An interesting point of the trial arose when Ransom's counsel entered a surprise plea of former jeopardy. Ransom's testimony in his own defense was the last given in the trial by the defense.

The decision of the jury concerning jeopardy was because of a former conviction of simple assault "in the same transaction." Dismissal of the charge hinged upon whether Ransom had struck Higgins with a steel rod. No one else saw Ransom hit him with the rod, as Higgins claimed. Ransom denied doing it.

The paper specified that 600 spectators jammed the seats and aisles of a large courtroom, and predicted selecting a jury would be a difficult task, with many not wishing to sit on it. The regular panel for the week had been exhausted.

The lack of acceptable jurors necessitated two deputy sheriffs hurriedly picking up more in the downtown area. Out of two more groups of ten, only two of each were acceptable, as most had read of the case and already formed opinions.

When Ransom's defense sprang the surprise plea of former jeopardy, it was contended that if facts established that his also was only a case of simple assault, charges would be dropped.

In Higgins' testimony, he claimed he was hit on the head with the steel rod. He did admit his boss told him to write what he did.

Another witness testified Officer Lynch took it away from Ransom and put it on the restaurant counter. This witness also said he saw no gun on Ransom.

Henry was put back on the stand where he was told to recite his career from the time he was age 19 until his resignation as chief of police.

"He said at the time of the assault he was in the city as a witness in a case in the Criminal District Court...He saw Higgins standing in front of Dudley's and ran over and hit him. He chased him into the restaurant and down the front of the counter where he says he hit him several licks. He said he called Higgins a character assassin...He swore he never hit him with anything but his fists.

"Ransom said that Higgins as a reporter had written untruths about him while he was Chief of Police," stated the newspaper article.

Headlines reported later that Ransom was fined $100 and given a jail sentence of 60 days for pistol toting. His case would be appealed. This was the decision of the same jury that the previous day acquitted him of the charge of aggravated assault.

When court was reconvened the next day, the room was packed with an even larger crowd than before. Discussion centered on Ransom carrying a pistol out of Fort Bend County where he was a deputy sheriff. A law was cited about this. Apparently so obscure was it that even the judge had not heard of it.

Horton, the acting night clerk who was put on the stand at last, testified that when Ransom was outside the building he told Horton he was not going anywhere. Horton said Ransom put his hand back to his right hip pocket. "I didn't see a gun," he admitted. "I then went after my own gun."

This was when Jules Baker came to his friend's defense and shot Horton in the neck.

Ransom's defense lawyers said that Henry believed he had the right to carry his pistol elsewhere. As the jury did feel he honestly thought this, he was acquitted.

Jonathan Lane, one of Henry's attorneys, had delivered a powerful punch near the end of the trial, as quoted from the Friday, November 7, 1913 paper:

"Do you mean to tell me that this jury did not believe Ransom thought he had a right to carry a gun, when even you, Judge of this Court, believed that he did, when I, practicing law for 25 years believed it, and when every Sheriff and Deputy Sheriff in the State of Texas believed they had a right to carry a gun anywhere in the State until the right was questioned here and this verdict rendered Wednesday?

"Let the announcement of the verdict in this case go forth across the State and with one blow you cripple the entire constabulary force of the State. The country will be overrun with horse thieves, robbers, and criminals of all sorts until those people who now seek to slander and traduce a man of the character of Henry Ransom will get upon their knees and beg men like Ransom and his type to save and deliver them."

The final paragraph in the newspaper article contained an astounding revelation: the prosecuting attorney himself, Richard Maury, at an earlier time had been charged with not just simple assault—but assault to murder—believe it or not—the same newspaperman!

History writes that, with the sounds of dueling pistols a few short years prior still ringing in their memories, men of those times seemed prone to settle heated arguments on the spot with their fists.

Beatrice, a high school student going on to college at this time, had been unaware of most of her father's somewhat stormy and dangerous activities inherent in his duties in law enforcement work.

All she knew at this time was that he planned to join the Texas Rangers again.

Henry's uncanny premonitions and so-called sixth sense, combined with his amazing marksmanship and astute judgment of character would serve him well in coping with the constant turmoil on the Border.

He was a valuable addition to the Ranger Force. The words "fearless" and "courageous" were applied by others in describing him. His brother-in-law, Tom Cooke, said he was "wonderful and fearless."

Too, he was so honest and genuine that he expected everyone else to be so, said his namesake nephew, who had the same thing said about himself in a book written about famous, highly respected sports figures.

After Henry's stint as special officer and chief of police in Houston, he added to his larger-than-life reputation for ability and deeds as a Captain in the Rangers.

Troubles on the Border were increasing. Local peace officers and the few Rangers stationed there had more than they could handle, without enough manpower to cover the vast distances along the line between Texas and Mexico. Texans, both Anglos and those of Mexican descent, on ranches and in isolated communities were being cold-bloodedly murdered during many raids by Mexican bandits.

The following description of typical turmoil in Mexico is from a newspaper clipping displayed at the Texas Ranger Museum in San Antonio. Neither name nor date were on it:

"On May 9, 1913, after a short but decisive battle with a garrison at Reynosa, Mexico, General Blanco was taking the town of Reynosa. Climbing upon the windmill tower after dark, we could see the red glow in the sky from the fires of the burning…town, which was about ten miles from Mission, as the crow flies. Citizens of Reynosa and surrounding territory seeking safety were crossing over to the Texas side by the hundreds. A straggling procession of men, women, and children carrying their meager possessions was followed by plodding 'viejitos' (old folks) leading their bleating milkgoats (that) clogged the roads leading inland away from the Rio Grande and Blanco. At that time Mission was crowded with refugees."

Some thought the pacifist policies of the Secretary of State William Jennings Bryan and President Woodrow Wilson caused or encouraged the guerilla activity on the Border in 1915. The Mexicans thought that the Americans would not return fire.

When Ransom joined the Rangers again, he was made Captain of his company. His training in the army, experiences in hand-to-hand combat, and directing men in his platoon equipped him, a man only 5'8" tall, for the public service of law enforcement, another career he pursued conscientiously.

At this time the Border was seething with criminal activity.

Guns were smuggled across the Border, stolen cattle driven back from Texas into Mexico, with people and arms constantly going back and forth.

Making matters worse were the Mexican officials on the other side of the Border who would not cooperate with the

American servicemen stationed there. Some were even suspected of aiding the bandits by giving them refuge and arms.

News gleaned from records in the Archives reveal the worsening situation the lawmen faced.

Rangers killed three bandits that August. In Cameron County, Texas, 14 Mexicans killed two Texans, a father and his son. The next day a young man was ambushed in his car and a watchman wounded.

Following that, the next day 60 outlaws battled U.S. troopers, Texas Rangers, and a sheriff and his men. A lone ranchman at San Juanito on September 24 killed four and wounded one of 12 bandits, fighting for an hour.

The Brownsville train a few miles north of the Border was derailed by bandits. A Brownsville citizen and the train's engineer were killed along with several soldiers on the train. Other passengers were robbed and more killed in cold blood. Rangers killed four bandits suspected of this crime when they were caught right afterward with articles stolen from the passengers, which was the rule of the game, at the time. One more U. S. soldier was killed nearby the next day.

Again, in October three troopers were killed and eight wounded when surprised in their camp by bandits. Another battle occurred in the following February and again in early May.

Mexicans killed three soldiers and captured two American civilians. The cavalrymen chased the raiders into Mexico to capture one of their officers. This was near El Paso. More raids began that June.

Almost constantly during these times, ranchers in remote areas had live stock stolen.

The group of only about two dozen Rangers was increased to work in the Lower Rio Grande Valley. It was said the bandidos feared one Ranger more than a company of U. S. troops who were "abiding by the rules of war" and the frustrating "watchful waiting" of Washington D. C.

Understanding Spanish was helpful, almost necessary for the lawmen. Many of their Mexican informants managed to communicate with their versions of "broken English."

Being on the Border so much, Henry absorbed by osmosis some of the kind of Spanish spoken by the Mexicans, known as "Tex-Mex." He needed to understand and speak it for self defense, if for no other reason.

When the Mexicans tried to pronounce certain English words, sounds they produced were as amusing as the Texans struggling to keep up with the rapid rate the Hispanics could rattle off their comments.

An example was the Mexican pronunciation of "the Rangers" that rolled off their tongues as "los Rinches."

Captain Ransom had a number of close Mexican friends, some of them being fellow Rangers. Convenient pipelines to their communities, they were valuable assets to him, warning of bandits' plans that happened to fall on their ears, dispelling rumors, giving directions to unfamiliar places.

The Rangers had to fight fire with fire sometimes. Return what the enemy gave plus more.

Henry had received a wire from the Adjutant General commanding him to go to the Border area and clean it up, "doing whatever it takes, and if you can't, I'll send someone who can." The Captain set about obeying the order.

Not only did his work not slow down but surged to new heights frequently. The Rangers' work was affected by strife within the Mexican boundary, partly because they were not allowed to cross it. Once a bandit escaped over the Mexican line, his Texas pursuers had to slide to a stop, extremely frustrating for the lawmen.

Keeping things stirred up on the Mexican side were Pancho Villa and Venustiano Carranza who, each with his own following, had been battling for control of Mexico. In September 1915 the United States recognized Carranza which irritated General Villa, who retaliated by taking seventeen Americans off a train in Chihuahua and killing them.

In March 1916, Pancho Villa went into New Mexico, killing eight U. S. troopers and ten civilians. General Pershing was sent into Mexico to get him but was ordered back after fighting men of both Villa and Carranza.

Finally all the National Guard of the United States was called out and readied for action. Governor James Ferguson and Carranza met at the International Bridge at Laredo. Several of the Rangers were present also. It is alleged that Captain Ransom was one of them.

A better understanding of the continued murders and other violence committed by the bandits can be acquired by reading the daily correspondence that went to and from the office of the

Adjutant General. He, then, reported to the Governor. A number of times the General accompanied his men to the major trouble spots and dutifully reported the specifics.

The collision of cultures increased the problems: the peaceful, home-loving settlers as opposed to the Mexicans, who were accustomed to revolutions, appearing to thrive on violence, some considering life cheap. It was a way of life for them, with others of their race begging for the fighting to stop.

Adding to the unsettling influences were a few of the people of German extraction who were having secret meetings, plotting and planning espionage with the Mexicans to help Germany win World War I. Spies from Germany traveled to Mexico to foment trouble, promising the Mexicans they could not only have Texas back but more adjoining land after the war was won.

Some citizens were noticing a few of their previously friendly Germans acting in strange, secretive ways. Rumors were flying making the people in sparsely settled communities uneasy and fearful.

Matters worsened when so many, including farmers, shop owners, and others, were deputized to carry guns for protection, the number climbing to as many as a thousand. Some were commissioned who did not have good judgment, not handling wisely the authority that came with the permits. This caused friction, but when the practice of commissioning untrained persons stopped, matters improved.

The outlaws enlarged upon their usual methods of retaliation by trying to discredit the lawmen, claiming, in an effort to turn public opinion against them, that they shot women and children.

The lies and rumors were counteracted by wise leadership. Archival records show that the Adjutant General, after any scrap between the Rangers and the bandidos, always arranged for a grand jury investigation if someone was wounded or killed. This succeeded in putting all the cards on the table, to make the cases publically clear-cut, honest, and aboveboard. He always had some of Mexican extraction on the juries also.

Right-thinking citizens appreciated the Texas Rangers, sometimes writing them thank-you letters expressing their gratitude when lawbreakers were caught, imprisoned, even killed.

The Rangers appreciated the acclaim given them by the grateful citizens, but rarely had time to acknowledge the kudos.

They had no time for holidays or vacations. Many joined the Ranger Force for short terms, then had to leave to take care of family matters or to help when someone was ill. Some had to take an extra job to make more money. When possible, many would return. These were the ones who loved their work, dangers and all, in spite of the low salaries.

Before Ransom's time in the Rangers, several who were quite harsh with the bandits were considered great heroes. Captain Leander H. ("Lee") McNelly, a dare-devil warrior of the South's Confederate Army, was one. As a Ranger he lined up corpses of murderers on the town squares to impress the others with what would happen to them. The job required swift, severe retaliation to prevent more senseless killing of innocents. McNelly received no complaints, certainly not from those whose family members had been murdered.

The difference in how things were accepted possibly could be attributed to the fact that a lot of people from the North were beginning to settle down in the Valley, and along the Border also to escape the harsh northern winters.

The Rangers were reminded that these people were not used to the sometimes necessarily rough pioneer ways. When they saw a Ranger with his guns, they might wonder what sort of country they had moved to, according to those who welcomed the newcomers to help populate the place and spend their money.

It was felt that public opinion might be changed if some of these complained, lacking experience or knowledge of local conditions. As true many times everywhere, the first to complain know the least, understanding nothing about unfamiliar situations.

The Texas Rangers, it was agreed, were to wear their coats so their pistols would not be visible, in order to prevent frightening some of the newer arrivals.

Armchair generals and others who live the life of a hothouse plant can scarcely be expected to fathom the kind of danger faced by the Rangers. Their accomplishments, even their very survival, seemed to be nothing short of miraculous. And some did not survive.

Many Americans outside Texas became upset and irate on hearing about the murders and robberies of their fellow citizens on the Texas coast. Men from many other states as well as Texas sent letters expressing the desire to join the Ranger Force. The answer was that they had to be Texans in the first place. Letters pleading for permission to join came from many of Mexican descent, written in Spanish or broken English.

Many offered to work for no pay. Some said they were organizing groups of volunteers. As the bandit wars worsened, the mail to the Adjutant General and the Captains increased accordingly.

Henry Ransom was spoken of as "one of the old time boys" by some who asked permission to join his company.

Wires and letters from those who were there tell the story vividly, reveal the colorful character of the writers, give one a distinct sense of the times. Next are numerous ones quoted word for word that almost place the reader back in time, to smell the gunsmoke, hear the shots of raiders and the Rangers, the thundering of their horses' hooves...

Burros with packs

CHAPTER XII

A telegram dated June 8, 1915, was sent to the Adjutant General: CUMMINGS AND SELF KILLED BANDIT THIS AM. RESISTED ARREST AND ATTACKED ME WITH A KNIFE. LEAVING FOR MARFA

The Adjutant General wired another Ranger: ARE BANDITS ON MEXICO OR TEXAS TERRITORY. HOW IS SITUATION TODAY. HUTCHINGS (No punctuation in wires. Periods added to make reading easier.)

An answer wired back the same day: BANDITS ON AMERICAN SOIL. SITUATION UNCHANGED

A letter to Adjutant General Hutchings dated July 13, 1915, from a Ranger Sergeant of Co. A in San Benito, Texas: "There are strange Mexicans being reported almost daily in this country and citizens of Raymondville and Lyford have been very much alarmed over a report that the Mexicans were going to rob the banks of these two places."

A letter from a young man age 20 who wanted to join: "I have thorough knowledge of bookkeeping and shorthand if that would help." Perhaps he could not shoot a gun but wanted to help in some way.

One letter was about "young men of a number of communities wanting to organize a group of Rangers if there would be a machine gun squad." Machine guns now fresh on the scene were on their minds!

A wire dated August 30, 1915 to a Ranger from his wife: CHILD REAL SICK. COME HOME IF POSSIBLE. The Adjutant General was generous about letting his men off to go to their families when they were in some sort of distress.

Letter from another applicant: "I pray to be one of your secret service men…"

At this time the Adjutant General's mail piled up while he was out with lumbago. Many letters also went to the Governor who transferred them to the General, adding to the stacks.

"What is (sic) the inducements as to pay?" queried one.

Another written in cursive: "I am rearing to get into action…"

Most letters were written in longhand, although a few were typed. Many sent telegrams. Words were misspelled; handwriting was not much to brag about sometimes, but all sounded sincere. Many professional men applied.

One telegram came that expressed great urgency, for some obscure reason: CAN YOU APPOINT ME TO THE TEXAS RANGERS ANSWER QUICK

Old veterans wrote wanting to fight on the Border: "Want to do more than sit by a water hole and slap flies!" said one.

Hutchings began his answer to one letter with this: "Napoleon was credited with stacking his mail for 30 days on the theory that by that time 75% would have already answered itself." His own mail continued to pile up during the times he made frequent trips to the Border or other places where his men were active.

He received a petition asking to be allowed to organize a "home guard." His answer was: "Take it up with your own sheriff." The Adjutant Generals were strict about not stepping into local affairs, as each kept reminding his men.

A letter came from a girl who stated she was an orphan and wanted her sweetheart back. He was on the Border in the National Guard, and would the Adjutant General discharge him?

Perhaps he was the one who wired about joining that had to have a quick answer.

On June 11, 1915, Texas Governor James E. Ferguson sent the following letter to President Woodrow Wilson:

"Dear Mr. Wilson: Again referring to our correspondence of some months ago, I beg to advise that conditions along the Mexican Border continue to grow worse. Each day brings new cases of violations of the law. The preservation of property rights has become exceedingly difficult. Marauding bands from Mexico make raids almost daily upon the property of our citizens. My people are appealing to me daily for aid to suppress lawlessness in every form, and which I am unable to give.

"I am, therefore, writing in hope that you might aid me to meet the situation. If you would advise that you could ask

Congress at the next regular session to appropriate Thirty Thousand Dollars for the maintenance of thirty additional Texas Rangers, I feel sure that Congress would make the appropriation with the same alacrity as when President Taft made a similar recommendation. With this assurance I can arrange here to finance the immediate installation of the increased force.

"Conditions could be materially helped if there were an increase in the River Guard force by the Federal Government.

"I assure you that this is with some degree of reluctance that I make this request, but I feel that the gravity of the situation makes such action on my part imperative…"

The Rangers were doing the best they could, as shown by Captain Ransom's Scout Report for the month of July 1915. It showed that he had traveled a total of 1,582 miles during that month going to San Antonio, Harlingen, San Benito, Hempstead, Austin, Brownsville, and Houston "seeing parties and making arrangements," as he described his duties. He also mentioned investigating the burning of railroad bridges.

A letter dated July 22, 1915 sent word that Sheriff A. Y. Baker of Hidalgo said bandits were still in the country, with conditions so bad that many ranchmen were moving their families to town.

On the same day, the Adjutant General told Captain Sanders of Del Rio or Captain Ransom of Harlingen that Miguel Gallardo would apply for a position in the Force. He came highly recommended.

Caesar Kleberg, Kingsville, wired the Adjutant General July 24, 1915: CONDITIONS NO BETTER. RAILROAD BRIDGE BURNED AND TELEGRAPH AND TELEPHONE WIRES CUT SATURDAY NIGHT

A wire dated July 26, 1915 from Hutchings to Captain J. J. Sanders: RANSOM HAS DUVAL JIM WELLS NUECES KLEBERG ZAPATA HOGG BROOKS WILLACY STARR HIDALGO AND CAMERON COUNTIES. REMOVE MEN REMAINING IN YOUR COMPANY OUT OF THESE COUNTIES. WHEN RANSOM ENLISTS HIS MEN AND LOCATES THEM AT POINTS WHICH HE DEEMS BEST THEN LOCATE YOUR MEN IN YOUR TERRITORY TO BEST ADVANTAGE.

The Adjutant General sent Sanders another wire the same day: HOW SOON WILL NEW COMPANY BE OPERATING.

CONDITIONS NO BETTER. SUGGEST YOU RUN UP TO
KINGSVILLE. WHERE IS CAPTAIN RANSOM. KEEP ME
ADVISED OF HIS AND YOUR LOCATION. HUTCHINGS

A thought-provoking wire from Sheriff Vann of Cameron
County dated July 26 to Hutchings: I WOULD LIKE FOR YOU TO
STATION NEW RANGER COMPANY D AT ALICE OR SAN
DIEGO AND RETAIN CAPTAIN J SANDERS AND HIS MEN
WHERE THEY ARE AT PRESENT. CAPTAIN SANDERS AND
HIS MEN ARE DOING GOOD WORK HERE NOW. HOPE THIS
WILL MEET WITH YOUR APPROVAL. WILL FOLLOW WITH
LETTER

Here is a clue Vann does not want Ransom in his county.
He is not the only one. The two men were not on friendly terms.

A letter addressed to Captain Henry L. Ransom, Harlingen:
"My dear Ransom: This will introduce you to my good friend,
Colonel Henry Hilliard, who at one time had the good fortune to
be a citizen of Austin; at the present he is less fortunate inasmuch
as he lives in St. Louis. He is still considerably interested materially
in Texas, and particularly in those counties in which you operate.
Any courtesies you may extend to Colonel Hilliard will be very
much appreciated by me." No signature.

Captain J. J. Sanders sent a wire dated July 27 to Hutchings:
RANSOM AND I HAVE JUST RETURNED FROM SEBASTIAN
WHERE BRIDGE WAS BURNED AND WIRE CUT. HE IS AT
HARLINGEN AND WILL TAKE CHARGE THE FIRST

Hutchings sent a diplomatic answer to Sheriff Vann July 27,
with the subject being distribution of the Ranger Force.

"1. His excellency, the Governor, has directed Captain
Henry Ransom to operate in the counties of Duval, Jim Wells,
Nueces, Kleberg, Jim Hogg, Willacy, Starr, Hidalgo, and Cameron.

"2. Captain Ransom and Captain Sanders are investigating
conditions in that territory, and as soon as Captain Ransom is
informed on such conditions and has his company enlisted will
take charge of that territory and Captain Sanders will withdraw the
remaining members of the company and operate in other territory.

"3. Captain Ransom will, of course, take station at such
point as may seem to him best and may from time to time change
to meet changed conditions.

"4. I'm very glad that the work of Captain Sanders and his men is commended by you, and feel quite sure that such commendation will be merited by Captain Ransom and his men."

In a wire from Hutchings to Captains Sanders and Ransom, he said he was advised that a certain Mexican that lived southeast of Raymondville and an Anglo president of a bank and stock raiser may be giving aid to the gang of bandits said to be operating in that vicinity.

Some crooked Americans in that area were known to be collaborating with bandits in cattle theft and other crimes.

Reading some of the Rangers' monthly reports brings home the absolute truth about their seemingly impossible accomplishments, these being original and filed in the State Archives of the De Zavala Building in Austin

An example of how much was done in one month, July 1915, by R. W. Aldrich was described in his report. He traveled 1,288 miles, inspected cattle, after going to San Benito to arrest two Mexicans, one wanted in another county, one wanted for horse stealing. He accompanied a sheriff and a posse to look for a band of outlaws, then went on to Raymondville to take J. M. who had attacked two white women (a sheriff's wife and another) in broad daylight, was shot by citizens, taken to a hospital to be patched up, and thence on to jail in another area to prevent his being lynched, arriving at 5:00 a.m., after traveling 126 miles.

They called at a ranch to look for a bandit gang then watched roads all night. The Rangers scouted with a posse to Filipino, Besera, Monado, Llescas, Rusias, Tres Nonas, and Lipanes Ranches in pursuit of banditos. One evening they answered a rush call from citizens at La Bote about part of the bandits seen there. That night they returned to San Benito for a saddle, a total of 132 miles. The following morning they left early to get an Indian tracker, then went with a posse and 36 men of Troop B, 12th Cavalry to search through a big brush pasture where a gang was supposed to be, without results.

They scouted through Besera, Gran Genio to Santa Roma Ranch where they watched the wells all night. A horse had been taken by bandits from this ranch the night before. The next day the Rangers went to the Zapata Ranch where three horses were stolen, then back to Santa Rita Ranch.

At this time they sent their horses back to Raymondville and went by train to Harlingen.

Another day in July they were told a gang supposedly headed for the Rio Grande, so watched the railroad crossing all night.

Next they went 76 miles to arrest F. C. for stealing and forgery. This was July 10. On July 11 they returned to Raymondville to look for a gang of bandits that robbed a store in Stockholm that day. Here they took a trail where the gang had cut telephone wires, to follow them on foot for eight miles.

The trail was lost on the Tiniente Ranch, but they stayed all night there at the request of Mr. Thompson, for his protection. Then they scouted through three other ranches, which was 23 miles. On July 13 they had a call from Sturer's Ranch saying bandits camped close there, but none were found when they arrived. After scouting for trails, they left their horses in the evening and returned to Raymondville by auto, after which they returned to San Benito to find orders to come to Del Rio.

This takes one only to July 15.

If the reader is worn out wading through this, think how fatigued the Rangers must have been, doing it all and most of it on horseback.

County Judge W. L. Yates of Brownsville wrote to the Adjutant General on August 3, 1915: "One man killed and four wounded in fight, none of bandits accounted for. Indications are that they will escape in the dense brush.

"The whole country is infested with armed men. Hold-ups which have been of nightly occurrence are now happening by day. The bandits in a fight this morning were armed with Mausers (and) act with remarkable facility and organization for bandits. Any overt act by the United States Government anywhere in Mexico would this time be ruinous to the Lower Rio Grande Valley.

"The distance to Rio Grande City is 120 miles. One regiment is utterly inadequate to protect even the towns. I cannot wire all I know for obvious reasons. Don't give publicity to this."

A letter from the Adjutant General, who was at Rockport at the time, was addressed to the Governor on August 4: "Sheriffs of Nueces, Kleberg, Jim Wells, Duval, Brooks, Jim Hogg report conditions quiet. Sheriff of Starr County reports if bandits enter along river with no protection, acts would be committed before Sheriff could be notified. Strong patrol of Rangers should be along river.

PHOTOS

102 E. HOUSTON ST.,
SAN ANTONIO,
TEXAS.

Cpl. Henry Ransom just back from Philippines (where he served twice)
after an honorable discharge

Two of Henry's sisters, Victoria Adelaide (Ransom) Davis (above), and Cora (Ransom) Waggoner (right)

Another of Henry's sisters, Mary (above), and Henry's Uncle Hamilton and Aunt Kate Ransom (left), who raised Henry when he was orphaned

Austin Bryan Cole, his wife Susan (Habermacher) and family (Martha Ella not born yet). Photo by Louis Rice, Victoria, Texas

Austin Bryan Cole on cattle drive.
This photo was taken in a studio in South Dakota.

One -room schoolhouse, probably at Hartsville when Henry attended or when Beatrice taught there

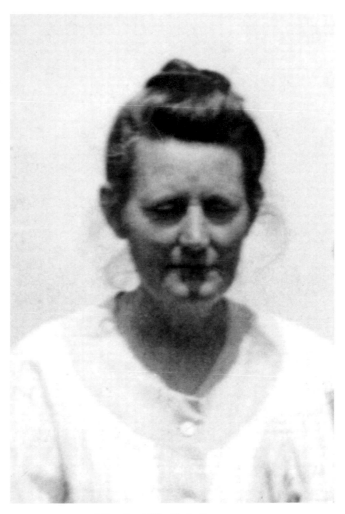

Martha Ella Cole Ransom,
Captain Ransom's first wife and mother of Beatrice
(photo taken later, after their divorce).

Captain Ransom's Texas Ranger badge. 1-1/4″ diameter gold with engraved letters that are filled in with blue paint and a pin on the back.

Texas Rangers Jules Baker (left) and Henry Ransom (right).
Photo donated by Mrs. Olene Baker Chapman, daughter of Jules.

Photo of the Texas Rangers of Co. A in Colorado City, Texas, 1905. Left to Right: Ivan Murchison, N.P. "Doc" Thomas, R.B. Baker, Henry Ransom, Capt. Frank Johnson, Preston Weston, Sgt. Billie McCauley, Thomas B. White. Source: Texas Dept. of Public Safety, 5805 N. Lamar, Austin, Texas 78773. Copy from: The Institute of Texan Cultures, San Antonio, Texas.

Henry Brown Ransom and sister Ina Aylor Ransom, children of Henry's brother Will Ransom. The little boy rode with his uncle, the captain, when he did target practice. He also listened to all his accounts of his adventures, and remembered it all!

Ruby Lee, Henry's daughter from his second marriage

*Sheriff Jack Yarbrough of Nolan County and
long-time friend of Henry Ransom*

Henry Ransom, next to last on viewer's right. Jules Baker is on the far left. Must be all Rangers (with shaved heads!). This has to be a studio shot — note the bank teller in the background with pistol in hand. Can anyone identify the others?

Henry's "Little Bee",
daughter Beatrice Ransom, age 16-18.

*Henry Ransom's daughter Beatrice, holding her daughter —
who became the author.*

"Sheriff of Cameron County reports situation very alarming. Bunches of bandits in various parts of the county. Suggests sending five companies National Guard to help control situation.

"Bates reports over 100 bandits from Mexico operate in the county. Citizens very much excited. Unless more federal troops sent very advisable to send several militia companies. All ranchmen ready to do all they can to aid militia with scouts.

"Ransom reports two or three well-organized bands of outlaws operating Cameron County. Sincere cooperation of all forces most needed. Bridge burned and wires cut last night on Brownsville railroad 8 miles north of Harlington. Ambush planned by bridge burners. Caesar Kleberg and Jim Wells say situation seems serious and asked me to meet them in Kingsville Thursday morning. I have courteously declined account prior engagement, but of course am subject to your wishes anytime. Hutchings."

Sheriff J. C. Guerra of Starr County sent a wire August 4, 1915 to the Adjutant General: SHOULD BANDITS AND THIEVES ENTER THIS COUNTY AS IN CAMERON OUR PEOPLE ALONG THE RIVER WOULD HAVE NO PROTECTION. ACTS WOULD BE DONE BEFORE THE SHERIFF AND DEPUTIES COULD BE NOTIFIED. STRONG PATROL OF RANGERS AND DEPUTIES SHOULD BE PLACED ALONG THIS RIVER

Captain H. L. Ransom wired the Adjutant General also on August 4: CONDITIONS BAD IN CAMERON COUNTY. SEEMS TO BE TWO OR THREE WELL ORGANIZED BANDS OF OUTLAWS OPERATING IN COUNTY. TO THE BEST OF MY OPINION WHAT IS MOST NEEDED IS COOPERATION OF ALL PARTIES WHICH I AM TRYING TO SECURE. BRIDGE BURNED AND WIRES CUT ON BROWNSVILLE RAILROAD EIGHT MILES NORTH OF HARLINGEN SOMETIME LATTER PART OF LAST NIGHT. AMBUSH PLANNED BY PARTIES THAT BURNED BRIDGE

The Adjutant General received more wires from Caesar Kleberg and others who were all alarmed, including Sheriff Vann of Brownsville suggesting that the National Guard be sent.

Another who wired him at that time was L. M. Bates of Brownsville: BEST INFORMATION OBTAINABLE OVER ONE HUNDRED BANDITS FROM MEXICO OPERATING IN THIS COUNTY. CITIZENS VERY MUCH EXCITED. FIGHT YESTERDAY RESULTED ONE DEATH FOUR WOUNDED NO LOSS ON

BANDIT SIDE. IT WOULD BE VERY POPULAR MOVE AND
VERY ADVISABLE TO SEND SEVERAL COMPANIES OF MILITIA
DOWN. MOST ALL MEXICAN RANCHMEN IN THIS SECTION
ARE READY TO COOPERATE AND DO ALL THEY CAN TO AID
MILITARY WITH AID OF SCOUTS AND MEXICAN TEXAN
RANCHMEN WHO KNOW THE COUNTRY AND THE PEOPLE

News from Laredo came to the Adjutant General in a letter
dated August 28, 1915 from the District Attorney John A. Walls.
He spoke of how on the surface in Laredo matters appear quiet
and peaceful but he does not believe that. He has been gathering
intelligence from reliable sources. "My old time Mexican friends
tell me that the American government must either recognize
Carranza or fight. The better class of Mexicans tell me that our
government will recognize Carranza and thus virtually acknowledge we are not prepared to fight Mexico."

Walls also stated, "Our Mexican newspapers are the greatest
source of trouble but the law is inadequate to reach them.
Incendiary editorials easily excite the Mexicans and create race
prejudice. I have prosecuted these newspaper men for libel and
have secured convictions but now they avoid the libel law and
continue to publish highly colored editorials which bode no good
for the community. I have no doubt there is a disturbing element
in Laredo that is holding secret meetings. Many automobiles from
San Antonio loaded with strange Mexicans have arrived here lately, always in the early hours of the morning, but what this mission
is, I have not been able to ascertain. I am satisfied these mischief
makers are fairly well supplied with money."

Monthly reports continue, no matter how much battle action
the Rangers endure. In Captain Ransom's "monthly return" of Co.
D is listed his inventory of "public property" used by his company. The following, listed in good condition, gives a clear picture of
their necessary supplies: 10 field cots, 18 blue blankets, 2 gray blankets, 3 pack saddle blankets, 2 sets pack saddle breeching, 5 water
bags, 1 camp outfit, 1 Det. Cap. outfit, 3 cases cartridges 30 cal, 300
.45 cartridges, 3 halters, 1 9x16 tarp, and 3 pack saddle bags.

Sheriff Vann of Cameron County wired Hutchings
September 2, 1915: BANDITS BROKE OUT AGAIN LAST NIGHT.
BURNED RAILROAD BRIDGE BETWEEN BROWNSVILLE AND
SAN BENITO. SHOT INTO TWO PARTIES OF AUTOMOBILES.

SHERIFF AND CAVALRY CAMPED TONIGHT ABOUT SIX-
TEEN MILES NORTH OF BROWNSVILLE

Governor Ferguson received a wire on September 3, from
Sheriff John Morine of Van Horn: AS THERE IS CONSIDERABLE
EXCITEMENT IN THE COMMUNITY OVER THE KILLING OF O
AND COMPANIONS IN THIS COUNTY BY SHERIFFS POSSE I
RESPECTFULLY REQUEST THE PLACING OF A FEW RANGERS
IN THIS VICINITY TO COOPERATE WITH ME IN RUNNING
DOWN OF MEXICAN BANDITS DEPREDATING RANCHES IN
THIS COUNTY WHICH IS SPARSELY SETTLED. RANCHMENS
HORSES IN DANGER OF BEING STOLEN AT ANY TIME.
PLEASE ANSWER

Gordon Hill wired Henry Hutchings on September 4: CAN
YOU COME DOWN IF NECESSARY. SOME ACTION MUST BE
TAKEN TO BREAK UP BANDIT ORGANIZATION. ANSWER

Hutchings heard also on September 4 from Sheriff W. T.
Gardner of Dimmit County: "For the protection of Asherton, Crystal
City, and Carrizo Springs and one hundred fifty miles of border adjacent to these towns, all of which are in striking distance of the river,
each having a population of one thousand, sixty percent Mexican
and each of said towns being on the west side of the Nueces River,
we feel that we are in danger and have been threatened.

"We ask that you station two Texas Rangers at Carrizo
Springs where they will be in easy reach for any emergency that
may arise. We have had no trouble but the work is growing so
much of late I can't control such a large border front.

"Two large bunches of horses and mules have escaped
through here, smuggled and stolen. There is running a train of
jitneys and many Mexicans are moving about very suspiciously at
night. There is surely something brewing in this country. We are
expecting something to break out soon. We have organized a home
guard. I need some help."

Captain Sanders wrote Hutchings on September 4:
"Everything is quiet at Norias just now, but the families of all
Mexicans employed on the ranch here left again, the last one on
the evening train yesterday. They have undoubtedly had information of some kind which caused them to leave.

"The hands helping a ranch foreman in the area heard
shooting and refused to go into the brush to see what was going
on," he added. "All left immediately heading to Raymondville. He

said this would indicate a band of bandits were either forming there or camping there in that neighborhood, too."

The Adjutant General wrote Captain Henry Ransom, who was in Harlingen, on September 4: "Sheriff Baker at McAllen wanted me to leave Rangers there instead of going to Rio Grande City. Could not do this. Can you give Baker any help?"

In a wire to Gordon Hill on September 5, Hutchings said: READY TO GO ANYWHERE ANY TIME ON GOVERNORS ORDERS

A letter came to Hutchings from Ranger Lester Ogg, who had eye problems and was not able to work. He asked if he could be retained if possible as he was getting better. He had been riding with Captain Ransom. A typical Ranger, he did not want to submit to human frailties.

When one Ranger, Sergeant T. N. Reneau, became quite ill, the other Rangers worried about him and kept current on his condition, reporting it to the Adjutant General. Captain Ransom conferred with his doctors. The medics were uncertain about Reneau's problem, saying he possibly had a "particle" of malaria or typhoid and he could not go back on duty for about a month.

"So we decided to let him go on to Houston," reported Ransom.

"Thought he would be better satisfied there and wouldn't worry so much as he could be with his daughters and friends." He did have friends there, as he had been on the police force when Henry was Chief of Police.

The Texas Rangers, a closely knit group, really cared about each other. They were appreciated by outsiders also. Caesar Kleberg of the King Ranch wrote on October 2, 1915 to Henry Hutchings: "I thank you very much for your kindness and consideration to me and to the Ranger force. Indications are that the present troubles will be with us for a considerable period and quite possibly winter will accentuate them."

Captain Ransom wired the Adjutant General October 20, 1915: COME DOWN HERE IF POSSIBLE. I NEED YOUR HELP IN CONNECTION WITH WRECKING AND ROBBING OF TRAIN NEAR BROWNSVILLE

The General penciled on the bottom of the wire his reply for the secretary to send back: RESPECTFULLY REFERRED TO THE GOVERNOR FOR MY INSTRUCTIONS

He continued to receive letters from many men elsewhere who wanted to come fight the bandits, saying they knew the Rangers and the military were doing the best they could but there just were not enough of them. One was a former major in the Texas National Guard who said he would recruit a number of others with him.

Another wrote saying that Captain Ransom was necessary, as without him, the writer felt "our people will take matters in hand and that is a situation to be avoided by all means."

Some were so outraged about this Brownsville train wreck and robbery that they begged to be allowed to help, with no pay, and furnishing themselves with whatever they needed.

The Governor received another letter: "I am willing to serve my state at any time that I can. If my service is needed, I will join for no pay. I am at present employed and will resign. I am twenty-one and can talk Spanish real good. I'm an old cowboy and have been with the bandits since this trouble started. Hoping I will be given a commission as a volunteer Ranger..." What he meant by "being with the bandits" was not explained, possibly a word or two left out by error.

Captain Ransom wrote Hutchings from Harlingen on October 24, telling of enlisting another man.

"Please have Colonel Stockton ship me two Ranger carbines by Express. Would like very much to have some soft point cartridges for our rifles if they can be furnished to us. Yours to command..."

On the 25th Ransom wired Hutchings: DETACHMENT OF AMERICAN SOLDIERS FIRED ON BY MEXICAN BANDITS EARLY LAST NIGHT NEAR PLACE OF WRECK. DON'T KNOW WHETHER ANY BANDITS WERE KILLED OR WOUNDED

He sent another wire on the 26th: WILL SUBMIT THE FOLLOWING FOR YOUR CONSIDERATION. FIRST THAT DETENTION CAMPS BE ESTABLISHED AND MAINTAINED ALONG THE BORDER BY THE FEDERAL GOVERNMENT SECOND THAT ALL SUSPECTS BE HELD IN SAID CAMPS UNDER GUARD AND WORKED WHEN NEEDED FOR SANITARY PURPOSES AND TO CUT RIGHT OF WAYS THROUGH BRUSHY PLACES ADJACENT TO RIVER TO MAKE PATROL DUTY MORE EFFICIENT

Hutchings wrote the Governor on October 28 listing Ransom's suggestions:

More Rangers

Take off semi-martial law

Put on martial law to military road

Put on martial law Cameron and Hidalgo Counties

Get federal government to notify Carranza to adequately patrol his side of Rio Grande or tell him U. S. will

Some danger of Texans taking things in their own hands regardless of neutrality laws

Small rewards

Seal up river

Secret Service

The Scout Report of Captain Ransom, Co. D, for October 1915: "Scouted from Pharr to Harlingen to investigate a murder, arrested men and turned them over to sheriff of Hidalago County, went to Edinburg, then to Pharr for trial of prisoners. Went to Austin from Harlingen to confer with Adjutant General, from there to Hempstead (348 miles). On 10th scouted Harlingen to Mission with Rangers Edwards, Glick, and Brunner to camp at Pharr. Then back to Pharr, Harlingen, on to Kingsville, attended another trial at Harlingen, then investigated wrecking and robbing of train."

On the 19th: "Scouting through brush searching for Mexican bandits. By trailing and making careful investigation we learned that part of the band of the Mexicans crossed the River southwest about six miles from place of wreck. A number of the trails were followed east from the place of the wreck to Mexican shacks and into the brush going in the direction of Brownsville."

October 23, 1915: Went to Brownsville to meet Adjutant General. Went to scene of wreck then back and forth to Brownsville, Harlingen, Villanueva, and vicinity, then Norias, camp at Harlingen, then La Cuna Ranch to investigate report of parties being fired upon. 31st scout was to Harlingen to Pharr and return. Total arrests 3. Total miles traveled this month 1,813."

This was followed by Scout Reports by each man in his company, all appearing to be in his handwriting. First was T. N. Reneau, now able to be back in the saddle. He did take time later to go to Houston once for medical treatment but returned and is in the scouting business again. He traveled 1,165 miles that month doing Ranger work.

This time the monthly inventory included 15 field cots, 1 cook stove, 2 cap outfits, 2 pair handcuffs, 2 more bags for packs, 1 letter file, and 2 bill files, along with 2 cases of Ball cartridges .30. 1500 distributed to members of Co. D, Ranger Force.

The Captains carried files for letters and bills, with all business records organized and meticulously kept. Nothing was haphazard, including carefully kept inventories of equipment and documented number of miles covered.

The courtesy, loyalty, and consideration the men showed their Captains and the Adjutant General made the Ranger Force a remarkable, well-oiled machine that accomplished much in spite of sparse funding, small enrollment, and huge areas to cover. The men did a lot with what they had, making them the respected law enforcement group they have always been.

What better way to understand, to share the Rangers' experiences — hair-raising, poignant, occasionally comical — than by reading what they actually wrote during these perilous times?

Their shades hover over the reader's shoulders as the words flood off the pages into the senses, spiriting one away into their nebulous world of gun smoke, camp fires, and lonely trails through miles of brush.

Governor Ferguson received a letter in Spanish dated November 2, 1915 from Albino G. Garra, a Mexican American living in Columbus, Texas. He said he has lived in Texas 14 years, is married with a family, and offers his services to the Governor to help fight the bandits.

Letters pertaining to railroad passes and warrants of authority were sent to the Adjutant General. When a Ranger left the Force, these had to be accounted for and returned to the office in Austin.

Captain Ransom reported the following in a wire November 9 to the General: RANGER BERT VEALE LEFT FOR HOUSTON ACCOUNT SICK MOTHER. RANGER J L ANDERS ATTENDING FEDERAL COURT AT LAREDO ACCOUNT WITNESS. I WOULD LIKE TO GO HOME FOR A DAY OR TWO

Hutchings replied November 10: YOU CAN GO HOME FOR A FEW DAYS. LEAVE RENEAU IN COMMAND

He sent another wire to Captain Ransom November 12: REPORT TO AUSTIN PRIOR TO RETURNING TO YOUR HOME STATION

Then on the 14th Hutchings sent another wire to Ransom: RETURN ALL PASSES FOR_____TO THIS OFFICE QUICK

No clue was given or in a later follow-up to explain what was happening and the reason for the rush. Ransom knew but we never will.

Apparently a Mexican named D. L. was killed in Reynosa and some of the Rangers were blamed for it. After carefully investigating the matter, the Adjutant General sent the following letter to Governor James Ferguson: "Sir, I have the honor to acknowledge receipt of letter of the 10th inst., accompanied by letter of the Honorable Secretary of State of the United States to your Excellency of date November 5, 1915, also the latter letters being returned herewith.

"Scout Reports of Captain Ransom's Command — the only organization of the Ranger Force operating in Hidalgo County, the only county in Texas within rifle shot of Reynosa — show detachments were in camp at Pharr and Harlingen on October 12, 1915, and from neither of said stations would a rifle shot carry to Reynosa.

"On September 12, 1915, Your Excellency directed members of the Ranger Force to not expose themselves to view from the Mexican side of the river and in compliance with the directions since that date no Rangers have been adjacent to the Rio Grande."

Copies of a letter dated November 20, 1915 from Hutchings were sent to Captains J. J. Sanders, J. M. Fox, and H. L. Ransom. The subject was "Summary Executions of Mexicans."

"1. By direction of His Excellency, the Governor, you are given the following instructions:

(a) To prevent the execution of all Mexicans except by due process of law.
(b) To notify city and county officers and citizens generally that any unlawful execution of Mexicans will be at their peril.
(c) To promptly report to this department all casualties, with names of witnesses.

"2. Acknowledge receipt of this letter."

After the previous episode in which Rangers were blamed wrongfully, the General felt such a note of caution and reminder was in order, to prevent possible problems in the future.

Captain Ransom heeded the General's request with a letter dated November 24, 1915: "I hereby acknowledge receipt of yours of November 20th in regard to summary execution of Mexicans..."

The Rangers' horses sometimes rode a train

CHAPTER XIII

James B. Murrah, President of the Sheep and Goat Raisers Association, wired Governor Ferguson November 25, 1915: WE HEARTILY ENDORSE A STRONGER RANGER FORCE AS BEING ASKED FOR BY SENATOR HUDSPETH AND SHERIFF ALMONDS

Next day a wire came to the Governor from Johnston Robertson of Del Rio: EDWARDS COUNTY IS INFESTED WITH GOAT THIEVES AND OUR RANCHMEN ARE SUFFERING GREAT LOSS WE NEED A RANGER TO COOPERATE WITH OUR SHERIFF PLEASE GRANT THE REQUEST OF THE RANCH-MEN AND SEND US A RANGER WE NEED HIM BADLY

On November 26, the Governor wrote Henry Hutchings: "Dear Sir, I enclosed you two telegrams in reference to depreda-tions against sheep and goats out in Edwards and Val Verde Counties. It might be a good idea to send a couple of Rangers there to cooperate with the sheriffs."

Captain Ransom wrote Hutchings the following on the 27th: "Today about noon Ranger Clive C. Hurst let his pistol go off acci-dentally while placing it in his scabbard. The bullet entered the fleshy part of the thigh and ranged downward. Dr. Leitzritch dressed wound but would not locate bullet. Don't think it will give him much trouble. Everything quiet in regard to bandit trouble in this section of the Border. Ransom"

Hurst had just enlisted 15 days earlier and probably felt he would never "live down" this embarrassing accident.

A letter dated November 27, 1915 came to Mr. Ed Lassiter, Brooks County. It must have been sent to the General for his infor-mation as it was in his correspondence file. It was signed "Sincerely your friend," but only initials are legible.

"Dear Mr. Lassiter," wrote L. C., "I have three or four Mexicans that stay on the other side of the river, who act in the Secret Service Department for me. They have been reporting to me for the last three or four days that five or six hundred bandits on the other side of the river are fixing up a raid on this side.

"I know that D. L. R., B., and R. have been in Matamoras for the last three weeks, and cross the Rio Grande River above Rio Grande City, and make a raid out in your country. Their purpose is to get horses and do a lot of robbing and stealing.

"They have been figuring on a raid in our country for the last two or three weeks, but conditions in our country are so well guarded and looked after that they have decided to go further up the road. The Carranza people on the other side of the river have done nothing so far towards putting down or arresting the bandits on the side of the river, but to the contrary are doing everything to aid them.

"Last Sunday we ran into five bandits near the south of the Arroyo Colorado, and they told us they were looking around seeing how conditions were and that they intended to make a raid this week which goes without saying that they will not be able to make a detailed report.

"Now, Mr. Ed, I am writing you this and you can take it for what it is worth. I know that they are fixing to do something on the other side of the river.

"I am going to send a copy of this letter to Captain Sanders at Alice."

The Adjutant General sent a letter in formal style, which he used sometimes, to Captain Ransom. He dated it November 26, and stated: "From," "To," and "Subject," followed by two points:

"1. Transmitted herewith are copies of letters from Mr. Whitehead and Colonel Coombs, with reference to Mr. Harry Scullin, and carbon copy of my reply.

"2. If Mr. Scullin finds it practicable to report to you, take him in charge and do the best you can for him."

"My dear Captain," wrote Harry Scullin on December 10 to Ransom, "I have decided to leave here December 20. If you are to be away, I would appreciate it if you would leave word at your headquarters when I can get in touch with you."

Thus began an unusual episode for Captain Henry Ransom.

An interesting diversion in the routine of the Border turmoil came to Henry in the person of Harry Scullin, president of his

Scullin Steel Company of St. Louis, Missouri. His ambition was to leave the concrete canyons of the big city to serve with the Texas Rangers.

He arranged to be away from his business for an adventure not for the faint-hearted, heading toward the smoke and blood of South Texas. He was sent by the Adjutant General to be a guest of Henry, who had been, and would continue to be for some years, in the thick of the Bandit Wars.

For a month that included Christmas Harry Scullin "was" a Texas Ranger, fulfilling a dream that many throughout the country could experience only vicariously by avidly absorbing daily accounts in the newspapers.

He rode with this famous group of scouts as Ransom's company answered calls for help, tracked down bandits, brought them to justice, and camped out at night in harsh terrain of mesquite thickets, cactus, and greasewood in counties on the Border.

At night under the stars or in the scant and infrequent rain of the area, he, too, bedded down, sometimes on the hard ground with a saddle for a pillow. He ate the grub the Rangers cooked over their fires, sharing the hardships and excitement.

Scullin arranged for a return "vacation" the next year. An educated, courtly gentleman of refinement, he appeared to have the time of his life in 1915 and 1916, which was during some rough times with bandits. Perhaps the following clues will cause some kin of the admirable and courageous man to surface. It is hoped they will.

His listing in the Who's Who in St. Louis in 1930-1931 states that his residence was 521 South Broadway. He was born October 6, 1867 in Leavenworth, Kansas to John and Hannah (Perry) Scullin. He married Julia Woodward, and their children were two daughters, with only their married names listed: Mrs. H. P Green and Mrs. Eugenia Sullivan. He attended St. John's College (Fordham, N.), received a B. A. from St. Louis University. The man became chairman of the boards of numerous organizations. For this much information, the author is indebted to Leland Hillingoss of the History and Genealogy Department of the St. Louis Public Library.

Captain Ransom's Scout Report for November 1915: "Scouted from Corpus Christi to Harlingen. At Harlingen working on monthly report, enlisted Albert Billingsly, scouted to Bishop, arrested D. N. and returned to Kingsville and placed him in jail.

Scouted from Kingsville to Brownsville with prisoner and turned him over to Sheriff in Cameron County. Scouted from Brownsville to Harlingen. Scouted to Kingsville, arrested L. L. (Mexican), returned to Brownsville and placed prisoner in Cameron County jail. Returned to Harlingen November 8. Scouted to Brownsville with Captain Sanders and Sheriff Scarborough to work on Case. (Enlisted Clive Hurst November 9). Scouted to Harlingen November 10. Nothing to report. November 11 scouted from Harlingen to San Antonio. Scouted from San Antonio to Houston November 13. At Hempstead (home) November 14. Scouted to Simonton, Fort Bend County, and returned same day. November 15 scouted Hempstead to Austin. November 16 attending business with the Adjutant General's Department and left for Harlingen. November 17 arrived at Harlingen. Scouted to Pharr and returned twice two days in a row, then November 22 scouted to Hebbronville. November 23 scouted from Hebbronville to Harlingen. November 24 scouted to Brownsville and returned 25th to 29th at Harlingen. November 30 left Harlingen on scout to Hebbronville. Total miles traveled 2,317.

His monthly inventory was almost the same as before, with the addition of more cartridges issued to men in his company and two nose-bags added for the horses.

M. T. Mosely of Corpus Christi, in a letter of December 2, 1915, tells Hutchings of going with two other Rangers, Aldrich and Erskin, "trying to run in a bunch of cow thieves…several days trying to catch them but we had no luck." He had worked some with Captain Ransom, adding that he would go back to work with him some more.

Ransom sent a letter December 1, 1915, to Hutchings saying he was returning railroad passes and warrants of authority of Private_____, "who was discharged from the Ranger service December 9, 1915, for getting drunk and conduct unbecoming to an officer. At present, Company has ten members, including myself, Sergeant T. M. Reneau and Privates Bills, Billingsly, and Veale at Pharr, Hidalgo County. Private Craighead at Hebbronville, Jim Hogg County. J. L. Anders on sick leave in Marlin. Clive C. Hurst (the man accidentally wounded) at home near Odum, San Patricio County, John J. Edds, M. L. Rountree, and self at Harlingen, Cameron County. Ranger L. C. Bills will leave this evening on business of personal nature for Comanche County. Yours to command…"

Captain J. J. Sanders, Company A, Alice, Texas, wrote on December 12 to the Adjutant General: "Your much appreciated letter granting me a two weeks leave of absence was received yesterday and I wish to thank you for the favor and for the many other kindnesses shown me during the years I have served under you.

"I wished to go home at this time very much, as my wife is not feeling at all well, but unfortunately, I fear that I will be unable to do so on account of conditions at San Diego.

"Judge Taylor and District Attorney Leslie, both appointees of Governor Ferguson, came to see me Friday night and told me they feared serious trouble there, that when the grand jury was examining the books of the county, Sheriff Tobin and State Senator Parr entered grand jury room and demanded that the audit be stopped or they would seize the books.

"Foreman Dubose refused to accede to their demands and they took the books away. The Judge stated that he must have officers to execute his orders and requested that myself and my command come to San Diego and remain until his court adjourns, which will be in about three weeks.

"I am much disappointed at not being able to avail myself of my leave, but if possible, I will go home for Christmas dinner anyway."

On December 13, 1915, Captain Ransom wired the General: WOULD LIKE TO GO TO RICHMOND AND HEMPSTEAD TIME TO RETURN HERE BY TWENTIETH. DON'T WANT TO BE AWAY DURING HOLIDAYS

Hutchings, December 13: HENRY RANSOM APPLICATION FOR LEAVE APPROVED

This was another Christmas Henry had to spend away from home and family.

Hutchings wired Captain Sanders, Company A at San Diego: ACTING GOVERNOR APPROVED YOUR ACTION TAKEN AT REQUEST OF JUDGE TAYLOR

Near Christmas of December 1915 Henry saw his family at home in Hempstead for a short time.

Ruby Lee knew he was coming home and ran down the road to meet him, as usual. He would stop his horse, lift her up to ride behind him the rest of the way to the house. At this particular time he rode a big, beautiful dappled gray, Ruby said.

He was known to ride the finest horses available and to give them the best of care.

For treats for Jonathan, Henry always saved little packets of sugar cubes from the hotel dining rooms where he stayed when not camped out in the open.

After an early holiday visit with Anna, Ruby Lee, and Jonathan, Henry trekked back to his camp near Harlingen. He couldn't stop all the evil activity, but he and his men did their best.

In Brown County there was gambling, bootlegging, and prostitution in Sheriff Vann's area, which came out in later testimony in a court case. One memorable incident that set the area on its ear was when a county commissioner was caught smuggling in a big load of "booze."

The Adjutant General always had every altercation involving one or more Rangers investigated thoroughly, employing grand juries in the county where the action took place. There would be at least one Mexican on these grand juries and maybe more where the Mexican population was higher.

The mere presence of Texas Rangers gave others confidence. Many citizens followed the lawmen's careers with great interest and pride, repeating colorful anecdotes about their favorites.

"A Ranger will charge a buzz saw," commented one person confidently. This and the remark concerning "one Ranger for one riot" live on, being attributed to various men and situations.

Overly ambitious reporters contributed to the supply of tales, slightly stretched sometimes, that would be embroidered upon numerous times as they were circulated.

One Ranger asked a newspaper reporter why he didn't check the facts before writing up an article. Why did he write such lies and sensational stories?

Without hesitating, the reporter replied, "I don't have to! I don't have time! Why, I get $4 apiece for these stories!" Clearly money was then, as now, a driving influence.

Lawlessness on the Border continued with no pause, running over the boundary of the Rio Grande, spreading like a tipped over bucket of bloody violence. In 1916 Pancho Villa with 400 men crossed the Border, raided Columbus, New Mexico, killing 16 citizens and burning part of the town.

President Wilson the next day ordered a force into Mexico to capture Villa and his band. Brigadier General Pershing was sent from San Francisco to command the punitive expedition into Mexico.

Carranza, instead of cooperating, objected to the U. S. Troops coming in Mexico and notified Pershing his invasion would be resisted. The American soldiers were withdrawn.

The United States recognized Carranza's government.

Pancho Villa and his followers were chased out of Mexico City by Carranza's chief general. Carranza considered Pancho Villa a bandit, did not trust him. Villa took refuge in the mountains of the northern states of Mexico.

On March 13, 1916 Adjutant General Henry Hutchings sent the following telegram to Captain J. M. Fox, Company B, Marfa: HUDSPETH AND DALE EL PASO TELEGRAPH THAT CONDITIONS IN EL PASO VERY SERIOUS. THREATENED UPRISING OF MEXICANS IN NEW MEXICO IN VICINITY OF EL PASO AND FROM EL PASO TO THE NEW MEXICO LINE. TELEGRAPH SENT AFTER CONFERENCE WITH SHERIFF. THEY ASK FOR TWO COMPANIES OF RANGERS AND THAT THE GOVENOR COME IN PERSON. THE GOVERNOR DIRECTS A DETAILED REPORT BY WIRE ON CONDITIONS AT EL PASO IN ORDER THAT HE MAY PASS ON THE ADVISABILITY OF SENDING THESE TWO COMPANIES

A lengthy wire dated April 14, 1916 to the Adjutant General came from Peyton J. Edwards and Captain J. M. Fox: OUR INFORMATION FROM JUAREZ REPORTS THAT CARRANZA OFFICERS IN CONSULTATION HAVE AGREED THAT THEY WILL EVACUATE JUAREZ BY TRAIN LOAD ATILLERY ON FLAT CARS AND SHELL US AS THEY LEAVE. NO DOUBT THIS IS THEIR PLAN BUT WHETHER THEY WILL DO THIS OR NOT CANNOT SAY NOR WHEN IT WILL TAKE PLACE. MEXICAN OFFICERS ARE INFLUENCING SOLDIERS BY TELLING THEM OUR SOLDIERS UNJUSTLY KILLED MANY WOMEN AND CHILDREN AT PARRAL. REPORTED IN JUAREZ THAT OUR SOLDIERS AND CARRANZA TROOPS FIGHTING TODAY NEAR PARRAL. SHOULD JUAREZ DO THIS IT MAY TAKE PLACE AT ANY MINUTE. THE ONLY BATTERIES HERE ARE FOUR GUNS AT FORT BLISS FIVE MILES FROM EL PASO AND SEVEN FROM JUAREZ WITH EFFECTIVE RANGE OF THREE

AND ONE HALF MILES AND WILL TAKE AT LEAST ONE
HOUR TO GET INTO POSITION FOR ACTION. THIS INFOR-
MATION WAS GIVEN GENERAL BELL AND HE MAY BRING
ARTILLERY WHERE IT BE OF SERVICE TO PREVENT THIS.
GENERAL BELL HAS BEEN ACTIVE AND TAKEN PRECAU-
TIONS TO PROTECT CITY AND BORDER UNDER HIS CON-
TROL BUT IF HE DOES NOT BRING THIS BATTERY WHERE IT
CAN GET INTO ACTION AT ONCE YOU ARE TO USE YOUR
INFLUENCE TO HAVE IT DONE

An interesting letter dated April 20, 1916 came to the
General, who is also in charge of the National Guard: "We have
organized in Galveston one thousand Negroes who desire to tender through you their services to the United States in case of a call
for Volunteers by the President. These men represent the pick of
the colored men in Galveston and are all enthusiastic to assist in
maintaining the Glory of this Country.

"Among the men enrolled are many who served the country
in the regular army in both this country and our foreign possessions.

"All these men ask is that each company he officered by
men of their choosing and that all officers above captain shall be
white men of ability.

"We would ask as a favor that you advise us at your earliest
convenience if you will accept our offer so that we may advise our
men at our next meeting."

With address of 2609 Market Street, Galveston, Texas, it was
signed by Charles Lemonds, W. E. Wales, C. J. Williams, Gus
Dupont, John Ward, and W. E. Judy. No information was found
about the outcome of this courageous offer.

A letter dated April 28, 1916 from the State Department in
Washington, D. C. was sent to the Governor of Texas with details
about individuals smuggling arms and ammunition from the U. S.
for use in Mexico. Suggestions for tightening up security with customs officials on permitting exportation of explosives for industrial
purposes and munitions of war were given. It was signed by
Robert Lansing.

A letter this time to Hutchings dated May 5, 1916 from E. B.
Spiller, Secretary of the Cattle Raisers Association of Texas was
about Mr. H. L. Roberson who had been a Texas Ranger a number
of years..." and is now a field inspector with this group. He had
done excellent work and there are cattle thieves eager to get him

out of the area. He has been assaulted twice and only wounded. This is to ask for a special commission for him same as those held by Frank Hamer and F. A. Moseley who are doing the same work as Roberson."

Sheriff W. E. Gardner of Carrizo Springs sent a wire on May 9, 1916 to the Adjutant General: REQUESTED BY CITIZENS OF DIMMIT COUNTY TO ASK FOR MORE PROTECTION ON BORDER OF ASHERTON AND CARRIZO SPRINGS. BOTH ARE RAILROAD TERMINALS. WHAT PROTECTION CAN YOU GIVE HUNDREDS OF REFUGEES IN ONION FIELDS HERE

On May 11 H. T. Fletcher, Manager of the 02 Ranch wired the Adjutant General: RANCH IS SITUATED IN CENTER OF BIG BEND COUNTRY AT CROSSING OF ROADS FROM ALPINE TO TERLINGUA AND PRESIDIO TO MARATHON. ON ACCOUNT GOOD BUNCH HORSES AM APPREHENSIVE OF RAIDS FROM MEXICANS. IF YOU WILL STATION THREE MEN AT YOUR HEADQUARTERS WE WILL FEED THEM AND MOUNTS AND FURNISH REMOUNTS IF NECESSARY. THIS RANCH EXTENDS WITHIN THIRTY FIVE MILES OF RIVER

A wire to Governor Ferguson same day was sent by Sheriff D. S. Barker and County Judge Howell Johnson: GREAT APPREHENSION OF DANGER FELT HERE AND ON PECOS RIVER THIS COUNTY ON ACCOUNT INFLUX MEXICAN REFUGEES. SEND TWO MOUNTED RANGERS AT ONCE. ANSWER

Letters and wires continued to flood in, calling for help from the small Force of Rangers.

One dated May 22, 1916 to the Governor from Sheriff J. C. Adkins of Willacy County and County Judge Avery T. Searle: "Having addressed a letter to the Adjutant General, we respectfully call your attention to our need at this place for several Rangers.

"We are in the midst of a very large expanse of unprotected territory, extending for forty miles to the South and for twenty miles to the West, where Mexicans and revolutionists can and do pass and go at will through the brush. We feel that under present disturbed conditions the State will do well to station five or six Rangers here."

A. C. Riegar, Indian Gap, Texas, wrote on May 26, 1916 to the General saying he just received a wire from Captain Ransom advising him to report to the Adjutant General at once for service. He has to have a few days to arrange to be gone and to equip himself. Riegar wants to know if he is to come on horseback or by rail and then get a horse.

A letter written on May 29, 1916 on "John A. Hulen" letterhead to the Adjutant General came from the Filipino boy, now adult, that Hulen adopted and brought back to the U. S. after the Spanish-American War: "I am very anxious to be with General Hulen while he is in the service, especially when he is ordered across the Border in which case he will need a confidential aide, interpreter, and also one who can look after him personally, administering the little things for his comfort; and at the same time I want to join in the service, so that I can be detailed to him.

"It occurred to me that you might have a vacancy. Will you please see what you can do for me, in order to accomplish this purpose?

"I am a third year man at the Rice Institute at present and having been reared under military atmosphere more or less I feel able to meet the necessary requirements.

…Rudolf Hulen Fernandez"

Also Eugene, a son of General Hulen, joined the Texas Rangers but was killed by bandits in May 1916.

The Adjutant General occasionally received a letter that was totally irrelevant but served an important purpose: it gave him a laugh that he could use during those grim times.

A prime example: "I want you to appoint me Judge Advocate. Of course, I couldn't afford to accept it, if it took me away from home and my law practice, but it just occurred to me it is a little honor that you would like to confer upon me as one of your most loyal friends. I would be glad to have the appointment for the dignity it carries with it."

No evidence was found that such action was taken as requested. The poor fellow was left without the dignity he craved.

On June 11, 1916, Hutchings was in Harlingen with the National Guard. He commented in a letter a few days later that sitting in a swivel chair at his desk with all of the Guard on active duty on the Border was rather hard to endure.

Parts of a long letter from W. T. Gardner, Sheriff of Dimmit County to Hutchings follow: "We have had no serious trouble here yet. I made an effort to catch the seven bandits who got away at Webb…when three were killed. I went to the place yesterday at daybreak and a shower of rain had put out all trails…

"What we need here is the Rangers that you have at Eagle Pass as we have good roads from here to the border to any ranch between here and the Rio Grande. We could reach any within two hours and autos that can get six or seven men at any time to go and ten of us can take care of any band less than 50. We need this protection so we could take care of anything from Minerva to Eagle Pass and still have the towns of Carrizo Springs and Asherton protected as well as Catarina Ranch where there are many good horses and a fine commissary, a fine place for them to make a raid.

"The Rangers are the only people that can do this work."

A letter from a Mexican, whose initials are T. R. that was dated June 20, 1916 came to the Adjutant General. It was on letterhead of "Texas Library and Historical Commission." Where did he obtain that?

"Permit me to make you a statement. I am a man, a workman. I lived near Brownsville and I had to flee on account of bandits. One J. S. is a companion of A. P. and L. L. R. last year at the time of the attack on the train during which they burned the railroad bridge and when he attacked the ranches one S. was in agreement with P. and L. L. R., advised them on the movements of the troops and the rangers. On account of that they did not seize hold of the bandits. I escaped myself or else they would have killed me. S. lives in Brownsville. S. is a bandit. He has 4 charges of robbery and smuggling. S. is a friend of the bandits on the Mexican side who came to rob near San Benito. I declare this to you because you are the chief one in authority in Texas. And you may inform Brownsville and you will see that S. has 4 charges against him on account of robbery and smuggling. He has a $500 bond for each one and goes free continuing his robbery. S. ought to be in the penitentiary, hanged, in fact, etc."

Sheriff J. S. Scarborough, Kingsville, sent the following dated July 5, 1916 to Henry Hutchings: "We had a meeting at the King Ranch this P. M. with Captain Sanders, Caesar Kleberg, Charlie Armstrong, and others in regard to the Mexican situation and to see about having some special Rangers appointed in Kleberg County and also Willacy County. I haven't but about five deputies in Kleberg County and I would like to have a few special Rangers appointed. The names I am sending you are seven good reliable men of Kleberg County, who are all men of families, ages ranging from 35 to 48 years.

"You will do me a great favor by appointing these men and I am sure that all of the best citizens of this county will appreciate same.

"Pink Barnhill and D. V. Stilwell, who you appointed last fall as special Rangers, say that Barnhill is in Cameron County on the King Ranch and Stilwell has joined Captain Ransom's company."

General Hutchings wrote the Governor on July 8, 1916 that the appropriation by the 34th Legislature for the Ranger force in suppression of lawlessness and crime was "practically exhausted." This was for the fiscal year ending August 31, 1916.

He applied for $10,000 more to meet necessary expenses maintaining the present force. A note at the bottom said: "Approved for $10,000. Governor of Texas."

Harry Scullin of St. Louis wrote Hutchings July 10, 1916: "If you will remember, last winter you very kindly allowed me to join Company D, Ranger Force at Harlingen. At that time I was unable to make as long a stay as I anticipated owing to pressure of business compelling me to return home, and just as I was about getting a little hardened, I had to leave, which I regretted very much.

"I am arranging my affairs to get away for about a month, commencing sometime during the latter part of August, and I wondered if I could impose on your good nature and if it would be possible for you to let me try this game again, either with Captain Ransom, or with the Company operating in the Big Bend country.

"I suppose you wonder why I would not prefer taking a good rest at some summer resort, but for the reason the call of the wild was born in me, and I must say the frontier always appeals to me. With very kindest regards..."

Charles Armstrong wrote to the Adjutant General July 11 mentioning the meeting with the others including Kleberg, and they decided that, on investigation, they found the Mexicans were thoroughly intimidated. Local officers with several Rangers could take care of any situation. To be prepared they would like several special Rangers appointed.

Hutchings received a short note in July with no name on it: "I am here in Tulsa at the Tulsa Hotel so when you get ready to go into Mexico, count me in." Hutchings must have known who his friend was.

On July 13 Hutchings answered Harry Scullin that Ransom was in his office that day saying he would be glad to have Scullin return. However, the General noted that there was nothing at that moment but troops in the lower part of the Rio Grande Valley, but there was a better chance for action this time in the Big Bend District. He suggested that Scullin visit Captain Fox and his Company in that area and see some of the locations made prominent by newspaper accounts.

Scullin's gracious answer, written July 21: "I am very glad indeed that I conducted myself in a sufficiently proper manner so that Captain Ransom was willing to have me pay him another visit. I note that you suggest that this time I go with Captain J. M. Fox of Company B in the Big Bend District and I am very glad indeed as that was my preference."

He asked for some kind of temporary commission, as he might be called to account by some of the soldiers for being armed.

In another letter Scullin said that he hoped to arrive in Marfa by September 13. The Adjutant General allowed him to enlist in Captain Fox's company, then gave him an honorable discharge at the end of his month's visit.

A letter of July 19, 1916 to Governor Ferguson was signed by a number of men living in Candelaria. They wanted some protection, feeling they were at the mercy of the bandits and that a marauding band of them would be certain to come up the river to attack the town of several merchandise stores, a flour mill and a cotton gin.

The following names were at the bottom of the letter: Bill Newton, Merchant; B.M. Vick, M. D.; M. H. Shelton, Postmaster; J. R. Grady, Merchant; S. E. Burton, Rancher near the Border; D. H. Hunter, Merchant; A. S. Warren, Ranchman on the Rio Grande; A. J. Sowell, Merchant; J. H. Gray, Butcher; J. J. Bailey, Hotel Keeper; George W. Floche, Builder; Hicks Gray, Merchant; Valentine Douglas; M. D. Asche, Merchant; George Mene, Physician; D. O. Howard, Justice of the Peace; Dal Dean; L. E. H., Hotel; Edwin Trimble, Tonsorial; Howard Bell, Wagonmaster; Vincent Snelies, Garage Man; T. Everette; C. O. Finley, Ranchman; W. E. _____, Carpenter; J. A. Skipper.

A Saddle Waiting for Action

CHAPTER XIV

The Adjutant General's usual answer to applications to the Ranger service was that the Force was running "on deficiency" and when a vacancy occurred, no new enlistment was made.

On July 20, 1916 J. L. Anders applied for a special Ranger commission, mentioning as references Sheriff Frank Hammond of Houston and G. A. Taft, General Superintendent of the Southern Division of the Wells Fargo Company.

Another person applying to join the U. S. Infantry, this would be through the Adjutant General as well, was born, reared, and educated in Switzerland and had served in the Mountain Infantry there as a Captain. At this time he had become an American citizen. His beautiful handwriting resembled calligraphy.

Judging from their reports and letters, the best handwriting of the Texas Rangers was that of Captain Fox, when he was not in a hurry. He used his pen staff to produce near-calligraphy also.

Henry Ransom's was neat and consistent, with very few misspellings, and had a relaxed Spencerian flow to it. However, as bandit problems increased along with other stress he was eventually under, his writing began to show the strain of his work and worries.

The Adjutant General heard from a boy aged 15 who said he wanted to organize a troop of Bicycle Scouts, ages 15-18, adding that their scoutmaster had moved away. He said they "could get soldier suits." The Adjutant General's formal reply: "Receipt is acknowledged of your letter of the 7th instant. This department has no jurisdiction or connection with the Boy Scout movement."

One applicant wrote Hutchings from his home in Rhode Island, saying he really was a native Texan. If he made the trip down to join is not known.

Another letter arrived from the Mexican American living in Columbus. It was dated July 30, 1916. He wrote of being loyal to Texas, saying he would give the rest of his blood in his body if necessary to obtain peace in the State. He waits for an answer to his first letter, hoping he can help. Although the courteous Hutchings faithfully answered his mail, and must have replied to this man, no copy was in his correspondence files.

Hutchings wrote the Governor on September 7 telling him that the Ranger Force entered the new fiscal year with four captains, four sergeants, and 56 privates. Appropriation for the year was $30,000, adding that it cost approximately $1,000 a year to maintain a Ranger. Would he view with favor the gradual reduction of the force to keep more nearly within the appropriation?

Sheriff Peyton J. Edwards wired to the General September 8, 1916: I STRENUOUSLY PROTEST AGAINST TAKING THE RANGERS AWAY FROM YSLETA AND ESPECIALLY ANY REPLACEMENT OF THESE RANGERS BY OTHERS AT THE PRESENT TIME. YSLETA CENTRALLY LOCATED ON THE RAILROAD AND TWO PAVED ROADS. THE MEN NOW STATIONED THERE ARE ACQUAINTED WITH THEIR SECTION AND THE CITY AND ARE OF MORE BENEFIT THAN NEW ONES WOULD BE. AM SATISFIED THAT SHOULD NEW ONES BE PLACED THERE YOU WOULD RECEIVE SOME PROTEST ABOUT THEM AS SOON AS THEY BEGIN TO PERFORM THEIR DUTY. THOSE ASKING THEIR REMOVAL DO NOT REPRESENT THE LAW ABIDING CITIZENS. YSLETA AND VICINITY ARE INDIGNANT AT YOUR TRANSFER ORDER AND BEG YOU TO RESCIND IT

The Adjutant General's answer wired to the Sheriff: I REGRET THAT YOU AND OTHER RESPONSIBLE CITIZENS SHOULD BE INDIGNANT AT CHANGE OF STATION OF ENLISTED MEN ON RANGER FORCE. THE ORDER WILL NOT BE RESCINDED. HUTCHINGS

On September 28, 1916, the General sent a letter to all his commanding officers pertaining to discipline of the Ranger Force:

"1. Considerable adverse criticism of the Ranger Force has recently reached the Governor and much of it from sources worth most serious consideration.

"2. Some of our friends believe that in enlisting Rangers too much stress is laid upon the record of the applicant as a man killer and that such a record is taken as proof of bravery. A very necessary qualification for a Ranger is bravery, but the killing of a man is not necessarily proof of the possession of that quality. As a general rule, men will not be enlisted in the Ranger Force who have been unfortunate enough to have had to kill their fellow men; exemptions to this rule will only be made when the facts are laid before this department and special authority for such enlistment is given.

"3. Ranger Captains are directed summarily on the spot to discharge any Ranger under the influence of liquor or any Ranger unnecessarily frequenting saloons.

"4. A large majority of the Ranger force are good men and performing invaluable service; Ranger Captains are directed and will be held responsible for the prompt discharge from the service of any or all men who may bring reproach on this service.

"5. Commanding officers will acknowledge receipt of this communication. By direction of the Governor."

In 1917 when Governor Ferguson organized a new company of Texas Rangers, it was felt more were needed to combat the serious bandit problem. First, he appointed Henry Ransom Captain of Company C and he was to enroll his new men himself. He had been Captain of Company D when he entered the Rangers the second time in 1915.

Another letter that describes colorfully the conditions the Ranger had to deal with is dated January 2, 1917 on Hotel Hamilton stationery, Laredo. Addressed to Captain M Johnson, Quartermaster of the Rangers, it is from Captain W. M. Ryan.

"Please express me two rifles .10 Government account of Rangers Jim Chessner and L. B. Carter, also 1,000 rifle cartridges and 1,000 .45 caliber Colt's pistol cartridges and try and get me some blankets before I go to stealing. We are about to freeze to death and can't buy any here to keep warm with. Please rush this order."

Because of lack of money some of the Rangers in Captain Ransom's company were mustered out in February, 1917.

A. C. Riegar, Comanche, Texas wrote on February 4, 1917 to Hutchings: "If because of the break with Germany, Border conditions become such that you recruit the Ranger Force, I want to ask that you suggest my name to either of the Captains that can use me. Prefer Captain Ransom on account of my former 'enlistment' in connection with which I wish to say to you that we got my boy out of his trouble and he is now somewhere in Mexico as interpreter and driver for an official out of the office of the Secretary of War in Washington.

"I am now situated so that I can start on the first train out after receiving Commission and transportation."

J. F. Fagan, Brakeman with the I and G N Railroad, San Antonio, wrote the following to the General on March 14, 1917: "On 3-11-17 in going over the top of train between Heafer and San Antonio my papers blew out of my pocket and I could not find my Ranger Commission papers. They were in Company C. Please send me a duplicate of my papers."

Unfortunately no mention was made about why Fagan was "going over the top of the train." The reason could be fascinating, and maybe a different story!

The annual booklet published by the Adjutant General's Department pertaining to regulations governing the Texas Rangers dated August 16, 1917 again spelled out the particulars at that time concerning the make-up of the Companies, the pay schedule, the length of terms of service, the accounting of supplies and equipment, the legal powers of the Rangers, and other important details, part of which is included here.

In this issue, which will show a few changes from earlier ones. The pay of officers and men was as follows: captains $125 a month, sergeants $60 a month, and privates $50 a month.

Men volunteering for the service were in for a term not exceeding two years.

Each Ranger, as always, furnished his horse, horse equipment, and clothing with the State to pay for a horse killed in action.

The State was to furnish each member of the Force with one improved carbine and pistol at cost, to be paid for out of the Ranger's first month's salary, and provide rations for the men, the camping equipment, ammunition, and forage for the horses.

The commanders of the companies were to enlist whatever number of men authorized, depending on appropriations.

Only such men as were courageous, discreet, honest, of temperate habits, and respectable families would be enlisted.

At this time the Ranger Force was organized thusly: Companies A, B, C, and D would each have one captain, one sergeant and 20 privates.

These assignments were made: Captain J. J. Sanders to Company A, Captain J. M. Fox to Company B, Captain H. L. Ransom to Company C, and Captain Jerry Gray to Company D.

Furthermore, each company commander would "on the last day of each month" forward the muster rolls and pay rolls of his company to the Adjutant General. He also would tender a monthly report of all work accomplished, including character of scouts made and number of miles traveled.

Being organized, with all regulations spelled out, resulted in an efficient, well-respected organization, in the best of "fighting order," necessary in those bandit-infested times.

They were perilous indeed for the Rangers, adding World War I to the turmoil on the Border.

Germany was actively courting Mexico, their infesting of that country washing over the Rio Grande to endanger Texas.

Not only were the Texas Rangers trying to win the bandit wars, they were also thrust into the boiling intrigue of problems generated by the Germans determined to undermine the United States through her vulnerable back door.

The American President read the sensational Zimmerman-Carranza note before the U. S. Congress. In the note, Zimmerman, the German Minister for Foreign Affairs, promised Mexico financial aid and the states of New Mexico, Texas, and Arizona if she would declare war against the United States.

This telegram was deciphered by the British Cryptographic Bureau early in 1917, just before America entered the war. Then the Germans knew the latest code between her and Mexico had been solved. They had to come up with a new one. American code breakers had tried the German code first in Spanish and German but found it in English.

Border counties of Texas already bloody with bandit crimes now had to deal with more Mexican chicanery fomented by politicians jockeying for positions of power. The Rangers picked up numerous clues about mysterious messages coming and going that they gave to authorities involved in wartime security of the U. S. Real mysteries, the sources of the coded messages, were difficult to track down.

A young genius named Herbert O. Yardley worked as a clerk in the Code Room of the U. S. Department of State, the room with its closed shelves stuffed with thick files of telegrams.

There were long flat tables that held stuttering wireless equipment. Several clerks worked with specially constructed type-writers capable of making at one time 15 copies of a telegram.

Yardley was puzzled as well as fascinated when observing numerous people from lowly clerks to highly placed officials who routinely visited the room to peruse messages coming in or to look up older ones to review.

He began to wonder if our diplomatic codes were safe with so many eyes going over them. Also he asked himself why did not the United States itself have a bureau for the reading of secret diplomatic codes and cipher telegrams of foreign governments as other countries had.

This brilliant fellow read all he could find about cryptography. When he located the best available, it turned out to be a U. S. Army pamphlet on cipher solution. He was amazed on discovering how easily he could solve the examples given, terming them "simple."

Also he discovered he could decipher quite quickly those coming in from foreign countries, and began work on a system more difficult to solve.

After some concentrated study, he presented his memorandum, titled "Exposition of American Diplomatic Codes," to his shocked superior. He figured out this new science for himself, then asked to be released from his job.

While he had been working in Washington on this problem, one of the Texas Rangers, designated as a special operative, was busi-ly conducting undercover work on the Texas Border and in Mexico, searching for the hidden receivers of messages from Germany.

Yardley wanted to leave the State Department to join the War Department, knowing the Army would need cryptographers. Major Van Deman, "the father of military intelligence" in the Army, was impressed, so Yardley was allowed to set up America's own bureau for reading foreign cryptography. This was in 1917 when the young man was 27.

At this time messages to be de-coded flowed around many areas of the world. Americans were hearing wireless messages sent out by a powerful German wireless station near Berlin that had no address or signature included, yet were repeated over and over again nearly every day. It was felt they were intended for German secret agents in some neutral or hostile country a long distance from Berlin.

The undercover man working with the Governor and commissioned a Ranger was adept at spying and setting up a network of informers on both sides of the Rio Grande. Clues he compiled no doubt aided in locating the source. Messages to the German Minister in Mexico were being received in Chapultepec.

Decoded, one message was "For German Minister, Mexico, Bleichroeder. Any time ready for loan negotiations. At present remittance from Germany impossible, meantime firm places ten million Spanish pesetas at your disposal in German Overseas Bank Madrid. You are authorized to offer this preliminary amount to Mexican government in name of Bleichroeder for three years, interest six, commission half per cent on supposition that Mexico will remain neutral during war. All good arrangements left to your discretion. Please reply. Foreign Office Bisshe. General Staff Political Section Berlin number hundred."

Another message decoded: "Telegram January two and telegraphic report S. Anthony Delmar via Spain received. Please suggest President (Mexico) to send to Berlin agent with fuller power for negotiations of loan and sale of raw product. Do not embroil yourself in Japanese affairs because communication through you too difficult. If Japanese are in earnest, they have enough representatives in Europe for the purpose. Foreign Office Bisshe. Machinery plans for rifle manufactory can be put at disposal. Details of machinery, technical staff, and engineer for aircraft could be arranged here with the authorized man of President (Mexico) to be sent by him for negotiations about loan. We agree purchase arranged by Craft (Kraft) in Japan of ten thousand rifles, etc., wished by President. General Staff Political Section."

The United States tuned in for more messages, but the wireless went suddenly silent. The code had been broken, so it was changed. Then the messages began again. This meant more work for Yardley's MIS which also became known as the "Black Room."

Thanks to Herbert Yardley's genius and dedication, the U. S. became second to none in this new science, expanded by the man who devoted his life to the endeavor.

Yardley's riveting book, THE AMERICAN BLACK CHAMBER, describing his ideas, discoveries, and eventual successes, explains in detail the important work accomplished by his remarkable ability.

Excited citizens were stirred up by rumors of German spies' activities in South Texas as well as actual threats and vandalism in some of the scattered communities. The Rangers coped with these along with the rest of the turmoil.

Back on July 30, 1917, Captain Ransom had an address in Austin, which he sent to Beatrice so their letters would not be lost. He started serving as a bodyguard for the Governor, who was under fire with impeachment proceedings that would continue for two months. Henry traveled with him during trips over the State, also staying at times at the family's ranch in Bosque County. Ferguson's daughter spoke so well of him in a book she authored some years later.

Ferguson's troubles accelerated when he would not approve part of the University of Texas' budget because some professors would give no accounting for certain funds used in the past. They orchestrated a veritable vendetta campus-wide that was duly recorded daily in the Austin press, dredging up instances of alleged corruption in his administration.

He continued to refuse his approval unless he was told how some missing funds were used. The professors inflamed the news media on and off the campus, instigated large student protests that paraded around the Governor's mansion, embarrassing and frightening his two little daughters.

Ferguson was impeached, with William P. Hobby, who had been re-elected Lieutenant Governor in 1916, assuming the position of Governor.

In August 1917 Henry Hutchings was Adjutant General but in a letter dated October 6, 1917, Brigadier General Hutchings stated, "I have been appointed in the National Guard and am no longer Adjutant General."

James A. Harley, former State Senator from Seguin who lost re-election, was appointed in Hutchings' place by Governor Hobby.

This could be the stage being set to move Captain Ransom, as Hutchings, a good friend of Henry's, would not approve of any adverse actions involving him. The General would suspect ulterior motives.

Henry Ransom wrote from Austin on August 17 to Beatrice, saying, "If you don't get a school, come stay with us. Don't work in the fields any more."

She must have gone back to her mother after getting her teacher's certificate to wait for a position to open.

He had been amused at Bee's tale about how, with no alarm clock, she woke up on time each morning for an early class when living in the dormitory in San Marcos. She devised her own system by tying a string to one of her big toes, with the other end fastened to a bedpost. When she stirred in the morning, the toe would be pulled and she would wake up. She claimed her invention never failed.

Henry looked forward to hearing her updates on progress in school and college. She completed courses with flying colors, and soon accepted her first job in New Ulm to teach grammar schoolers, her favorite age group.

Later she taught at the Hartsville School, where her father had attended, and stayed with cousins who saddled her horse for her every morning. She rode sidesaddle to the small school where she taught several grades in the same classroom. She spanked a little boy for standing on top of the piano when she left the room for a few minutes. Later, when grown, he joked about how thoroughly Miss Ransom switched him for his naughty deed.

Ransom wrote her on Texas Ranger letterhead August 10, 1917 "My dear B—Your letter received and sure glad to hear you have a place so close to home. Enclosed find a check for ten dollars to help you out…Write me as often as you can. With lots of love, Dad." The envelope was addressed to Beatrice at Wallis, a red two cent stamp gracing its upper right had corner.

Speaking of letters, one of the new Adjutant General's first was from Captain J. J. Sanders, written October 3, asking permission to purchase a pair of mules and a wagon for Ranger use. He says he needs them very much as Border counties are so thinly populated that accommodations are not available. They must carry provisions, bedding, and feed with them while on scouts.

Harley, the new Adjutant General, wrote to J. M. Fox at Marfa on October 8: "You are advised that this department would like to have a personal record on every member in your company pertaining to his honesty, sobriety, integrity…if any previous service as a peace officer prior to his enlistment in the Rangers, his efficiency as a peace officer…in fact all pertinent data that pertains to the above subject. Kindly comply with the above directions at your earliest convenience."

General Harley wrote October 11 to Captain Ransom, Company C the following: "You are hereby directed to proceed at once with your command to Ysleta, 12 miles east of El Paso, to be stationed at that point until further orders from this Department.

"You may communicate with the Sheriff at El Paso and if it is his wish, you may station one man in his office."

On the same day he sent a copy of the following to both Captain Ransom and Captain Fox: "It is the intention of this Department to co-operate with the National Government in the execution of the selective service law in Texas.

"You are instructed that no claim for exemption will be made in behalf of members of the Ranger Force who registered June 5th and have enlisted as Rangers since the first day of April A. D. 1917. Such men will be discharged from the Rangers when they (are) ordered to report for entrainment to Camp Travis."

Clyde Butrill wrote October 12 to Judge A. M. Turney in Abilene: "There was another bunch of horses stolen here night before last…We trailed them to the river and had to quit. They are safe just as soon as they get on the other side. Something has got to be done…sixty seven head of horses, including freight teams, that I know of, have been stolen here in the last six months. It is just like Indian times when a man turns a horse loose, he don't know whether he will ever see him again or not. If we could follow them across, I think we could soon break it up. If you will take it up with the higher-ups maybe we can have an understanding with the Mexican government whereby we can follow them across."

Captain J. M. Fox, Company B, Marfa, to Captain H. D. Griffits, Austin: "Dear Sir and Friend, what's the matter with passes for Frank Patterson, Max Newmann, Ben F. Pennington? Am in need of them badly. Please spur up a little and see how quick you can get them and I will buy you one some of these days. Just came from the river. We were expecting a fight between the Nesters and the Carranzistas but it failed to mature. Will be in about Monday or Tuesday if anything happens. Regards to all and especially the stenographer."

While in Ysleta, Captain Ransom sent a letter in October to Harley in Austin: "Subject: Members of Company C, Ranger Force

"1st: Sergeant Sam McKenzie and Privates C. C. Hurst and W. H. Koon arrived here on 10-12-1917.

"2nd: I arrived here with three men...Privates W. S. Miles, J. B. Nalls, and R. M. Miller on 10-17-1917 p.m.

"3rd: Looking for Privates W. E. Hodge, J. C. Perkins, and A. F. Gholson. The Rangers I had stationed at Snyder to arrive here on 10-19-17.

"4th: I left Private J. S. White at Austin with understanding that he must transfer or resign by November 1st. Yours to command..."

C. B. Hudspeth of Hudspeth, Dale, and Harper, Attorneys wrote the Adjutant General October 26: "Dear Jim, the little town of Clint is situated twenty-one miles east of El Paso. Formerly there were four Rangers stationed at this place...the little town is only two and a half miles from the River. Mexicans constantly depredate from one side to the other, as you are aware from your experience on the Rio Grande last summer...

"There are two nice little banks in the town and several mercantile establishments and, in fact, it is the most thoroughly American town east of El Paso." He asks for two more Rangers.

"Please take this matter up at once, Jim, because this is my constituency and I never call upon you except when they need protection. A petition of some 200 citizens is being forwarded to you."

Constable J. P. Barkley, Kent County, wrote Governor Hobby on October 29, 1917 the following: "I am writing to you relative to B. B. P., a Ranger who was in this county about 30 days ago and who left the county without paying his board bill, his phone bill, his garage bill or money borrowed from the bank at this place, then took off with him a pair of $20 boots new that I let him wear while here and he won't talk to me when I call him by wire and won't answer my letters...Trusting that you will take this matter up with him and have him to adjust his obligations with the people at this place and to return my boots."

The boots were returned unscathed and all bills paid.

On November 6th, Captain J. M. Fox wired Harley: WILL BE ON RIVER TWO DAYS EIGHTY MEXICANS RUN OVER TO THIS SIDE WANT TO LOOK THEM OVER

A Ranger who did not want his name mentioned wrote Governor Hobby asking for more Rangers to be sent south of El Paso as many cattle are put out to graze on the side of the Rio Grande, and cautions that Rangers are to double their vigilance.

He understands, he says, there are factions in that area friendly with the Villa bunch in Mexico.

A report on Wells Fargo & Co. Express stationery came to the General and also to the Captain of Company C that reveals examples of the pay rate in those days.

"As a Special Ranger in Eagle Pass my earnings last month by Wells Fargo money: To Spofford $2.00, To San Antonio $6.00, to Spofford $2.00, Night Guard $2.50. Business not good last month. No arrests so far last month. I stopped two rows. All doing nicely. All hunters are out trying to get a buck. Your obedient servant, W. L. Donelson."

On November 19, 1917 Captain Ransom wrote the General "I herein acknowledge receipt of letters and instructions regarding expense accounts and distributed among members of my Company as per your request. Report Ranger R. M. Miller absent on account child very sick. His home is near Paint Rock. Have been requested by Sheriff Harry Moore of Hudspeth Co. to enlist one Jim Carter of the county to be stationed at Sierra Blanco. Advise me in regard to same. We are expecting Villa to attack Juarez real soon. Yours to command…"

On the same day Ransom wrote to Captain H. W. Griffits: "Dear Griff, please ship me one thousand pounds of those hard point rifle cartridges and one tarpaulin. My freight finally arrived. Will furnish you a list of all State property on first of month unless otherwise advised. Griff, hurry ammunition. I believe Villa will attack Juarez pretty quickly. Best regards to all. Your amigo, Captain H. L. Ransom."

The Adjutant General wrote to Captain Ransom at Ysleta November 2, 1917, telling him that "owing in the very near future the entire Ranger Force will be reorganized and enlarged, it is desired that no new members be enlisted until further notice."

Captain J. J. Sanders, Company A, stationed in Alice wrote on November 27 to General James Harley: "I just returned from the Border last night and I find quite a lot of uneasiness among the citizens on the immediate Border on account of Mexicans crossing from Mexico on this side in small bunches. They have been planning on the other side to kill the two Rangers stationed at Los Ebanos.

"Upon arriving at the Donna Pumping Plant and being informed by the officers and best citizens of the country that there had not been but one case of smallpox, neither on this nor the other side for over twelve months as far as they knew, and as there was nothing for these men to do at this point, I moved the two men I had stationed at Donna to Los Ebanos and camped with them with the two Rangers stationed at that place.

"The killing of Deputy Sheriff Martin at Raymondville Saturday night last has created a considerable uneasiness in that community. I was not notified of the killing until about twelve o'clock Sunday. I immediately went to Raymondville and took up the trail of the three Mexicans that killed Martin, losing the trail yesterday near the River, and being thoroughly convinced that they had crossed into Mexico, I returned to Alice. I think that they will return to this side in the near future, as they are prominent local politicians at Raymondville.

"On the strong solicitation of Mr. Caesar Kleberg I am today sending two men to be stationed at D...I will try to be in Austin about Monday or Tuesday of next week."

Captain Ransom received a curious, unsigned letter dated November 28, 1917, addressed to him at Ysleta.

"My dear Captain, General Harley requests me to have you report here Friday morning, the 7th of December at 10 o'clock. Hoping to see you at that time, I remain very sincerely yours..."

No signature. Do "My dear..." and "very sincerely" sound suspicious?

This unsigned letter, the second he had received with no signature, had no address of the sender included. No record exists of who sent it, nor is anything available about what was discussed during the appointment on that December 7, 1917.

Mission at Ysleta

CHAPTER XV

Captain Ransom was to receive the following telegram on November 30, 1917: REPORT TO THIS OFFICE AS SOON AS POSSIBLE. A wire came back to Harley: WIRE UNDELIVERED PARTY LEFT FOR AUSTIN LAST NIGHT

Captain Jerry Gray wrote November 30 to Adjutant General Harley: "I saw the District Attorney, Hugh Carney, today and found out that it wasn't a murder case at all they want us to work on. But is 'Bootlegging,' 'Gambling,' and 'Bawdy House,' which are running wide open in the eyes of the local authorities, here. Carney seems to think they are in the deal or at any rate the greater part of them.

"I think what they need here is a private detective instead of Rangers. He wants us to stay here fifteen or twenty days and buy whiskey from the Bootleggers, get in with the Gamblers if we can, and the last work to close the Bawdy House.

"Fact is, General, the District Attorney wants us to do the work that the local officers should do and know about and he says are in the deal and we cannot take them in our confidence.

"The District Attorney has cautioned us to be very careful and not let them know who we are, as they are apt to gang up on us. He also is of the opinion we are going to have to kill two or three. Now if we are to clean up the town, we can sure do so in grand style, but the local authorities here are going to help frame against us and of course you know what that will mean. If you think it advisable for us to do this work here that the officers the people elected should do, please send me Andrews, Young, and Saulsberry. If you send them, ship rifles by express and tell them to come in quietly with SMALL hats on. If you should wire me any instructions, send them over the McKay or Postal, as the District Attorney said Western Union will tip us off."

Walter F. Rowe wrote Harley the same day: "While Captain Gray was over to see the District Attorney today I went off and tried to find out what I could and found as follows: I got in with a one-legged bootlegger and he had no whiskey but went out to get me some and I with him. The boys were of the opinion I was an officer and would not let him have it for me. While talking with this bootlegger he told me the Chief of Police was in the game and all his men were assisting him. Fact of the thing is the whole town is one large nest of crooks including officers and all, and it will take very drastic means to convert them as well as time and money. Will the State stand for expense of buying the bootlegger at $2.00 per pint?"

Another interesting letter, dated December 3, 1917, if from G. W. Waddell to General Harley: "I see in the papers you have appointed four new Ranger Captains and will raise a company for each. I wish to ask you if there is any age limit to the man who is expected to enlist—if not, I would like to join. I am 69 years of age but in good health and very good eye sight. I enlisted the last year of the Civil War. Joined Captain Sam Wilbourne's Company under the command of General Bee who was stationed near the mouth of the Rio Grande River. I lived for 30 years out on the head of the Colorado River. Went out there in 1876 where the country was covered with Buffalo and the Indians raided the country every light moon. Have lived here in the Valley 3 years. Should I be per-mitted to join what would I have to furnish myself with and what pay would I get? Hoping to receive a favorable reply. I am respect-fully G.W. Waddell."

No record can be found concerning an answer to the remarkable man's offer. His descendents should be popping their buttons with pride.

Monthly report of Special Ranger, W. L. Donalson, Eagle Pass: "Collected from two soldiers for Mr. K. Stine checks they had raised on First National Bank. Bill settled. My fee was $8.00. Wells Fargo money guard $3.00 per day. One night guard at offices $2.50. Spofford guard $2.00. Arrested two Mexican lieu-tenants of army for abusing U.S. Quarantine Inspectors. Everything going nicely so far. I am riding every night looking for a man dressed in Women's clothing. He has been after several men and women. I am doing all I can against lawbreakers and stopped several fights. I made cash this total $24.00. P. S. if you need my services at any time wire me orders."

Adjutant General Harley wrote to H. J. Ellis, Owl Drug Store, El Paso, explaining the Ranger policy, saying he regrets not being able to assist in enforcing local laws.

"It is not our policy to use the Ranger Force to usurp the powers of duly appointed officers. We only send Rangers to assist in Local conditions when requested to do so by officers. We cannot afford to give the impression that we are endeavoring to run the affairs of any community as we must look to local authorities to co-operate with our Ranger Force. People have the right to elect their own officers and are only entitled to such protection and enforcement of laws as they themselves desire. This is a sound democratic principle. People have a right to govern themselves and must be allowed to do so or else appeal to the federal government. Regretting that our policy conflicts with the granting of your request..."

Notes of interest from some of the correspondence: In some letters Ranger Bates was spoken of as "fearless, coolheaded, sober, and industrious."

Harley wrote to his Ranger Captains "No new Rangers are to be taken in for in the near future the entire Ranger Force is to be re-organized."

The letters between Rangers and the Adjutant General were quite formal, using such terms as "I beg to acknowledge..." Some, including Henry Ransom, signed off by saying "Yours to command..." However, Henry Ransom omitted the phrase in the last few letters of his life.

A wire dated December 1917 was sent to the Secretary of State, Washington, D.C. from H. P. Blocker, American Vice Consul in Charge: W B WETHERSBEE AMERICAN CITIZEN AND OWNER SAN GREGORIO HACIENDA REPORTS THAT TWO AMERICAN EMPLOYEES BY NAME LEE SHARPE AND SPECK SELLERS EVIDENTLY WERE KILLED OR KIDNAPPED BY CATTLE THIEVES OPERATING ALONG THE RIO GRANDE. BOTH HAVE BEEN GONE SIX DAYS. WHEN LAST SEEN HAD STARTED DEER HUNTING. HACIENDA AND ADJOINING RANCHES HAVE BEEN SEARCHED BUT NO TRACE. MEXICAN COMMANDER MILITARY FORCES HAS DISPATCHED TROOPS TO AID SEARCH AND ONE BAND EIGHT MEN ENCOUNTERED BUT THEY DENY HAVING ANY

182   *Captain Ransom, Texas Ranger*

KNOWLEDGE OF AMERICANS. WILL REPORT FURTHER
DEVELOPMENTS LATER. EMBASSY UNADVISED

Adjutant General Harley wired Ransom in Ysleta: MOVE
RIGHT AWAY IF YOU WANT TO. ADVISE US

Henry's reply same day: COGGINS AND JONES CASES
CONTINUED. WOULD LIKE TO MOVE AT ONCE IF IT MEETS
WITH YOUR APPROVAL. ANSWER

Another wire that day from Ransom to Harley: PLEASE
TRANSFER R M MILLER INSTEAD OF TRANSFERRING W H
KOON AS MILLER IS BETTER QUALIFIED FOR BORDER DUTY

Seth B. Orndorff of El Paso sent a letter to Harley the next
day: "I wish to thank you for the attendance of Captain Ransom
and his men here in El Paso. They have rendered me an invaluable
assistance and I have found them willing to help in any way that I
requested them. They seem to be a sober, steady lot of men and
willing to do their duty." The sheriff has learned that Henry is
leaving the area.

On December 14, 1917, a wire from Harley came to Ransom:
LEAVE THREE RANGERS TO BE TRANSFERRED AND THREE
OTHER MEN FROM YOUR COMPANY AT YSLETA IN CHARGE
OF CAMP UNTIL RELIEVED. THEY WILL REPORT TO YOU AT
ABILENE

Captain Henry Ransom is being moved, his camp broken
up. What does this mean?

The same day Ransom wired Harley back: PLEASE ADVISE
ME WHEN THE THREE RANGERS WILL BE TRANSFERRED
AND WHO THEY MUST REPORT TO. ALSO WHO WILL TAKE
CHARGE OF THE CAMP AND STATE PROPERTY HERE

Ransom wired from Ysleta that day to Harley: WILL LEAVE
TONIGHT FOR HEMPSTEAD ON ACCOUNT OF DEATH OF MY
FATHER-IN-LAW. PLEASE ANSWER NIGHT LETTER AT ONCE

The Assistant Adjutant General wired back: GENERAL
HARLEY SAYS TO GO ON TO HEMPSTEAD

Assistant General Woodul wrote to Captain W. W. Davis, El
Paso, December 19, 1917: "You are instructed to enlist five good
men and immediately proceed to Ysleta and report to Captain
Ransom whom you will relieve.

"You will receipt for such State property as you receive
from Captain Ransom, giving him a receipt and sending us duplicate of same.

"He will transfer two men from his company, which will give you seven men. You will not recruit any more men until you have had further instructions from this office.

"You will cover the same territory that Captain Ransom covered and follow out as best you can such suggestions he may give you.

"Major N. and party found the bodies of Seller and Sharpe in a cave about seven miles from where they were camped. They were found about 7:30 this morning. Will see you the 24th." This was written in a beautiful Spencerian hand.

Captain Ransom sent the following wire to General Harley while still at Ysleta December 21: WILL LEAVE HERE FOR SWEETWATER TOMORROW MORNING

Now headed for Sweetwater, he misses yet another Christmas with his family.

A letter about "Mexican scheming" dated December 24, 1917 came to the General's office, to Walter Woodul, Assistant Adjutant General, from W. M. Hanson, Special Agent at that time in San Antonio.

"All the different heads of the anti-Carranza revolution in Mexico will consolidate within the next 30 days and will choose for a leader a man who if successful will at once declare his purpose of protecting foreign interests in that Republic, and his sincere friendship for the United States and our Allies, declare war on Germany if it is so desired by the U. S., and in all things be governed by the advice and wishes of this Government. They will not accept a single dollar from Pro-Germans and in all things will work to stifle all German intrigue in Mexico, and put down all such bands who contemplate raiding over the Border.

"Villa will retire from his command within a month after they get started. Their only idea is to re-establish their old constitution, and overthrow Carranza who they claim is playing into German hands and who will continue to the point of intervention, unless stopped quickly.

"They do not fear any danger in the oil fields of Mexico, as General Pelias will come in with them, and continue to give security in that section. They claim that if any raiding is done along the border it will be by Carranzistas, and not them.

"The above, General, is my latest information, and I believe it is positively true, but of course we must take into consideration that fact that it is Mexican scheming, and very often their plans miscarry.

"Consider your source of information strictly confidential, for I do not want anyone outside yourself and General Harley to know that I furnished it, for it would prevent me from getting any more."

Woodul sent a letter December 26 to Captain W. W. Davis in El Paso: "Replying to your telegram in which you state you had not received my letter of instructions, I wrote to you to report to Captain Ransom with the number of men you reported to follow his advice as much as possible, and to take over his property there.

"Now, Captain, it is essential that you keep your men out of El Paso as much as possible. They are not to go in unless they just have to or are called by the local authorities. El Paso is large enough to get along without assistance of the Rangers unless they call for them."

Captain Cunningham wired Harley from Eagle Pass December 28: HAVE CORRALLED BUNCH OF INDIO RANCH GOATS ACROSS RIO GRANDE RIVER. THINK WE CAN RECOVER STOLEN PROPERTY IF YOU WILL GRANT PERMISSION TO CROSS RIVER

The reply from Assistant Adjutant General Woodul the next day: SEND TWO MEN TO ALPINE TEXAS RIGHT AWAY TO JOIN OTHER RANGERS

So now he has lost two more men.

Another would-be Ranger, Gully Cousert of El Paso, wrote Adjutant General December 31: "I am writing in regards to my application to the Ranger Force, as Captain Henry Ransom told me he has put in my application for same.

"Owing to recent trouble with Mexicans in Big Bend country I understand there will be more Rangers put on. If you have a place for me I would like to enlist. I am well acquainted with border country from here to Del Rio having worked on different ranches in that country.

"I am not in the draft age limit. For other references I refer you to Harry Moore, Sheriff, Hudspeth Co., Oscar Lotta, Sheriff in Kimble Co., Captain Monroe Fox or Captain Ransom and Seth Orndorff, Sheriff of El Paso Co."

Read the paragraph below and smile. Do not miss the part about baking powder!

"Section 10. The amount of rations and forage shall not exceed the following, to-wit: for each man's daily allowance, twelve ounces bacon or 20 ounces beef, twenty ounces of flour or cornmeal, two and two-fifths ounces of beans or peas, one and three-fifths ounces of rice, three and one-fifth ounces of coffee, three and one-fifth ounces of sugar, one-sixth gill of vinegar or pickles, one-sixth ounce candies, one-third ounce of soup, two-thirds of an ounce of salt, one twenty-fourth of an ounce of pepper, four-fifths ounces of potatoes, sixteen twenty-fifths of an ounce of baking powder. Forage for each horse shall not exceed twelve pounds of corn or oats, and fourteen pounds of hay per day, and two ounces of salt per week, provided that when in case of emergency the members of said force are employed in such duty that is impracticable to furnish the rations herein provided for, each member of said force so employed shall be allowed for his necessary actual expenses for such subsistence not to exceed one dollar and fifty cents ($1.50) per day; and provided further that when it becomes necessary to move the members of said force from one place to another by railroad, the actual necessary expenses of such transportation shall be paid." (from annual report)

All this and to be shot at, too.

The Quartermaster, appointed by the Governor, with duties of commissary and paymaster, would rank and receive the pay of a captain.

For further edification, Governor William P. Hobby wrote the following summary on Border Conditions in 1917-1918: "On account of the 'draft,' thousands of slackers and deserters have escaped into Mexico and established themselves on the Mexican side of the Rio Grande River. As a rule, these people have very little to eat, no money, and no work. They have to live, and as a result our citizens have been and are suffering from their depredations on the Texas side of the river.

"Knowing the country as they do, these refugees give information to the bandits infesting the border as to when they can depredate to the best advantage. Being in such destitute circumstances they often act as guides to the lawless element. While we have prevented such lawlessness, there is much work still to be done. Our Ranger Force is inadequate in number to protect our people notwithstanding the fact that they are working day and night.

"Mexico has been depleted in every resource, especially in horses, mules, and cattle. Therefore there is a ready market for all that can be stolen on the Texas side and smuggled into Mexico. Because we have not received much assistance from Mexico in recovering animals and property stolen and taken over into that country, there is little fear in detection or punishment. If it was not for the Ranger Service people could not live in security within 10 miles of the Border. This country is developing wonderfully and the people demand better protection.

"Mescal and other liquors are very cheap in Mexico, probably $2.00 to $3.00 per gallon. The same class of people who do the stealing and often commit murder on this side of the Border smuggle and sell this liquor on the Texas side for $3.00 to $10.00 per quart. Therefore this proves a very lucrative business for the lawless element. The magnitude of this traffic is inconceivable. During the last few months two Rangers and custom guard have lost their lives assisting the local and Federal officers to capture outlaws.

"The above and other bad conditions, especially along the Texas-Mexican Border, make it necessary that a large Ranger Force be retained during the year 1919. Unless this is done thousands of our citizens will be left at the mercy of this lawless element, thereby entailing great suffering and financial sacrifice. It is very probable that unless they have more protection it will become necessary for them to leave their homes and seek security in the interior as was the case in 1915-1916.

"To cope with this situation it is necessary to have the very best men Texas affords. In order that we may secure this class of men we must pay them at least the same wages they might earn in less dangerous pursuits. The Department of Justice and United States Intelligence Bureau pay their men from $100 to $200 for like work. Salaries in the immigration and other departments are as shown above. The work is not nearly so dangerous as that of the Texas Ranger.

"In justice to the men, therefore, I believe members of the Ranger Force should receive the same pay as those paid for like work. The cost of living was increased to a big extent and most of these men have families (all of them have someone depending on them), and I am very much in favor of raising the salaries of the present force for the coming year at least.

"I am also in favor of increasing the Ranger Force, in the event it becomes necessary, for the protection of Texas life and property.

"In handling the Ranger Force during my incumbency there have necessarily been some unpleasant features. Perhaps at times things that seemed to us right and proper did not meet the approbation of everyone, but under your direction I have earnestly endeavored to establish a policy that was both humane and just to all concerned and at the same time uphold the dignity of the law and the honor of this great State.

"In the enforcement of the law our activities were not confined alone to the border section of the State. From every section of Texas calls were made upon our force for assistance, especially during the war. In every instance we have complied with the request, thereby resulting in our being compelled to keep a number of our men at the State Capitol ready for any emergency. At this time we have stationed in Northwest Texas a force for the purpose of keeping down feuds and lawlessness.

"Loyalty Secret Service Department: In January, under authority of a special act of the Thirty-fifth Legislature, I authorized the establishment of a Loyalty Ranger Force to consist of approximately three picked men from each county in Texas. Captain W. M. Hanson was appointed captain of these forces with headquarters at 618 Frost Building, San Antonio, Texas. Later one sergeant and two assistants were appointed to assist him.

"The duties of this force were to act as a secret service department for the State and to work in conjunction with all Federal, State, County, and Municipal officers in the execution of all State laws, especially House Bill No. 15, better known as the 'Hobby Loyalty Act.' Through the assistance of the loyalty secret service department this office has been kept advised as to Mexico revolutionary activities carried on, principally outside of San Antonio, and in the border counties in Mexico and this State.

"The loyalty secret service department has been of great assistance in the successful prosecution of the war and in the alleviation of unsettled conditions along the border. The following are copies of some of the letters received from the United States Intelligence Department, Department of Justice, and commanding officers in the Southern Department, U. S. Army, complimenting the Ranger service of this State, especially the loyalty officers, for their valuable assistance.

"There were 583 cases investigated by the Secret Service Department, covering the following offenses: disloyalty, draft evasion, bootlegging, assault on government witnesses, desertion from the U. S. Army, aiding and abetting deserts and slackers, accepting money to keep drafted men out of service, violations of House Bill No. 15, known as the 'Hobby Loyalty Act,' failure to register, cattle stealing, burning of cotton by suspected pro-Germans, alien spies, securing data in Mexico as to wireless stations, general anti-American activities in Mexico, and many other irregularities." (Reproduced from the holdings of the Texas State Archives.)

Well done. In earlier days, Hobby had worked for newspapers, beginning in Beaumont, Texas, then in the circulation department of the Houston Post, advancing to Managing Editor, and becoming one of the owners of the Post.

In a letter to J. W. Favela, Laredo, the Assistant Adjutant General listed the locations of the Ranger Captains.

Captain J. J. Sanders, Alice
Captain J. M. Fox, Marfa
Captain H. L. Ransom, Sweetwater
Captain Jerry Gray, Austin
Captain W. L. Barter, Del Rio
Captain Carroll Bates, Marathon
Captain Charles F. Stevens, Edinburg
Captain Roy W. Aldrich, Austin
Captain W. M. Ryan, Laredo
Captain W. W. Wright, Laredo
Captain W. W. Davis, Ysleta
Captain K. F. Cunningham, Eagle Pass

Rangers stationed in Sweetwater always stayed at the Wright Hotel. Henry Ransom was transferred to Sweetwater in December 1917. Ensuing events may reveal clues about the real reason his company was disbanded and he was sent to that area.

Captain W. W. Davis again wrote the General on January 10: "In reply to your letter of the 4th...I did not intend to ask if I should help the officers of El Paso, but it was in regard to bootlegging to soldiers in the valley. All officers in the valley are Mexicans except one deputy sheriff stationed in Ysleta. I do not allow my men to go to El Paso except on business.

"Wade has been to El Paso twice as a witness. Oden ate Christmas dinner with his family. Robinson was up one day to move his wife here. Lowenstein to get a pair of glasses, that is all. I have three men at Fabens and four here. I do not let my men take a drink, and told them if they did, they would have to quit. I do not believe in peace officers drinking.

"We ride every day. There has been only one case of horse or cow stealing since we have been here. Three horses had been stolen. We recovered the horses but did not get the thieves.

"I bought 480 rifle cartridges and one hundred pistol cartridges, about one hundred rounds of rifle for each. We had a report of fighting across the river below here and as we were short of ammunition I thought best to wire you. Things are quiet here but people are more or less alarmed as there are plenty of Villistas all along the border and they have no food and sooner or later will come across to get it. We work with the River Guards all the time and investigate all rumors but they are not very definite. Would you please send me stationery of all kinds I will need as I have none. I would like to come to Austin sometime this month and have a talk with you and find out more definitely just what to do."

During this time nothing much was heard of Captain Ransom, now stationed at Sweetwater while conducting an investigation, his company disbanded, equipment scattered among other companies. He is away from the Border, where some people wanted him. Away. Far away.

Adjutant General James Harley wrote on January 30, 1918 to Senator Morris Sheppard, Washington, D. C.: "My dear Senator-the newspaper reports of the last few days carry General Order No.6 by the Director General of the Railroads, which in effect prohibits the use of, and orders the cancellation of, all Railroad passes throughout the country. I am taking the matter up with you in the interest of the Texas Ranger Force with a view to having you use your best efforts to have Mr. McAdoo understand the necessity of modifying his order to the extent of exempting Texas Rangers.

"As you know, the Texas Ranger is an officer of peculiar and varied duties and besides doing State service, he is also doing an additional service in providing peace along the border. His duty is not only that of a State peace officer but he differs from (them) in that part of his work is a work that should be done by the federal government for his principal duty is to protect the international border between Texas and Mexico. There he spends his time moving from place to place as the exigency of the occasion demands. Raids are very frequent in the border section of the country and it is often necessary to move from a dozen to two dozen Rangers from one point on the border to another in order to prevent a raid by Mexican bandits from across the Rio Grande.

"In addition to this, the Texas Ranger is called upon and it is necessary for him very often to ride on trains along the border to prevent their being attacked and the passengers robbed. If this order goes into effect and he is compelled to pay to ride upon trains when doing the Railroad Company a very valuable service, the Railroad will lose his protection and it will very often result in failure to prevent outbreaks and depredations at different points along the border.

"In addition to the work done upon the border, the Texas Ranger has been used by the Supervisor of the Draft in Texas for the purpose of escorting trainloads of raw recruits to camps and keeping peace among them. Their duties have also been to assist the federal authorities in the suppression of the Farmers' Protective Alliance in some sections of the State and in this they have accomplished a great deal of good.

"The Legislature of Texas at its last session did not provide an appropriation sufficient to warrant the State in paying transportation of the State Rangers, and if the Director of Railroad now cuts them off from railroad passes which have been furnished them it will very materially hamper their operations and handicap both the State and federal authorities in keeping the border cleared of bandits and bandits' raids.

"Thank you in advance for anything you can do."

Also on January 31, Captain J. M. Fox wrote Captain Johnson in Austin the following: "Please send me some more Winchester cotterges (sic) as we might run out have been using a good many lately. Making a run tonight. Looks a little bad on river at present."

Captain Stevens wrote February 4, 1918, to General Harley: "I beg to report that Sunday, February 3, Sheriff A. Y. Baker called on me and stated that Governor Hobby had wired him that there was to be horse races at Mercedes, and that trouble was expected there and that he wanted the races stopped.

"So I telephoned the two Rangers stationed at Mercedes to stop the races. I also telephoned the two Rangers stationed at Harlingen to proceed to Mercedes and to assist the Rangers there to enforce the law. The races were stopped — without trouble."

Notice that no letters or telegrams to or from Captain Ransom exist or are available for some time, not since he was transferred to Sweetwater. Ranger work continues over the State but nothing is heard concerning him.

One Ranger wrote on February 2, 1918: "Politically Governor Hobby is very strong in this District, and when the time comes, if he wants anything done in Medina County, or in Goliad County, let me know, as I have some men in my company whose friends and relatives have considerable influence in those counties.

"Of course, we are not taking a hand in local politics in this District."

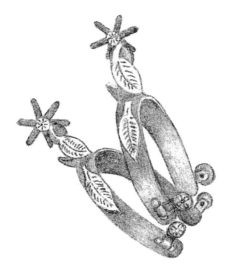

Spurs Handy But More Humane With Easy Rowels

CHAPTER XVI

The Special Agent, W. M. Hanson, had an innate sense of humor that bubbled to the surface on numerous occasions, in spite of some of his grim assignments. His letter of March 1, 1918 to the Assistant Adjutant General is an example.

"I herewith beg to hand you my February 1918 account. Please do not fail to see that this has IMMEDIATE attention for although 'Hooverising' in every conceivable manner, frijoles and beans must be secured for the family. Please rush back to me for I may leave any moment for the border."

Captain W. W. Davis, who took Captain Ransom's place on the Border, wired General Harley on March 3: MEXICAN GUARDS CROSS LINE. RANGER AND SOLDIERS KILLED SIX. FIGHT LASTED FIVE HOURS. FEELING BETTER EXCEPT FOR MORE FIGHTING. CAN I ENLIST SIX MEN. WOULD LIKE TO GIVE PENNINGTON ANOTHER CHANCE. MADE GOOD IN FIGHT. EXPRESS ONE THOUSAND RIFLE CARTRIDGES

This telegram was 20 days late. Were these men left without ammunition? According to the date stamped on it on receipt at the Adjutant General's Department, it came March 23. Why so late? Was this investigated or did someone set the date stamp wrong?

Still no correspondence is available from or to Captain Ransom in Sweetwater. What is the reason?

An American citizen, a Texan of Mexican descent, in business in San Antonio, confided in the undercover agent, Captain Hanson, who reported his findings to both Harley and Hobby. This businessman had inside knowledge from Mexican natives who talked freely to him, believing him to be one of them.

The patriotic American closed the letter by offering his services "for all things tending to uphold the honor and dignity of our glorious STARS AND STRIPES."

Captain W. L. Wright, Company K sent Harley the following detailed report on the bandit raid March 7, 1918 of the East

Ranch: "I left Laredo on the morning of the third, with six of my men, Connolly, Hutchinson, Pullin, W. D. Wells, Monroe Wells, and J. P. Perkins. We arrived at Hebbronville on the evening of the fourth. I found that grass was good, so I decided to rest ourselves and horses a day or so. Mr. Henry Edds furnished me a place to camp and a room over his office to sleep in. So on the morning of the 7th, about half after four o'clock, a Mexican came and called for me. He told me that the bandits had taken the East Ranch, that is robbed it, and he didn't know but that they had killed everybody on the place, about thirty miles from Hebbronville.

"I at once got Mr. Edds and Mr. Thompson together and I told Mr. Craighead, the Sheriff and Mr. John Droeper. Mr. Thompson furnished us a truck to haul our saddles in, and Mr. Edds furnished cars to haul my men, so we were on the road to this ranch in less than thirty minutes after we got the information. We arrived there in less than two hours. I left W. D. Wells, one of my men, in charge of my mules and our horses with instructions to follow us, as I knew that the horses on ranches were weak and wouldn't amount to much. As soon as we arrived and learned what happened, I at once made arrangements to follow their trail.

"After the bandits had robbed the ranch and store of Tom East, they went from there to what is known as the San Antonio Viejo Ranch. They also robbed this ranch. Mr. East didn't have any horses at his first ranch, but had sent after some that they claimed to be good ones. I left instructions for him to follow us on these good horses, and we went to the San Antonio Viejo Ranch and got horses there but they had been ridden the day before and were not good to start with. So I left instructions there at the old ranch, when these fresh horses reached there for them to follow us at once, as I was certain the ones we were riding wouldn't go very far.

"We took the trail at this ranch and Mr. Thompson and Mr. Edds following us in their cars. I sent them to Rio Grande City to notify the soldiers and also my men there that the bandits were coming in that direction. We trailed them about 25 miles in a direction of Roma...about 15 miles above Rio Grande City. They quit the Roma road several times but would always come back. At the Charcalargo Ranch they went to a windmill, about a mile from the road, where they lost some Mauser cartridges.

"Before I go further I will give you the names of the men who were with me on the trail on horseback. My six men I already mentioned above, Tom Mosely, who is Cattle Association Inspector, Dudley Stilwell, who is employed by Mr. Edds and is a special Ranger, Mr. John Droeper, and a Mr. Franklin. This composed the crowd that was with me on the trail.

"They struck the Javali Ranch, which is about 25 or 30 miles from Roma, on the Rio Grande. After they had gone into the Javali Ranch about half a mile, they turned direct to the right into the brush, a dense thicket, known in the Southwest to be the thickest brush on the border. It was so thick we almost had to go in single file.

"We had our Winchesters in our hands, as we thought maybe they might be near, as the trail was hot, and all at once we were within 20 feet of them. They commenced shooting as they got on their horses and before you could snap your finger, they were all running, and we after them. After they ran a short distance, they scattered in bunches and the men also scattered to follow them, as there was no time to give orders. There were about eight stayed together for awhile, and ran in a southwesterly direction. Tom Mosely, John Droeper, Dudley Stilwell, and my man, Mr. Pullin, and I got after these eight. We ran them about three miles, they shooting back over their shoulders, and we shooting at them. We don't know for certain how many were killed. I know two were killed. We found one and buried him, the other one that I saw fall from his horse, shot, we could never find. In other words, we didn't have time to hunt them as were hot on the trail of the others. The boys think we killed several others, but I can't say we did.

"I am certain that we wounded several, as we found blood on their horses and saddles that we recovered. We crowded them so close that they threw away everything. They lost pistols, Winchesters, five of them lost their hats, two of them were bought at Hebbronville. The Captain of the band, at least we thought him to be the captain, was riding a black paint horse he had stolen at the ranch. This was a very fine horse and had been fed grain all winter. He led the bunch of eight that I was after. His horse was much faster than the rest. One of them wounded the horse in the left thigh, just a flesh wound, and I am most certain we wounded him, too. He got away from us that evening in that pasture.

"The next day we trailed this one that went through the fence to the Rio Grande and where three of the horsemen crossed the river. We found the black paint horse on this side. A Mexican told us that this horse came to a little well to get some water the first time he saw him. Yesterday my _____(illegible) who I have now at Salinenio, found the saddle, that he had also _____(illegible) at the East Ranch in an old house near where the horse was found, and also found in this same house…blood on some boards, it looked like he had been sitting down there.

"My men have the horse and saddle in our camp at Salinenio. They had the bullet extracted from the thigh by a government veterinary. The horses we were riding, when the chase was over, were completely given out.

"Mr. Tom East didn't follow us with the fresh horses as he had promised us…the horses never reached us in time to do us any good. My horses and wagon and mules reached us at one o'clock in the morning, after having been driven 55 miles. Mr. Edds and Mr. Thompson furnished me two Mexicans to drive my horses behind the wagon. Mr. W. B. Allen furnished his truck and driver to haul my hay and oats to the El Javali Ranch, where we were camped that night after the chase.

"If Mr. East had followed us with his horses, as I instructed him to do, I am almost certain that we would have been able to have captured or killed every last one of those bandits. They would not surrender at all, as I hollered at them to throw up their hands, and the other boys did, too, to surrender, but they paid no attention to our request. It seemed that they would rather die than surrender. Mr. Henry Edds had instructed a little Mexican boy to stay about a half mile behind us on the trail with a car, so in case he was needed to carry messages, he would be on hand. I wish to state now that it turned out that he was a very much needed man after the chase, as he knew the country and knew where we were at; we didn't.

"So I sent a note by this Mexican to Roma, where he struck Mr. Edds and Mr. Thompson, with Sgt. J. J. Edds and three of my men and brought them to this El Javali Ranch, and also brought us some provisions…there wasn't a living thing in that whole country but the brush and prickle pear, not even a rabbit.

"The next morning after the chase we all had fresh mounts, so we trailed the other six to the Rio Grande. We captured seven horses and two mules, also the same amount of saddles, bridles, spurs, some Winchesters, and pistols.

"I wish to say in conclusion that the State of Texas owes to Mr. Henry Edds and Mr. Oscar Thompson many thanks in this chase alone, for the services they rendered in running down these bandits. Had they gotten away with this booty, it would have encouraged many others to do likewise. And I am certain that this will teach those that got away an everlasting lesson. I also want to mention to you the gallant services that Mr. Tom Mosely, John Droeper, Dudley Stilwell, and Mr. Franklin rendered us. They showed skill and bravery in running these bandits through the thick brush.

"Several of the boys, after the chase, didn't have enough clothes on to hide themselves.

"I believe this to be a correct statement of the whole affair. I know I am a poor hand to make a report of this kind, and I don't know if I've made it as it should have been made out but I have done the best I could."

At the end of a letter from another Ranger to the Adjutant General: "It looks like Governor Hobby will carry El Paso County overwhelmingly."

Again, politics rears its ugly head. It appears rules can be forgotten. Walter Prescott Webb, in his book about the Texas Rangers, mentioned that some were used to "politic" for Hobby's election.

On March 8th, Adjutant General Harley sent two wires, the first below to Captain Will Wright, Laredo: REPORT EAST RANCH RAIDED LAST NIGHT AT HEBBRONVILLE IF YOU CAN ASSIST IN RUNNING DOWN THE BANDITS DO SO AT ONCE

Captain Wright was already "running down the bandits."

Captain J. J. Sanders, at Alice, received the next wire below: IT IS REPORTED HERE THAT ROBERT EAST RANCH AT HEBBRONVILLE WAS RAIDED LAST NIGHT REPORT CIRCUMSTANCES AT YOUR EARLY CONVENIENCE IF YOU NEED HELP WE WILL SEND IT I AM WIRING STEVENS AND WRIGHT

Activity on the Border is still hot also, with Captain Ransom out of the picture, stationed in Sweetwater doing who knows what. No correspondence to or from him yet during this time period was found in the Adjutant Generals' files in the Archives.

Next is a description from a different viewpoint, at the T. T. East Ranch. This is by Mr. East himself.

"Thursday morning I was at a round-up, about three and one half miles south of the ranch, at what I call the Old Ranch, and as I had to send a message to town, Terry Downs, my driver, took my wife to the ranch to phone the message…and as they came up to the barn, there was a car there with the curtains all up…two men and one woman, Mexicans, were in the car. The men had coats drawn up over their faces so as to disguise themselves, but one of the fellows did pull the cover off his face enough so she could see him. They came up from the west, saying they were from Mission and inquired about the road to Hebbronville…they told him the road was about one mile away, and that they could not go through there as that was not a public road, but he paid no attention to them and went through anyway. My wife told me this when she got back and said it looked awful suspicious, but I did not think much of it at the time.

"That night when we got through with the cattle, about 7:45, we left the Old Ranch in the car for the headquarters, and arrived there about 8 p.m.

"To get to the garage and house…you come up a lane from the South and go through a gate about 25 yards, then through a gate in the barn, and into a gate from the North, about 25 feet from the barn, into the enclosure around the houses. As I went to shut the barn door and to open the other gate, I saw four men with guns run to the other gate…they threw their guns down on my wife and driver. Then I heard them say 'Buenas tardes' and 'las armas' meaning 'good evening…the arms' which they gave them, three rifles and one pistol that were in the car. They did not see me as the light of the car was shining in their faces and I was behind the car. I ran out about a hundred yards west and jumped a fence and stopped, listened and figured on the best thing to do.

"The one thing I knew I had to do was to get help as soon as possible. My cow outfit was camped at the Old Ranch, and I started for there on foot, to get horses and men and send for help. I got there I guess about 9 o'clock, and got the boys out after the horses, about 75 head that were in about a 100 acre pasture and got them mounted, after sending the men, with the exception of Jourdan Franklin, the boss, and three Mexicans to the brush, and turning out the horses in the big pasture. I sent one Mexican to another ranch of mine about 15 miles from there to get Dudley Stilwell, the Special Ranger, who works for me, and Tom Mosely. One Mexican I sent to

J. P. Reed's ranch to get two guns for Franklin and myself and the other to W. P. Allen's ranch to phone to Hebbronville for help.

"Claude McGill of Alice and Steve Franklin, my ranch manager in Hidalgo came up to the ranch in Oscar Thompson's car, and as they got within a few feet of the gate the bandits fired on them about 10 or 15 shots and they stopped. Then the bandits made them get out then searched them and took everything of value, and took them to the house where they already had Will Franklin Sr. and Will Franklin Jr. and their wives under guard. This was about 7:30, about half an hour before they got my wife and driver.

"They then put all of them under guard and proceeded to ransack the place. They took everything they could carry away, including all of the guns, of which they got seven, and merchandise. Then they left part of the men to guard the people at the ranch, and the balance took and went to Hebbronville, saying they were going after whiskey and rob the bank. They got just within a few miles and got scared and came back to the ranch and made the ladies cook them something to eat…went through the store again, and got everything else they forgot the first time.

"The reason they stayed there so long, they kept saying I would be back after awhile. They told all the people there they were not going to hurt them if they did not try to do anything, that Stilwell and I were the ones they wanted. They left the ranch about 3 a.m. and passed right close to me, as I had gotten my horse in the brush, and crawled up as close as I could to see what I could see.

"They left the ranch and went South to the Old Ranch and took a saddle there and several pairs of leggings and some fresh meat and coffee. My wife said as they went into the gates, the first fellow she saw was the man she saw in the car that morning, and he had a gun leveled right at her. In all they took about $1200 worth of stuff at the ranch, including the two horses and the saddles.

"The Rangers, under Captain Will Wright, Oscar Thompson, Henry Edds, and John Droeper got to the Ranch about seven a.m. Friday and got horses and took the trail…I brought my wife and Claude McGill on to Kingsville. The Mexicans could all talk English and said they were Texas Mexicans. We recognized three men in that bunch. They were all young men from 21-30 years old. They were very polite to the ladies and did not hurt them in any way, but punched the men around with their guns and talked of killing Will Franklin Jr., as they thought he was Stilwell, and did put a rope around his neck. They also said they were going to take Mrs. East away if I did not come.

"When they left, they made them all tell them 'Good-bye' and said if they sent after the Rangers, they would come back and kill them all.

"They left one of their guns and two old saddles. Their gun is a Mauser. Several more had guns just like the ones left…which is same as used by Carranza soldiers.

"If you wish any more information let me know and will be glad to furnish it if I can."

An early Model T

CHAPTER XVII

General Harley received a letter dated March 25, 1918 from C. E. Huddleston of Waco: "Mr. Williams and I are still on the job and getting along very nicely considering the long hours that we are on duty.

"…Mr. Miles of Captain Ransom's Company tells me that they received an expense allowance of $2.00 per day for month of February and would certainly consider it a personal favor if Mr. Williams and I could be allowed same, for expenses in Waco are equally as much as those in Sweetwater. Trusting that this will receive your prompt attention and with the very highest regards, always, for General Harley and his office as well as his personal aspirations…"

What might be the Adjutant General's personal aspirations? A curious remark…

Ransom has not been heard from or at least nothing has been put in the Archives at this point. It was said he was appointed an "inspector" of Texas Rangers to investigate some suspected wrong-doing, thus his company could be dispersed without arousing suspicion. However, he was really assigned to the Judge Higgins murder case in that area.

Just prior to this, Harley continued to receive more reports from Hanson, his undercover agent on the Border, who kept his finger on countless pulses.

These included assessments of how the voters felt about certain candidates and descriptions of his meetings with various groups working to get them elected or defeated.

The knowledge obtained from Hanson's letters to the General was that "the people" did not want Ransom down there any more, with no explanation about the reason. Perhaps none was needed. Both the General and Hanson knew why, so the latter did not need to put it in writing.

Incidents add up: 1. several of the Rangers reporting confidentially to both Harley and Hobby were drawn into illegally campaigning for the election of Hobby, who was serving out the term of Ferguson, after the former Governor's impeachment. 2. the letter telling about Parr and a sheriff coming in to boldly confiscate a box of ballots in spite of an election official's protests, and 3. Harley's apparent ignoring Ransom's several requests for additional men to help him in Sweetwater, his wires and letters being unanswered.

As far as is known, the fate of the stolen ballots was not told nor is there a record available of that letter from the Judge ever being acknowledged and answered. This occurred in the same area where numerous corpses resting in cemeteries were reputed to have been resurrected miraculously so they could vote.

Henry could not have been the knowledgeable, informed, and successful Ranger Captain he was and be unaware of the blatant political shenanigans in the Border counties. The politicians and their cohorts were uneasy with him there. Did they suspect he might blow the whistle on their activities?

In earlier days in the Rangers, he worked in the area, which he knew well, along with its people, and they were well aware of his incorruptible character.

Sweetwater, alleged at this time to be the state "headquarters" for a large cattle theft ring, echoed with clashes among various factions and outright feuding that had festered for some time. Gunplay was hardly strange in that part of Texas.

Could he have been transferred to Sweetwater for another purpose, such as to get him away from the Border? Speculation has it that had he been assassinated down there, an investigation might have turned up details of the operations of local political cliques. He had to be moved away from the Border and killed elsewhere, if that was the plan, in another dangerous spot less familiar to the public, and less known for political manipulation.

With an upcoming election, the politicians did not want to risk an upset of any kind. Hobby wanted to remain in the Governor's office.

Below is a quote from a letter written in April 1918, from Fred E. M. to Captain W. M. Hanson, Special Agent: "In compliance with my promise to you and General Harley relative to the candidacy of Governor Hobby in this county, I am more than pleased to state from a personal campaign made by me with our influential political friends that Governor Hobby will have the support of Starr County. A petition has been circulated by Judge M. and signed by all of the county officials and endorsed by_____. I believe by the time of the primaries I will have all that is to be had in the Hobby band wagon…I explained to our friends your desire of having all of them stand by the Governor for re-election (NOTE: Hobby was not elected in the first place, but as Lt. Governor took Ferguson's place when the latter was impeached)…I assure you, from present conditions, that any other candidate will not have even a look-in."

Of course Hanson was not authorized to hand out Ranger commissions. This was in the hands of the Adjutant General, Harley, who was appointed by the Governor, Hobby, who would have the final decision.

In another letter dated the same day, he asked Hanson for a Special Ranger appointment for Mr. D. C., "one of the strong supporters for our present Governor, Mr. Hobby."

Mr. M. added, "I am writing you separately a letter in connection with what I have done…in behalf of Mr. Hobby's candidacy in the county, so that you can show it to General Harley, as I promised you both when you spoke to me about this matter."

Letters and telegrams from others, as well as from Captain Ransom himself to Harley's office the last days of his life, and for some time afterward, are veritable clues from the coffin of the murdered Ranger. Simply read them in this chronological order.

Suddenly their contents add up.

Ransom's letters, including those to his wife, expressing last thoughts before he was killed, speak volumes, his handwriting an added clue.

The following important letter by T. W. of Austin to his brother, B. W., an attorney practicing law in Waco, describes the powder keg conditions under which Henry Ransom was working.

"Dear Brother, I returned from West Texas Sunday morning. My case at Baird will either be continued or the venue changed to Eastland County. In any event, it will not come up now, but I will probably have to go out there again in a few days.

"Conditions in that country are in a very bad shape and there were several other killings booked to take place at Baird. The man who actually shot Higgins has committed suicide, but he made a statement to one of the Rangers and later to the Deputy

Sheriff at Sweetwater telling who were the immediate parties that got him to do it and the reasons for it. Those two parties implicated by him are two notorious outlaws in West Texas.

"Things are popping open out there now and matters are coming to light, but the trouble is that Capt. Ransom, or whatever his name is, has not enough men at his command to work on the situation. He seems to be a thoroughly competent man, well acquainted with conditions in West Texas and in this particular locality and knows the history of the men he is dealing with. He is a first-class officer, and, if afforded proper help, will save the lives of some other good men. If not, there will be further innocent parties to lose their lives in that country, and among them some of the very best and law abiding citizens there.

"Capt. Ransom ought to be given at least three or four other experienced men of his own selection in that country at this time. There is not another place in Texas that needs them half so bad. Of course, this letter is written to you personally, and I would not care for it to go out of your hands, because it is actually dangerous for a man to express himself about conditions out there.

"I want you to go at once and see General Harley and show him this letter and explain to him that I have just come back…and was out there for four or five days and that I know at first hand from the best people in that country just what that situation is and that it is in much need for competent protection as I have indicated above."

W.'s letter emphasizes that Captain Ransom is short-handed, needing more men. Why was he not sent more help especially after he, obviously under great stress, requested it?

General Harley usually answered letters and telegrams immediately on receipt, as evidenced by numerous previous ones. This time was Harley conveniently out of town, out of his office? On purpose? As far as is known, he did not respond in any way.

He must have seen the letter from W. from his brother, for it was preserved in his correspondence files.

Why did General Harley not take action after reading the above letter? Also Captain Ransom began writing to Assistant Adjutant General Woodul.

A letter dated March 28, 1918 from E.A. Hockaday to Captain Hanson, the Special Agent emphasized that the Border remain the usual hot spot.

A letter to Captain W. W. Davis, Ysleta, from Assistant Adjutant General Walter F. Woodul, written March 26, 1918: "As to Pennington, if he ever so much as touches another drop, you will immediately dismiss him from service and this goes for any of your men.

"Rifle will be sent to Frank Black. Special Rangers' commissions will go forward today."

On March 26, Ransom wrote Harley: "Dear Sir: Beg to submit the following report. In the Higgins murder or rather assassination, we have made three arrests. Bob Higden, Witt Luman, and Sye Bostick. Who hanged himself in the Sweetwater jail. It became absolutely necessary for me to hold Ranger Koon to help me in this murder. Will need Sgt. J. L. Anders until the Grand Jury gets through, which I understand will start investigation next two or three days. I need two more men awful bad. And I insist it is my wright (sic) to select them, as I am held responsible. Ransom"

Note the sense of urgency, the usual respectful closing, "Yours to command" missing and the cryptic use of only the Captain's surname. In previous letters his sentences have not been in fragments, as in this letter.

After requesting more men to help him, the final sentence is: "I have the wright to pick them myself," with the "w" added to the word "right," a definite indication of stress. He was in the Wright Hotel, the usual headquarters for Texas Rangers stationed in Sweetwater.

He will not trust anyone else to choose which others to help him, it being imperative that he be certain of their loyalty. Henry realizes he is in a precarious position.

The extra, unusual amount of pressure and force on his pen point as he neared the end of his letter might foreshadow the impending doom he must have felt.

Others who knew him well had expressed the feeling that he seemed at times to be almost psychic, appearing to sense the proximity of danger. This was never put in his own words, but surmised by others acquainted with past incidents and reports of witnesses to them.

Yet in spite of the trouble he must have felt was ahead, he took a few minutes to pen a note to his family.

"Dear Anna and the Kids, Just got in late last night and read your letter. Have got to go back to Kent County this evening. Hope the boy is better of the measels (sic). Be careful with him when he first gets up on account of pneumonia. Do hope he and Ruby's through with that stuff for awhile.

"In a hurry to get off. Lots of love to all of you. Write soon."

On the subject of letters, Hansen is now writing to the Assistant Adjutant General Woodul, instead of Harley. Is he aware that Harley possibly is absent from his office? How much more does he know?

Hansen to Woodul, letter dated March 26, 1918: "Following your instructions I called on General Ruckman this morning, he did not think there was much to report from Brownsville...He was...pleased that you was (sic) sending me there...He seems very sanguine that we are to have a lot of trouble along the border, and I told him every Ranger in Texas was subject to his call on all border raids...he was very much pleased.

"One of the leading stockmen of the Brownsville country told me that he had positive information that the Mexican Consul at Brownsville and the Colonel of the Carranza forces in Matamoros was having his cattle stolen and driven to their ranch about twenty miles south of Matamoros in Mexico and requested that I give it my personal attention when I arrived there which I will do, but will call Captain Stevens in so he will not get ruffled. I will send a man to their ranch to check it up, and as the cattle stolen were Jerseys we should have no trouble in locating them if there. A Mexican lieutenant from Matamoros gave him the information.

"I have a Mexican meeting me from Monterey at Brownsville to give me a list of the East raiders, their residence and the whole plot. I know it will be perfectly reliable. THEY WERE NOT TEX-MEXICANS BUT FROM THE MEXICO SIDE, and within next week I will furnish you the proof (sent there by a Military officer from that side.")

Captain Charles F. Stevens wrote March 27 to Walter Woodul: "Yours of March 25 received, in regard to T. J. L., who is applying for a commission as a Special Ranger, I do not recommend him for the appointment. He is a deputy sheriff at Harlingen and a few days ago he insulted a lieutenant in the U. S. Army. The Army officers have been very nice to me, and when my men are out on a scout and go into an Army camp, they are always invited to eat and their horses are fed. So far as Deputy Sheriff L. ever giving any of my men any assistance, I have never heard of it, and I have instructed my men to have nothing to do with him."

On March 28, Hanson, the Special Agent, wrote again to Walter Woodul, with the first two paragraphs being vague and requiring some explanation: "I beg to acknowledge receipt of your letter of instructions to the Ranger Captains, and I fully explained the future policy of this Department to Captain Stevens." What "future policy"?

"I also received yours of former date to Capt. Stevens and Capt. Wright, and Capt. Stevens is well pleased…I am sure Capt. Wright will be tickled to death. It was a very necessary move, and I hope to convince you good people that it is necessary to get Capt. Sanders nearer the border, and Capt. Ryan of Webb County to the Zapata line.

"Personal contact with the people here and Sheriff Vann proves to me that this portion of the border only has it in for Capt. Ransom and none others. Capt. Sanders is very popular here, and they say they knew who did the objectionable work here, but Governor Ferguson told that 'He had to appoint Ransom, and had no other place to put him.' I feel sure that I have healed the breech (sic) perfectly between the people and the Ranger service, by explaining the policy of the Department. It is very popular and will materially assist Governor Hobby and General Harley in the FUTURE. All we have to do now is make good."

What "policy" that would help Hobby and Harley?

"I had a long talk with Consul Garza today," continues Hanson's letter, "and it was very satisfactory to him. He gave me a full gallon of Mexican diplomacy and I returned the 'JUG' to the rim. Capt. Harrison heard the conversation and remarked that I was a 'bigger liar than he was' and that was 'going some' for I heard him also make a talk to the honorable Consul."

This letter contains an implication only, no details. To what "objectionable work" of Captain Ransom's did Hanson refer? Or was it Ransom's? Nothing showed up in reference to such a problem in all of the correspondence files of the Adjutant General.

Sheriff Vann could not be expected to say anything good about Ransom, for each had a hearty dislike for the other. Corruption, as stated by others earlier, existed in Vann's area of jurisdiction, and doubtless Ransom knew it. And Vann knew Ransom knew, probably.

Hanson's letter smacks of more political maneuvering. Vann's long-time opposition to Ransom was emphasized even more several years after Ransom's death when Vann "testified" at a hearing about the Rangers. It was instigated by a Mexican legislator from the Border area. Vann had to be reminded not to criticize a man in his grave who could not defend himself.

Political campaigning has been carried on behind the scenes in spite of regulations prohibiting such involvement of the Rangers. The veiled remarks of these "confidential" letters by and to the undercover agent and several Rangers make it clear there are two sets of rules. Hobby himself set up the "special operative" group, needed partly because of wartime, and appointed Captain Hanson as head. It had more than one use.

Close-mouthed Henry Ransom apparently did confide in his family, especially his brother, Will, that illegal "politicking" including the Parr influence, was rampant in the Border counties. Had Hutchings remained adjutant general, Henry might have spoken of this to him, but now was hesitant as Harley appeared to be involved also, or at least condoned the activities.

For certain some of the Rangers were being "used." It is well to remember that the Governor always appointed the Adjutant General.

The political leaders of South Texas probably feared Ransom was aware of their maneuvers and wanted him out of the way before he implicated people in prominent positions, affecting the outcome of the coming elections.

If former Governor Ferguson was quoted correctly in saying he "had to appoint Ransom" Captain of the new company of Rangers that was sent to the Border, and that he "had no other place to put him," this is strange. He respected Ransom and his ability. They had become well-acquainted when Henry served as Ferguson's bodyguard during the impeachment.

Before this, Ransom had received from the earlier General a command to go to the Border, and clean it up, no matter what method it would take to do. He added, "If you can't do it, I'll send someone else."

Ransom meticulously followed orders, perhaps too much so, to suit some who did not care to have the area so well "cleaned up."

At this same time in a letter to Harley, Hanson wrote: "This morning I met several leading citizens at the Chamber of

Commerce rooms and behind closed doors had a heart-to-heart talk with them. They feel...this section of the Border is and will be in great danger from the Mexicans of all classes and ...want more rangers. Satisfied with Capt. Stevens but want more...in the past they did not like Capt. Sanders for the reason he drank some. I assured them your policy was to fire anyone in the service that drank. They said 'Under that condition we would rather have Capt. Sanders and his men than any other companies you could send...That gave me a chance to outline your policy with reference to the Ranger service and I never saw a better pleased bunch and they requested me to say to you that they, to a man, were with you, ALL DOWN THE LINE..."

Hanson also mentioned "the breech" again, saying it had existed there for years.

As for the "new policy" of Harley's, it has not appeared in any of the correspondence or official papers outlining Ranger business. Why isn't the "policy" published for all to see? Why so secretive?

Is this a last minute ploy to get some voters in a good mood?

General Harley is leaving his post in several days, making his total time as Adjutant General only eight months. He was put there for a purpose. Guess what.

Hanson also told Harley in the same letter that he had talked with a Colonel Slocum,..."I then outlined your policy fully, and he said he hoped we would forgive him for formerly fighting the Ranger service, and asked me to make it public through the press, but I told him we were getting it to the people in a more substantial manner, and was keeping it out of the publicity columns...that pleased him...he said 'no politics in that.'"

A letter dated March 28, 1918 from Hanson in Brownsville, to Harley is a short report on the bandits' raid of the East Ranch. "This band was formed near Ochoa, Mexico, for the express purpose of raiding the Hebbronville bank and there they were to be joined by another band from San Diego, Texas...from there they were to rob other banks and ranches in Texas. They robbed the East Ranch, the Viejo Ranch, and concluded to return to the Border for safety. They were attacked at the Jabali Ranch by Rangers who killed one of the bands by the name of Palonesa.

After the fight they disbanded and crossed the river at a point called Alamo, near Roma, Starr County. The raiders were not Tex-Mexicans but all from the Mexican side..."

Captain J. M. Fox, Co. B, Marfa, sent a letter to Sergeant Cardwell, Austin, March 30, 1918: "Send us twelve or fifteen hundred steel point Winchester cartridges as we are running low and abut eight hundred rounds of Colt's .45 smokeless. Please rush as we are likely to have lots of trouble. Better send them by express so they will get here quick."

On the same day Captain Fox wrote to Major Woodul: "I...am asking should I keep my company up to full strength. I have sent for the man Dyches you told me to enlist but since I have returned I've had two men quit. Clint Holder had to go home on account of his mother who lives in Llano is old and a widow. W. K. Duncan also resigned. He is just a young boy and I guess thought it too tough. You know it takes a man with hair in his nose to stand the guff here and it looks as if the whole of Mexico is going to get on us now.

"O. C. Dow who has been a river guard for several years wants to join my company and I know he will make good and be one of the boys. With your permission I will enlist him. I am going to El Paso tomorrow to Federal Court. Can't say how long will have to be there. I wish you would wire me at sheriff's office El Paso Monday regarding the enlisting of men up to 16. The Mexicans are raising Cain across the river. The American soldiers had a fight with them and without letting anything out; the Americans got cleaned to a finish and whipped back to Texas. It looks awfully bad here at this time."

Familiar Sight — A Blooming Cactus

CHAPTER XVIII

Captain Charles F. Stevens, Company G. Mercedes, Texas sent a letter dated March 31, 1918 to the Assistant Adjutant General: "...I returned from Brownsville to Mercedes March 30th. On my arrival at Mercedes I received information that on the night of March 29th a man by the name of Dr. Richard Linder...who is a lieutenant in the German Army, had left his farm and was making for the Rio Grande River with the intention of crossing into Mexico. I immediately telephoned Colonel Sear, U. S. Army. He at once sent out patrols on the river and Dr. Lindner was captured... just as he was making arrangements to cross-over in a boat to Mexico. Proceeded at once to Dr. Lindner's farmhouse and there after investigation, I arrested a man by the name of Rev. Rooper who is connected with these Germans. I searched the house, taking all the writing of Dr. Lindner's and delivered Rev. Rooper and all papers to Colonel Sears. The Colonel was very thankful for what I did in the matter.

These men were taken as prisoners to Ft. Brown. This Dr. Lindner first came from Canada and I understand he was a prisoner of war in Canada, then crossed into the United States in Montana. From there he went to Seattle, Washington, then to Chicago, then to Wisconsin, then into Indiana, and from there down into this country. I think the Government will get a good trace on some of these German matters through the arrest of these parties and that there will be more Germans arrested in this section of the country. My idea of the matter: these men are part of a chain of spies who are operating throughout the United States and communicating news to the German Representative in Mexico and from there into Germany.

"Mr. Garza, Mexican Consulate, informed me that he was satisfied when certain Mexican Custom Officials were on duty on the Mexican side that there was always something stolen on the American side of the river. He asked me to come to Brownsville on Monday, April 1. I could watch on the American side and capture them, if they cross to steal anything on the American side..."

Captain Ransom sent the following letter dated March 31 to Major Walter Woodul Assistant Adjutant General: "Enclosed find warrant of authority of Ranger C. C. Hurst. He tendered resignation to take effect this date. Resigned of his own accord to accept Federal position.

"Hurst is one of the boys that was stationed at Ranger, Texas and I am very sorry to lose him. I am returning Mr. Box's letter to you thinking perhaps you could send some of the boys at Austin out there as we are all busy on this murder case. The Grand Jury meets at Clairmont April 9th and we will all have to be up there until they get through with their investigation which will last at least a week…Ransom."

Henry always writes to the General himself. Several preceding letters were addressed to Woodul.

Is it because he cannot get a response from Harley, the Adjutant General who customarily answered letters and wires the same or next day? What is going on?

The same evening, on March 31, Henry wrote to his wife: "Dear Anna and Children, Your letter received and was sure glad to hear Jonathan was doing well. I have been up in Garza and Kent Counties, working on that murder case. We haven't had rain here yet. I believe I'll buy another car, and am thinking about getting a Dodge…They are awful good cars. I want to take a vacation this summer and we will have a good car to go on a trip with. Glad you all had rain. Guess it helped Thomas' radishes. Will send you a check in next letter. Lots of love to you and children and best wishes to Nany and Thomas. Tell Jonathan Daddy was glad to get his letter…"

An interesting letter dated April 1 to the Assistant Adjutant General Woodul from W. M. Hanson, who signs his letter "Special Agent": "Kindly say to the General that I am notified that some of the Jersey cows stolen from Mr. Jessup are tonight in Matamoros and we will get them tomorrow…I think we will get them all before we quit. Never so well tickled (sic) people in my life. Getting these cows will carry the county for the Governor.

"Lawrence Bates has been here three weeks working for Ferguson. WE HAVE HIM ON THE HIP! He will not take one trick. Some DEMOCRATIC POLITICIANS ourselves, AIN'T WE! BOB COON the Ferguson orator arrived last night and he and Bates consulted several hours last night. This afternoon Bob came to my room and asked me what I was doing here. I told him catching stolen cattle and thieves. He replied that I was a "G-D-Liar, (joking, you know) that he had seen my footprints on every side track and pavement. He went home this afternoon and Bates is going tomorrow. Don't be uneasy. I will not make any breaks, every track is covered and Hobby stock at PAR!"

"PAR" in this letter may have a double meaning and also has to refer to the Parr political machine. It speaks loud and clear. The writer mentioned blatant hints, such as "every track covered," not realizing his remarks would one day be open to the public in the State Archives. All actors in the scene are long gone, but glaring light is shed on their plots, thanks to those who conserved the correspondence that came to and out of the Adjutant General's Department.

The intrigue continues on both sides of the Rio Grande, the International Boundary, as shown in the previous letter while the plot building against Captain Ransom reaches its climax.

He was killed on the second floor of the Wright Hotel about 10 o'clock the night of March 31, 1918.

He would have left shortly for Clairmont to deliver evidence he had collected for the Grand Jury's investigation of Judge Higgins' murder. Immediately after the shooting, his briefcase on a table in his hotel room disappeared, never to be seen again, witnesses said.

The following telegram was sent to Adjutant General James Harley, Austin: LONG AND MILLER WERE SHOOTING AT EACH OTHER IN HALL OF WRIGHT HOTEL. CAPTAIN RANSOM CAME OUT OF ROOM TO STOP SHOOTING AND WAS KILLED BY LONG. TROUBLE WAS OVER FAMILY MATTERS. RANGER KOON OVERTOOK AND CAPTURED MILLER ABOUT FIFTEEN MILES FROM SWEETWATER WHILE TRYING TO ESCAPE IN HIS AUTOMOBILE WHICH WAS WRECKED AND ALSO FIRED ONE SHOT AT LONG WHILE TRYING TO ARREST MILLER AND LONG. BOTH IN JAIL HERE. I WAS AT POST CITY WHEN TROUBLE HAPPENED. EVERYTHING IS QUIET. WOULD LIKE TO HAVE ONE OR TWO MEN. JUST IN RECEIPT OF MESSAGE FROM MRS RANSOM SHE WANTS BODY SHIPPED TO HEMPSTEAD. BODY LEAVES HERE FOUR TEN THIS AFTERNOON OVER SANTA FE TO ARRIVE HEMPSTEAD TWELVE TEN PM TOMORROW. SGT MCKENZIE 10:07 AM

Henry had collected enough evidence probably to put in the penitentiary close friends of men in high office. This paralleled the kinfolks' remarks on hearing of his death that highly placed politicians were involved. Will, his brother, was one of the very few he confided in and knew first-hand from him about the political intrigue on the Border, and South Texas in general.

According to descriptions by others Ransom's nephew, Henry Jr., judged the other man shot his uncle from the back, probably squatting down to shoot upward, to be purposely low himself, in case Ransom turned around suddenly. The coroner stated that the victim was first hit in the left shoulder, maybe indicating a split second impulse to turn to the left.

The coroner's official report: "Shot in the left shoulder 5" from spine on up through head. Killed instantly."

Early in the morning of April 1, at home in Hempstead Anna Ransom stood reading the telegram just handed her at the front door.

Shaken, her first thought was, as she said later, "What a cruel April Fool's joke to play on me!"

Then seeing the Adjutant General's name, she was struck by the horrible reality.

When able to speak, she called her brother, Tom, to handle the sad details for burial, then wired Austin to ship the body to Hempstead.

Headlines in big type flashed news of the tragedy to the front pages of newspapers all over Texas, and outside it, too.

Letters and telegrams of condolence began pouring in to Anna from bootblacks to the former Governor, James Ferguson. His wife sent a separate letter of sympathy.

The influence of Captain Ransom's character and integrity, and his fair way of dealing with others, had been noted, even in his youth. His heroism and yet modest demeanor were mentioned in the numerous newspaper accounts summarizing his life and service to the people of Texas.

In an article of the April 2nd issue of the Sweetwater paper, it was said he was considered one of the best officers of the Texas Rangers.

"He ranked high in the estimation of everyone both as an officer and a man," stated one article. He was termed "one of the great captains…The first time he was in the Rangers in 1905 he had earned a reputation as a man more feared by the lawless than anyone else.

If winning the bandit wars could be attributed to any one man, it should be Captain Henry Ransom, wrote a prominent historian in his book about the Texas Rangers.

From the Houston Post Wednesday, April 3, 1918: "Henry Ransom was known as one of the most fearless men in Texas. His life was largely one of service to the nation, the state, and the community.

"Many of his acts of valor have never been told because Ransom was not a talkative man and generally his silence was respected by his friends. Feared as he was by his enemies, he was equally well loved by his close friends."

Sigmund Byrd, in his column later in a Houston Paper, wrote of "Captain Henry Ransom, Texas Ranger and all-round peace officer, whom old timers called Houston's greatest police chief..."

Years later, Jonathan's wife, Dorothy, the daughter-in-law that Henry never knew, said "It was always strange to think about him being such a slight, small man when he did such big things!"

Sheriff Jack Yarbrough of Nolan County immediately wired his condolences, with a lengthy letter obviously pecked out by himself on a typewriter. He promised to write more later after investigation should reveal more details. He did write later but had no more information for her.

Yarbrough had wired the doctors in Hempstead receiving the body to remove bullets and apprise him of their caliber, mentioning the two kinds probably still lodged in it. No evidence surfaced indicating this was done.

The explanation given about this event was that one rancher's wife and a neighboring rancher were having an affair, and had been caught by her husband one day when he returned home earlier than expected.

When the wife's "lover" ran out to race off in his car, the husband jumped in his to give chase, shooting at the other man as they hurtled down the country roads. Finally the chasee ran out of gas, and leaped out of his car to dash on foot across a cotton field. The chaser stopped his car and ran after the other man, still shooting occasionally. It was said that when he ran out of ammunition, the other man realized it and turned around to chase the husband, who fled to his car and left.

All this melodrama in the fields was reported, it was said, by a so-called witness, who observed the commotion and stopped his car to watch the fun. Spoken of in this tale only as "the witness," his name was never revealed. What luck to have this handy person "appear." He had no witness himself.

Then, the tale continued, the husband decided the couple would be at the Wright Hotel. (Note: after this, they would meet again?) His wife had spoken earlier of going by train to visit friends. Allegedly she had waited at the hotel instead. Her husband suspected this much; it was claimed by those who had a ready story.

Later that evening the husband drove there, according to the story told later, to ask if his wife was registered.

Sure enough, he was given her room number. He said he hurried to the second floor and into a room next to hers, applying his ear to the wall to hear what he could. Ransom's room was across the hall, it was pointed out.

Soon the wife's lover walked out and the two men began shooting at each other.

If the other man actually came out of the next room, the two should have been within only a few feet of each other. Did they take the time to back up to make room for Ransom to stand between them?

However, both insisted that Henry stepped out in the line of fire, catching the lead that killed him instantly.

For him to act so foolishly was certainly out of character with his cautious, well-trained mind and split-second reactions.

For years he had been accustomed to dealing with outlaws who would have been happy to kill him had they been able to outwit him. He had survived all sorts of treachery while serving in the Philippines as well.

No one was skilled enough to outshoot him in a direct confrontation. A clever scheme had to be devised to make killing him appear accidental, including a woman and "hanky panky" to muddy the facts.

The role of the woman involved could be pure fiction, fabricated so the incident could be "hushed up." She could have been a good actress. In times past, an "unwritten law" existed—and perhaps followed these days—that bestowed upon a man the privilege or shooting another fellow who was dilly-dallying with his wife.

Yet after more than eighty years, descendants of the two men allegedly shooting at each other on the second floor hallway of Sweetwater's Wright Hotel contend this tale is true. However, they prefer that the details not be brought to light, even at this late date, claiming someone in these families might be hurt. They can be positive those in Captain Ransom's family were certainly hurt, the worst being his young children growing up without their father.

The author was assured by a descendent of one of the two firing at each other that a short notice in the Sweetwater newspaper about the Grand Jury meeting was all that appeared in print about the killing. This person insisted that not even the name of the Ranger was known and that no article about the tragedy appeared in any newspapers. This is untrue.

Ransom had his life cut short at age 44, with the other parties involved living out more years.

Who did kill Captain Ransom? Have enough clues been unearthed to solve this mystery?

From the Sweetwater newspaper, the "Daily Reporter" of April 3 a short item stated only the following: "The Grand Jury assembled this morning for the purpose of investigating the tragedy enacted in this city on Monday night. They have gotten down to business and the investigations are underway.

"Yesterday evening W. C. Miller was released without bond and Marion Long was allowed bail in the sum of $20,000 which was readily made. Both men are still in the city."

Captain Ransom's name was not mentioned in this article, but appeared in all the others.

However, not only did the Sweetwater newspaper later print long accounts of this episode, but many major newspapers over the State carried detailed articles about it plus much data about Ransom's life and career in law enforcement. The author obtained these numerous clippings.

Several incidents beg for explanation: if this was an accident, as claimed, why did Long and Miller flee the scene, Long even getting 15 miles away and crashing his car, as per the telegram from Sergeant Sam McKenzie to the Adjutant General?

Why did Koon chase the other two when he knew his shot — "accidentally" — killed Ransom? He claimed he thought he was being attacked and fired his gun, too. What made him think he was being attacked, when he hit Henry, who was not even in the fracas? Koon was staying in a room next to Ransom's room.

The bullets were not removed from Ransom's body to be examined to determine whose guns fired the fatal shots. No one ever complied with the Sheriff's request. Why?

Why was no death certificate found in the Nolan County records, where Ransom was killed? On some lists of all Texas Rangers, his name is omitted beside the dates he served. Why? The only photo of him on display with a wall full of others in a museum in San Antonio showed him as Captain with his company. His name had been changed. Were these errors or intentional? WHO WAS KOON?

Incidentally, the same photo is published with his correct name in a book about the Rangers. Also, thanks to Retired Texas Ranger "Geronimo" Preiss, Ransom's name has been restored in the photo in the museum. In several other places his name is left off, but these omissions are being corrected. Soon a large framed portrait of Henry Ransom will hang in the excellent Houston Police Museum, along with those of all the other Houston Chiefs of Police.

Apparently neither Long nor Miller was indicted. In an account of what happened, it was gossip that Marion Long's father, "a very wealthy man, was out a good bit to clear things up."

What had to be "cleared up" if Koon fired the fatal shot?

S. A. Hackworth, termed "Acting Adjutant General," sent flowers in his name from that office, being heard from for the first time. Apparently he was so new in that position that Henry knew nothing of him, addressing his letter to the Assistant Adjutant General because he had no response from Harley when calling for more help.

Some people well acquainted with Ransom and his habits continued to contend that he, with all his experience, would be too cagey to stick his head out into gunfire. This would not be typical action of his, they asserted. Others wondered if blanks were fired at first in the hall to make noise that would lure him out of his room.

On hearing nothing but wild rumors, a great nephew, Terrell Rogers, who later became a test block operator specializing in aircraft engines in World War II, went to ask Henry's widow if she knew what really happened.

Anna told him that a group of her husband's close friends in the Rangers called on her to convey their sympathy, adding that they knew how and why he was shot to death. They asserted that another Ranger had been paid $7,000 with which he shortly bought a house.

They urged Anna to have the matter investigated.

She refused. Perhaps she feared possible consequences of opening up the case. She may have felt her children might suffer some sort of retaliation.

A person of strong character and beliefs, Anna certainly was capable of seeking out her husband's assassins to see they were brought to justice. She, too, had been told that some involved in the plot were in high public offices.

Did she believe the barrage of denials of criminal intent? Had she been warned about dangers in digging for details? Was she threatened in any way?

The letters that follow are two from Sheriff Vann to Governor Hobby and to Captain W. M. Hanson, the special operative, both written the day Ransom was buried. They add a mysterious slant to the puzzle. Never had there been any love lost between Ransom and Vann, according to witnesses of past incidents.

Vann's letter to Governor Hobby: "I write you again relative to the appointment of E. W. Anglin as Ranger Captain. I notice there is a vacancy now and I wonder if you could not appoint him as per agreement while Judge Jones and I were in Austin some two months ago. As we stated to you, he is a good man and will make an excellent Captain and you promised us that you would appoint him as soon as an opportunity presented itself so if you possible (sic) can, would like very much to have him appointed as I know it will meet the approval of a great many people in this section."

Sheriff Vann wrote the following to Captain Hanson: "While in Austin some two months ago with my old friend Bill Jones, Governor Hobby promised us the appoint (sic) of E. W. Anglin of Harlingen as Ranger Captain in this section of the State. I presume you know Anglin, as I understand his mother is your cousin, he is a very good man and a very efficient officer and inasmuch as Captain Henry Ransom is dead I presume there will be a vacancy, so I would like very much to take this matter up with the Governor at an early date. Also with Adjutant General Harley, if you feel so disposed. I think he will make a very good captain and he has a great many friends in this part of the State..."

Captain Hanson sent the above letter on to Governor Hobby, with these additional remarks typed on the bottom, an intriguing caution that might imply a lot: "This is for your information. Advise no action be taken at this time. Hanson." Why not?

In a letter on a previous date, Vann wrote to Hanson complaining about the Rangers "avoiding" him. He accused them of not cooperating with him.

Hanson sent that letter also to Harley, with an explanation. He said he felt one particular Ranger mentioned by Vann could not work with him as "Vann turns the thieves loose faster than he (the Ranger) can catch them." Other Rangers had expressed the same complaint.

Another letter written the same day was the second from Sheriff Yarbrough to Henry's widow: "I wish to express to you my deepest sympathy in your bereavement. It has been my pleasure to know Captain Ransom on all sides of life; I have found him to be a gentleman of the highest type, loyal and true in the performance of his duty—a man who knew no fear. We, the County officers, feel we have indeed lost a true friend. May God comfort you in this hour of trouble."

In his other letter later he told her that one man's wife and another man were "pretty thick" and had arranged to meet at the Wright Hotel in Sweetwater "for the night." Some way her husband found this out. The woman had a room just across the hall from Captain Ransom. When her husband arrived, a porter took him upstairs to show him her room, then returned to the desk clerk, saying the man was eavesdropping. As the clerk was phoning the woman's room shots rang out upstairs. Some came from down the hall, it was said. Later the woman stated Ransom ran out in the hall and called to "them" to stop shooting various "tales" circulated.

Sheriff Yarbrough said Ranger Koon claimed he shot only once, thinking someone was trying to murder him, but he, the Sheriff, did not examine Koon's gun. Henry still had his gun in his hand, Yarbrough told her.

He wrote her that after investigation it was concluded Henry was shot "accidentally" by his friends, either Koon or Ransom's friend he knew in Houston.

The latter such "friend" was never named in the letter, in newspaper articles, or mentioned earlier by Ransom. Koon had accompanied him to Sweetwater, but never was it noted that another man was with him. From the correspondence, and lack thereof, with Ransom's unanswered requests for more help, even until the very last, the mention of another man with him appears erroneous. Perhaps he was the one who sneaked into Ransom's room to grab the briefcase of evidence? The Sheriff said he did not know the man's name, but that should have been determined in a thorough investigation.

The sheriff stated that some thought murder was committed when it was realized the two men involved came from Snyder, where some sort of trouble was brewing. He added that no one knew every little detail so this was about "as near as I can explain."

Before the funeral Anna's brother, Tom, went with her to the nearest river bridge with Henry's trunk of guns. She had insisted and he felt he had to humor her.

She hurled pistols and rifles off the bridge one at a time, intently watching each as it hit the water.

Patient Tom could stand it no longer when Anna finally snatched up the last one from the trunk.

He asked her for the rifle. She hesitated.

"Your son would want one of his father's guns, Anna. You know he should have one, don't you?"

Silently, she handed it to him and together they sadly left the bridge.

Condolences and floral tributes overflowed the rooms at Captain Ransom's home in Hempstead, where the memorial service was held at 2:30 p.m. on April 3, 1918. The body would be interred in the City Cemetery.

Letters and telegrams came from E. E. "Luke" Ransom, Ranger J. L. Anders, "Aunt Sallie," Mr. and Mrs. J. W. Moss, J. F. Wolters, Walter F. Woodul, Acting Adjutant General S. A. Hackworth, Sheriff Jack Yarbrough, Mrs. James E. Ferguson, former Governor James E. Ferguson, Ranger Sergeant Sam McKenzie, former Houston Mayor H. Baldwin Rice, Mr. and Mrs. Emett Johson, among others.

Floral arrangements were from Mr. and Mrs. Henry Hill and Ruby, Mr. and Mrs. H. Baldwin Rice, Mr. and Mrs. J. F. Wolters, Sheriff Burney Parker of Washington County, Mattie Norman, Mr. and Mrs. A. E. Rankin, Mr. and Mrs. J. L. Kasha, Mr. and Mrs. Jim McDade, The Adjutant General's Department of the State Capitol, Mrs. Claude Abner Searcy, and the largest, most elaborate from the Wells Fargo Co. and Express of Houston. Flowers also arrived from Mrs. W. H. Schindler, Mr. W. B. Ransom, Mrs. R. J. Ransom of Richmond, Mrs. Lou A. Hagan, Mrs. J. A. Dodd, and Mrs. Royal Raymond Urban.

At the cemetery in Hempstead, Beatrice stood to one side, alone in her grief. Ella may have felt her presence might be interpreted by Anna as an intrusion. She remained at home

Henry's brother, Will, and his family were in the large crowd, seated along with Vickie and his other sisters and their families. Near Will were Anna and the two children, Ruby Lee, age nine or so, and Jonathan, almost four years old.

Ransom's favorite nephew, Henry Jr., standing beside his own father, never forgot overhearing little Jonathan say, "When I grow up, I'm going to find the man that killed my daddy!"

Bee was clad in a long black coat, her thick dark hair contrasting with her fair complexion. Coiled high on the back of her head, it gave the impression of a crown, adding to her stately appearance.

The minute details of her father's funeral would be seared in her memory for the rest of her life.

She would recall the happy times that had been spent with him: riding beside him on the little "Sap" train, spending overnights in the sheriff's quarters in the Richmond jail, his leading Traveler to her, all saddled up.

Especially she treasured the moments when he had visited with her after the divorce. She would keep the frequent letters from him, the few photographs, and the small Bible he had brought her from the Philippines. She was grateful for the handful of newspaper clippings Aunt Vickie had just given her.

As Beatrice stood listening to the minister's final words, she visualized her father in her mind's eye, his bright blue eyes smiling at her as always when he said goodbye, just before leaving for duty.

After the graveside service, she stepped forward through the crowd, past the numerous floral offerings banked on either side of the closed bronze casket.

Gently Bee patted the side near a fall of flowers cascading over the top, her own blue eyes brimming with tears.

"Good night, little Papa," she whispered.

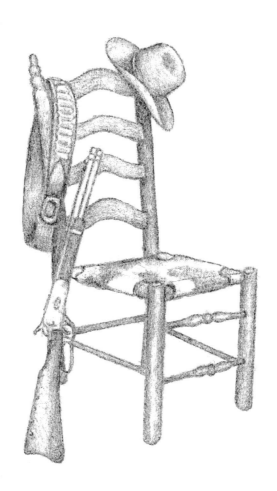

BIBLIOGRAPHY

Branda, Eldon Stephen, Editor, *The Handbook of Texas*, Vol. I and II, Texas State Historical Association, University of Texas Print Division, 1976

Brogan, Evelyn, *Famous Horses of American History*

Bruce, Florence Guild, *Lillie of Six Shooter Junction*, The Naylor Co., Publishers, San Antonio, Texas

Bryan, William S. and de Olivares, Jose, *Our Islands and Their People*, Vol. I and II, N. D. Thompson Publishing Co., St. Louis, New York, Chicago, Atlanta, 1899

DeShields, James T., *Tall Men and Long Rifles*, The Naylor Co., San Antonio, Texas 1935 and 1971

Dietrich, Wilfred O., *The Blazing History of Washington County*, Nortex Offset Pub. Co., Wichita Falls, Texas, copyright 1923 and 1950 by the author

Douglas, C. L., *The Men in White Hats*, South-West Press, 1934

Encyclopedia Britannica, 1935 Texas Edition

Genealogy Publishing, *Stephen F. Austin's Register of Families*, from the originals in the General Land Office, Austin, Texas, 1984, 1989

Gillett, James B., *Six Years With The Texas Rangers*, Yale University Press, New Haven and London, 1921

Haley, J. Evetts, *A Texan Looks at Lyndon*, Palo Duro Press, Canyon, Texas, 1964

Halstad, Murat, *The Story of the Philippines, Our New Possession*, Our Possessions Publishing Co., H. L. Barber Co., Chicago, 1898

Hedge, John W. and Dawson, Geoffrey S., *The San Antonio and Arkansas Pass Railway*, AMA Graphics, Waco, Texas, copyright by authors 1983

Lea, Tom, *The King Ranch*, Vol. I and II, Little, Brown Co., 1957

Lent, Joy, *Houston's Heritage*, D. H. White and Co., Pub., Houston, 1983

Nalle, Ouida Ferguson, *The Fergusons of Texas*, The Naylor Co., San Antonio

National Archives Trust Fund Board, Washington, D. C., U. S. Army Service Records

Ray, Worth S., *Austin Colony Pioneers*, Pemberton Press, Jenkins Pub. Co., Austin and New York

Russell, Hon, Henry B., *The Story of Two Wars, Our War with Spain and Our War With The Filipinos*, Vol. I and II, The Hartford Pub. Co., Hartford Conn., 1899

Schott, Joseph L., *Oredeal of Samar*, Howard W. Sams and Co., Indianapolis, New York

Scrapbooks of Early Houston, in the Texas Room, Julia Ideson Library, Houston

Sowell, A. J., *History of Fort Bend County*, W. B. Coyle and Co., Stationers and Printers, 1904

Sterling, William W., *Trails and Trials of a Texas Ranger*, University of Oklahoma Press, 1968

Webb, Walter Prescott, *The Texas Rangers*, University of Texas Press, Austin, 1985

Wright, General Marcus F., *The Story of American Expansion*, Vol. I and II, War Records Office, Washington, D. C., 1904

Yardley, Herbert O., *The American Black Chamber*, Blue Ribbon Books, Inc. 448 Fourth Avenue, New York, 1931

INDEX

Pat Hill Goodrich (Mrs. W. A., Jr.)
P O Box 418
Pinehurst, Texas 77362

U. S. Copyright Office
Reg. No. PAu 2-562-389
and TXu-1-011-045
Writers Guild of America East
No. 122054-00

CAPTAIN RANSOM, TEXAS RANGER
Captain Henry Lee Ransom
1874-1918

Author: Pat Hill Goodrich
Illustrator: Stonewall